THIRD EDITION

PROPOSAL DEVELOPMENT

How to Respond & Win the Bid

Bud Porter-Roth

The Oasis Press®
Central Point, Oregon

Published by the Oasis Press®
Proposal Development: How to Respond and Win the Bid
©1989, 1993, 1998 by Bud Porter-Roth

This publication is designed to provide accurate and authoritative information in regard to the subject matter covered. It is sold with the understanding that the publisher is not engaged in rendering legal, accounting, or other professional service. If legal advice or other expert assistance is required, the services of a competent professional person should be sought.

— from a declaration of principles jointly adopted by a committee of the American Bar Association and a committee of publishers.

Please direct any comments, questions, or suggestions regarding this book to The Oasis Press Editorial Department at the address below:

PSI Research
The Oasis Press®
P.O. Box 3727
Central Point, Oregon 97502
(541) 479-9464 *phone*
(541) 476-1479 *fax*
info@psi-research.com *email*

Porter-Roth, Bud
  Proposal Development: how to respond to a bid / Bud Porter-Roth. – 3rd ed.
    p.   cm.
  ISBN 1-55571-431-5 (pbk.)
  1. Proposal writing in business.   I. Title.
  HF5718.5.P67   1998
  808'.066658—dc21
                           98-21244
                           CIP

The Oasis Press® is a Registered Trademark of Publishing Services, Inc., an Oregon corporation doing business as PSI Research.
ISBN 1-55571-431-5 (Paperback)
Printed in the United States of America
Third Edition 10 9 8 7 6 5 4 3 2
♻ Printed on recycled paper when available

Table of Contents

Chapter 1 Organization

INTRODUCTION...1-3

TYPES OF PROPOSAL REQUESTS.......................................1-4

    Shopping Cart Approach..1-5

    Request for Information (RFI).................................1-6

    Request for Proposal...1-7

GENERATION OF THE RFP/RFI..1-8

PRE-PROPOSAL PREPARATION......................................1-11

    RFP Response Cycle..1-11

    Qualify the Opportunity 1-12

    Bid/No-bid Decision 1-16

    Outline the RFP 1-20

PROPOSAL PREPARATION...1-23

    The Proposal Team...1-23

    Work Space or the Warroom..................................1-24

    Developing the Winning Strategy............................1-26

    Proposal Kickoff Meeting......................................1-28

    Work Assignments...1-31

    Management Personnel...1-31

    Proposal Style Sheet..1-32

PROPOSAL ACTIVITIES...1-34

    Proposal Leader's Responsibilities..........................1-34

    Developing RFP Questions.....................................1-34

IN-HOUSE REVIEW...1-38

    Virtual Red Team...1-40

SCHEDULE..1-40

PROPOSAL ACTIVITIES...1-42

PROPOSAL DISPOSITION ACTIVITIES.............................1-45

ALTERNATE PROPOSALS...1-46

WRITING LEVELS...1-47

SUMMARY..1-50

Chapter 2 Proposal Contents: Overview

INTRODUCTION..2-3

PROPOSAL COVER 2-3

PHYSICAL ORGANIZATION OF A PROPOSAL.................................2-7

    Constants.. 2-7

    Variables.. 2-7

FRONT MATTER.. 2-7

    Cover Letter... 2-8

    Title Page.. 2-9

    Proprietary Notice...2-10

    Table of Contents (TOC)... 2-12

    Abbreviations List...2-14

ADDITIONAL FRONT MATTER... 2-14

    Compliance Matrix.. 2-15

    Exceptions List...2-16

    Bonds...2-16

    Buy USA Statement...2-17

    Minority, Small, Women-owned, and Veteran Business
    Enterprise (MSWVBE) Requirements......................................2-17

    Proposal Road Map..2-17

PROPOSAL ORGANIZATION.. 2-18

PROPOSAL FORMAT............ 2-20

    Style Sheet.. 2-20

Chapter 3 Proposal Contents: Essential Sections

INTRODUCTION...3-3

THE EXECUTIVE SUMMARY...3-3

    Who Reads the Executive Summary...3-4

    Development of the Executive Summary....................................3-5

    Summary...3-16

TECHNICAL SECTION... 3-16

    Who Reads the Technical Section..3-17

    Development of the Technical Section...................................... 3-18

Summary...3-24

MANAGEMENT SECTION...3-25

Who Reads the Management Section....................................3-26

Development of Management Section...................................3-26

Using Proposal Boilerplate Material.................................3-28

Summary...3-31

PRICING SECTION..3-32

Who Reads the Pricing Section.......................................3-32

Development of the Pricing Section..................................3-34

Organization of the Pricing Section................................3-35

Pricing Strategies...3-37

Summary...3-39

APPENDIX...3-40

SUMMARY..3-42

Chapter 4 Proposal Contents: Boilerplate Files

INTRODUCTION...4-3

TEXT BOILERPLATE FILES...4-4

Descriptions of Products or Services................................4-5

Company Services Provided...4-6

Corporate Descriptions..4-8

Reference Account Descriptions......................................4-12

Capabilities and Facilities..4-15

Previous Proposals..4-16

GRAPHICS BOILERPLATE FILES..4-17

Products or Equipment..4-19

Facilities..4-20

Headquarters Organization and Personnel 4-21

Reference Accounts...4-22

Cost/Pricing Information...4-24

Cover Artwork and Illustrations....................................4-25

USING BOILERPLATE FILES...4-25

INDEXING FILES...4-27

Written Files...4-27

Illustrations..4-28

DEVELOPING BOILERPLATE FILES..4-29

DISSEMINATION OF MATERIAL...4-31

MAINTENANCE OF THE BOILERPLATE LIBRARY.........................4-32

SUMMARY..4-33

Chapter 5 Proposal Contents: Illustrations

INTRODUCTION..5-3

THE ART OF ILLUSTRATIONS..5-4

    Types of Illustrations..5-4

    Sources of Ready-to-use Art 5-10

ILLUSTRATION FORMATS..5-12

    Landscape versus Portrait Orientation..................................5-13

    In-text Graphics...5-13

ILLUSTRATION STANDARDS...5-14

    Boxing Illustrations..5-14

    Type Styles...5-15

    Line Weight...5-15

    Figure and Table Numbers...5-15

    Illustration References...5-15

    Titles and Captions...5-16

    Punctuation...5-16

    Illustration Consistency and Orientation...............................5-16

ORGANIZATION 5-17

    Numbering and Indexing Artwork 5-18

    Master Proposal Art File..5-19

STORAGE OF ILLUSTRATIONS 5-20

SUMMARY 5-20

Chapter 6 Post-Proposal Activities

INTRODUCTION 6-3

SUBMISSION CRITERIA 6-4

    General Submission Criteria..6-5

    Specific Non-standard Criteria....................................6-6

PROPOSAL DELIVERY REQUIREMENTS........................... 6-8

    Delivery Date.. 6-8

    Delivery Conditions.. 6-9

    Delivery Method.. 6-10

POST-DELIVERY CONSIDERATIONS.............................. 6-10

PRE-CONTRACT STEPS... 6-13

    Question and Answer Period.................................... 6-14

    Oral Presentation..6-15

    Product Demonstration..6-17

    Reference Validation, Reference Site Visits,

    and Headquarters Visit.. 6-19

    Best and Final Offer (BAFO)..................................... 6-20

    Contract Negotiation... 6-21

INTERPRETING POST-PROPOSAL DATA.......................... 6-23

SUMMARY.. 6-24

Chapter 7 Evaluation

INTRODUCTION.. 7-3

IN-HOUSE EVALUATION... 7-5

    Rating the Proposal.. 7-5

    Developing the Evaluation Criteria..............................7-7

    Forming an In-house Evaluation Team.......................7-8

CUSTOMER EVALUATION.. 7-11

    The Evaluation Board.. 7-12

SUMMARY... 7-14

Chapter 8 Printing the Proposal

INTRODUCTION..8-3

METHODS OF PRINTING...8-3

SPECIALTY PRINTING...8-4

    Binder Tabs...8-5

    General Information..8-6

    Ordering Tabs...8-6

    Preparing Instructions for the Printer........................8-8

    Preparing the Dummy..8-9

TYPES OF BINDING 8-11

    Three-Ring Binder...8-11

    Acco® Fastener..8-12

    Plastic Comb Binding..8-12

SELECTING A PRINTER OR REPRODUCTION SHOP.......8-13

FINAL ASSEMBLY...8-14

Proposal Checklists

    Appendix A: General Pre-proposal Checklist.............A-1

    Appendix B: Proposal Writing Checklist...................B-1

    Appendix C: Pre-submission Checklist......................C-1

    Appendix D: Printing Checklist.................................D-1

    Appendix E: Evaluation Checklist for Proposal Team.................E-1

    Appendix F: Proposal Submission Checklist..............F-1

    Appendix G: Post-proposal Checklist........................G-1

    Appendix H: Bid/No-Bid Checklists...........................H-1

    Appendix I: Sample Forms...I-1

List of Illustrations

Chapter 1 Organization

Figure 1-1.   RFI/RFP Development Cycle 1-10

Figure 1-2.   Typical Proposal Flow Chart 1-13

Figure 1-3.   Sample No-bid Letter 1-19

Figure 1-4.   Typical Proposal Outline 1-22

Figure 1-5.   Basic Proposal Team 1-24

Figure 1-6.   Kickoff Meeting Agenda 1-30

Figure 1-7.   Proposal Status 1-32

Figure 1-8.   Sample Art Log 1-33

Figure 1-9.   Sample Request for Extension 1-43

Chapter 2 Proposal Contents: Overview

Figure 2-1.   Sample Cover Sheet... 2-5

Figure 2-2.   Sample Cover Sheet with Text Only.. 2-6

Figure 2-3.   Sample Cover Letter 2-9

Figure 2-4.   Sample Title Page 2-11

Figure 2-5.   Sample Proprietary Notice 2-12

Figure 2-6.   Sample List of Illustrations 2-13

Figure 2-7.   Sample List of Tables 2-13

Figure 2-8.   Sample Abbreviations List 2-14

Figure 2-9.   Compliance matrix.. 2-15

Figure 2-10.   Exceptions list 2-16

Figure 2-11.   Proposal Road Map 2-18

Figure 2-12.   Sample Style Guide for Abbreviations and Acronyms 2-21

Figure 2-13.   Sample Style Sheet 2-22

Chapter 3 Proposal Contents: Essential Sections

Figure 3-1.   Requirement/Response Format 3-21

Figure 3-2.   Assumptions 3-23

Figure 3-3.   Sample Project Management Schedule 3-33

Figure 3-4.   Pricing Outline 3-36

Chapter 4 Proposal Contents: Boilerplate Files

Figure 4-1.   Example RFP Specifications 4-6

Figure 4-2.   Sample Table for Maintenance Response Time 4-7

Figure 4-3.   Sample Class Description 4-9

Figure 4-4.   Sample Project Plan 4-11

Figure 4-5.   Sample Resume 4-12

Figure 4-6.   Sample Reference Account 4-14

Figure 4-7.   Typical Boilerplate Illustration 4-20

Figure 4-8.   Management Organization Charts 4-23

Chapter 5 Proposal Contents: Illustrations

Figure 5-1.   Placement of Figure Title and Caption 5-5

Figure 5-2.   Placement of Number and Title 5-7

Figure 5-3.   Example Table and Call-outs.. 5-9

Figure 5-4.   Tabular Information Presented as a Chart 5-10

Figure 5-5.   Sample of Computer-generated Artwork 5-11

Figure 5-6.   Example Art Log 5-19

Chapter 7 Evaluation

Figure 7-1.   Evaluation Guidelines 7-9

Figure 7-2.   Evaluation Checklist 7-10

Chapter 8 Printing the Proposal

Figure 8-1.   Binder Tab Order Checklist 8-7

Figure 8-2.   Sample Dummy Sheet 8-10

Preface

The purpose of this book is to provide you with a practical guide to writing and organizing sales proposals. Whether you are a novice or senior proposal writer, you will find tips and techniques that will be beneficial to you. Instead of discussing salesmanship 101, sales theories, and proposal war stories, this book focuses on developing a process for writing winning proposals.

A process may be defined as a method for achieving results that involves a number of identifiable steps and operations. For a process to be successful it must be repeatable—otherwise it is not a process as such and any results are only accidental. Being able to win proposals consistently is not accidental; it is the result of utilizing a well-planned process (and having a good product helps!). This book defines the basic steps that are a part of that process.

These steps include, but are not limited to:

- Having the discipline for a critical reading of the RFP
- Developing an outline of your proposal
- Planning and scheduling your resources and facilities
- Preparing a competitive analysis and using it
- Reserving time for a final review of your proposal

Having an easily applied process reduces wasted time spent in the mechanical aspects of coordinating a variety of disparate materials. Instead, you can devote time to a better understanding the RFP, developing a winning strategy, getting the right pricing, and working with the customer.

This book is a "soup to nuts" review of proposal writing and the proposal development process. This book is written with a best-case-scenario in mind and you may not have access to all of the resources listed. This book is useful not only as a writing guide, but as a resource itself to show management how professional proposals are resourced, managed, and written.

> *"There is never time to do it right, but there is*
> *always time to do it over."*

This is the third edition of this book. While the basic principles of good proposalmanship haven't changed, technology has given us new tools that allow us to work better and smarter. Current desktop technology allows the small to average user to produce a proposal that will compete on any level. This technology includes:

- High-quality laser printers
- Color printers
- Scanners
- Digital cameras
- Word processors
- Spreadsheet and statistical programs
- Illustration programs
- Desktop publishing software
- Groupware or collaborative software
- Internet resources

Today there is no reason why a smaller company or individual sales representative can't produce a professional-level proposal.

One of the major advances is the Internet. With the Internet, individuals and companies can easily share files, access boilerplate caches, collaborate in the development of a proposal, and create a virtual proposal center where such important items as the proposal strategy, competitive information, and answers to questions can be posted. This allows the team to be geographically dispersed and work regardless of the place and the time zone. For the more technologically advanced, computer teleconferencing and on-line whiteboards add to the tool bag.

These ideas and others are explored in this new edition. But, the tried and true principles of writing a good proposal remain, regardless of technology.

I hope you will find this book a valuable addition to your library and your bag of tricks for winning proposals. I will be happy to answer any questions, and will gladly accept suggestions and recommendations for future editions.

Bud Porter-Roth
Porter-Roth Associates
Mill Valley, CA

Organization

Next to having the proper solution,
good proposal organization is paramount.

Organization

■ INTRODUCTION

✑A proposal is an answer to a question.

Proposals and requests for proposals are generated in virtually every public and private business sector. A request for proposal (RFP) is a document that outlines a need and solicits proposals that explain how that need can be solved. A proposal, then, is an answer to a question. It could be as simple as a letter response for pricing in which a price sheet is supplied, or as complex as a multi-volume written response that has taken months to complete and additional months for the response to be evaluated. The most common types of proposals are sales proposals, which explain a product or service, and grant proposals, which request funding or resources for a project. This book will focus on the sales proposal.

RFPs are released to a number of potential bidders with the intent of developing a competitive situation that will produce the highest quality product at the lowest price. The following is taken from a recent California State RFP: "The purpose of competitive bidding is to secure public objectives at the lowest practical cost and avoid the possibilities of graft, fraud, collusion, etc. Competitive bidding is designed to benefit the public body, and is not for the benefit of the bidders."

Winning a competitive bid involves certain skills in developing, writing, and selling the proposal. Even with a superior product or price, it is possible to lose to a better prepared proposal.

✑Emphasis should be on completeness and clarity of content.

Proposal writing, like most projects, can be elevated to an art form in the right hands. Most customers, however, are looking for a clean, well-written proposal that clearly tells them what they want to know. A typical RFP preparation instruction will caution that, "Proposals should be prepared simply and economically, providing a straightforward, concise description of the bidders' capabilities to satisfy the requirements of the RFP. Proposals that are overly elaborate and use extensive embellishments, such as color illustrations, are neither required nor necessary. *Emphasis should be on completeness and clarity of content.*"

A key point to successful proposal writing is understanding RFPs — why they are written, how they are written, and who writes them.

In the course of this book, I will quote from a variety of sources — commercial and government RFIs, RFPs, and other documents — that I have found to be valuable in my career. I would like to share with you what I have learned from these sources and from my past experience.

■ TYPES OF PROPOSAL REQUESTS

To enable vendors to provide a proper technical solution, an RFP must represent a clear understanding of all the issues (Technical Section), it must provide a method for responding to and managing those issues (Management Section), and it must provide the vendor with an acceptable method for doing business (Contract and Price Section). Many RFPs are not successful because they fail to properly communicate one or more of the above issues and this results in a problem contract or no contract.

Developing and writing an RFP serves numerous purposes for the customer. First, the RFP process allows an organization or company to develop a detailed analysis of the problem or issue they are trying to solve. Second, when the operational problems are understood internally by the customer, they can be clearly communicated to potential vendors. Third, communications between all parties can be crisp, based on a mutual understanding of the requirements. Fourth, a contract between customer and vendor is more likely to be successful because expectations have been established and agreed upon.

✎An RFP helps set the expectations for both the customer and the vendor.

A poorly organized and confusing RFP can seriously undermine a company's market position and strength if the issues driving the RFP directly affect the primary business operations of the company. The purchasing process and installation of equipment will take longer, cost more than anticipated, and will probably not provide a satisfactory long-term solution.

Writing successful RFPs depends on a clear understanding of the forces that initiated and are driving the RFP. Properly organized and executed, RFPs are powerful tools for selecting the best solution and developing straightforward relationships with vendors. Preparing an unambiguous RFP depends on, but is not limited to, the following:

1. Recognizing a deficiency in current operations that could be resolved through the purchase of equipment or services

2. Developing a plan for understanding the problem

3. Identifying appropriate potential solutions

4. Developing and specifying the return on investment

5. Gaining visibility and internal acceptance of the problem and potential solution

6. Determining the projected budget

7. Building a project schedule

8. Selecting the project leader and personnel

⊯RFI responses provide the customer with multiple approaches to his problem.

Often, the customer will send out a "pre-RFP" or RFI (request for information) to test the technology waters. These pre-RFPs are described below, but their basic intent is to help the customer determine whether there is a technology solution available that matches the need. If we look at it from both the customer and the vendor point of view, why waste the time and money to send out an RFP if there are no products to fill the need. While this may sound unrealistic that a customer will do this, it is very possible because of what is called the "shopping-cart approach" to writing RFPs.

Shopping-cart Approach

⊯Requirements may not always correspond to products.

Many customers do their homework prior to writing an RFP (and of course some don't). The problem begins when customers take the best features from several products, combine them, and write that feature as if it were one product. This is like saying that you want a motor vehicle with the ride of a luxury car, the seating of a van, the fuel efficiency of an economy car, and the hauling capacity of a pickup.

Hence, it is good for a customer to "try-out" requirements in a pre-RFP and determine if vendors have the products available. I can not stress enough that RFPs are written by people who may not fully understand the technology or services they are requesting and it is up to the proposal writers to guide, explain, and shepherd the RFP writers and evaluators without speaking down to them or asking them to "figure it out."

For example, a records manager at a large law firm is asked to modernize the records system. Today, the paper-based system uses note cards to track documents by subject and location and the records manager only has a passing familiarity with computers, mainly used for word processing. The records manager has been tasked with researching and writing an RFP for a computerized records keeping system.

While this person, we assume, will do an excellent job of research, and will make every effort to understand the many different technologies that may apply, it is highly likely that the RFP will combine features and benefits from different products resulting in requirements for which there is no product set.

The bottom line is, help the customer to understand not only your product, but the technology and/or service.

Depending on the size and complexity of the project, the customer will normally use one of the following vehicles to convey his/her request.

Request for Information (RFI)

✍ *RFIs are used to gain information.*

An RFI is a way for the customer to determine what is available from the vendors he thinks are capable of solving his problems. It is also a way of determining whether or not the request is reasonable and if technology is available. If there is little interest or negative responses to the request by vendors, the customer returns to a study phase.

Typically, an RFI encompasses all of the requirements and is structured just as the RFP would be. It is important to not only put forth the technical issues, but to also list what is needed for project management, maintenance, training, and support. Thus, the potential vendors are allowed to comment on all aspects of the procurement and to establish for the customer what is possible and what is not possible—from the vendor's point of view.

Of course, customers are going to have to separate the wheat from the chaff, complaint-wise, so that the resulting RFP does not favor only one vendor or important requirements are deleted because one vendor could not meet them.

✍ *Not all requirements are reasonable.*

Customers try to ensure that a request is technically reasonable because of the cost of RFI preparation and the subsequent costs incurred from issuing the RFP. However, this is not to say that all RFIs will be fully thought through and without problems. Also, because of costs and time, the RFI is written such that a large portion of it is directly reusable in the RFP.

In responding to an RFI, one must be careful and try to prevent the customer from combining several features, a la´ the shopping-cart approach, into the final RFP. Close contact with the customer, and education when needed, may prevent this from occurring.

The following paragraphs were taken directly from an RFI:

[Our company] *is in the process of researching optical document imaging systems that support the document imaging needs of... The objective of this RFI is to obtain information about systems that are available from a selected set of vendors.*

It must be clearly understood that this RFI is being used as a vehicle to obtain information about potential optical imaging systems vendors. The RFI should in no way be interpreted as a contract (implicit, explicit, or implied), nor does it imply any form of an agreement to candidate vendors. In addition, no inference should be made that we will purchase and/or implement in the future, any of the optical imaging systems proposed by the vendors responding to this RFI.

In this case, the customer is making it very clear that an RFI is being released solely to gain an understanding of this type of technology (optical document management systems) and who the major vendors are. Establishing contact with the customer, getting him to your company for a site visit and technology demonstration, and writing a superior response to the RFI will help you gain the advantage over your competition when the RFP is released. Sometimes a customer is so impressed by a single company during the RFI stage that the RFP is bypassed and a contract is awarded.

Many companies only send the subsequent RFP to those vendors who responded to the RFI. Therefore, the RFI becomes an important document and ensures your place on the bidders' list for the RFP.

Lastly, an RFI may also be a way of getting vendors to write a free study of multiple approaches to the customer's problem. If an RFI is poorly put together, has little focus, and requires vendors to not only comment on requirements but also suggest and document alternate technologies, the vendor should properly gauge if this opportunity will bear fruit. Many RFIs and RFPs die on the vine and are never released because the customer has severely misjudged the technology, the implementation, and the cost. Thus, any time spent by the vendors has been wasted.

On the other hand, RFI work is the best place for a vendor to try to influence the customer's formal request and therefore develop and have the inside track when the RFP is released. An old proposal proverb goes something like this: "If you didn't write the RFI, don't bother with the RFP."

Request for Proposal (RFP)

An RFP is the next step by a customer and is usually the direct result of the RFI. However, some companies eliminate the RFI stage and employ a consultant or technology expert who will write the RFP without benefit of an RFI, as a cost-saving measure. In the RFP, the

Proposals usually become attachments to the contract.

customer very clearly, or at least to the best of his technical understanding and ability, spells out exact requirements that represent his problems, and requests vendors to provide formal proposals that can be negotiated into a contract. An RFP is considered a formal request because the winning response becomes part of the resulting contract. Statements made in a proposal must be supportable.

The following is taken from the Proposal Preparation Instructions of an RFP:

[This company] *reserves the right to award the contract according to the evaluation criteria... The vendor chosen for award should be prepared to have his proposal incorporated, along with all other written correspondence concerning this RFP, into the contract. Any false or misleading statements found in the proposal will be grounds for disqualification.*

Unlike an RFI, in which the customer is still fact finding, the RFP represents a decision to buy technology or services. Proposals submitted in response to an RFP often are incorporated into the contract as an addendum or exhibit in order to contractually obligate the vendor to comply with statements made in the proposal and provide legal recourse if the vendor cannot meet the requirements as stated in the RFP and agreed to in the proposal.

RFPs are significant opportunities for vendors.

An RFP represents a significant opportunity for vendors to sell their products, systems, or services. An RFP provides a stable set of specifications and requirements for vendors to work from, it provides them a platform for describing and promoting products, and it allows vendors a chance to interact with the sponsoring organization.

In summary, we can say that an RFP is a written document that represents a large amount of time, energy, and money spent by the customer to try to communicate an understanding of his business needs. The resulting proposal represents an interpretation of the customer's needs and a proposed solution, and involves the expenditure of a commensurate amount of time and resources.

■ GENERATION OF THE RFI/RFP

The typical cycle begins when the customer realizes that his company is no longer working efficiently, for whatever reasons, and a task force is assigned to study the deficiency. This task force identifies the problem or problems and recommends that a study be made, if time

An RFP identifies a problem area in a company that requires resolution.

permits, to determine possible resolutions. This study usually results in the writing of an RFI or RFP.

An RFI/RFP is a difficult document to write—more difficult than a proposal in some respects, because it is the initial definition of a problem by people who often do not fully understand the problem themselves or the best way to solve it. Writing the RFP will not only have to address the technical aspects of solving the problem, but also will have to address the political issue (IBM, DEC, or HP internal advocates) and territorial issue (which department owns the problem and buys the technology) associated with implementing new technology within a closed environment.

Like proposals, RFPs are written by committees.

Because of the time, effort, expense, and justification for getting new equipment, a proposal that does not respond directly to the requirements section of the RFP has very little chance of winning. Not only is the hard work that went into creating the RFP ignored, a team of people are asked to throw out months of work, and within the usual evaluation period of four to eight weeks, determine whether or not the technical solution will meet the requirements. In addition, the evaluators will have to study what impact the solution may have on other systems/equipment that were not documented in the RFP. It should be taken into account that the people who wrote the RFI/RFP will be the same people who will evaluate the proposals.

Proposals must follow the requirements to win.

Aggressive, innovative solutions that push the limits of the requirements (but stay with them) are what the evaluators are looking for and what should be proposed. However, if proposals are widely divergent from each other and the RFP requirements, either:

1. Vendors did not pay attention to the requirements

2. The requirements were not well specified

3. The customer did not do his homework

Contracts may not always be awarded.

If there is a wide gap between what is required and what is proposed, the customer will have little choice but to reconsider spending any further time or money on the project. Thus, vendors run the risk of alienating the customer by going too far beyond the basic requirements. This becomes the vendor's problem for either not educating the customer initially, or improperly deciding to bid on a project.

A response that is not consistent with the RFP requirements will do more long-term harm than not bidding in the first place. Figure 1-1 illustrates the typical cycle a customer goes through from developing an RFP to awarding a contract.

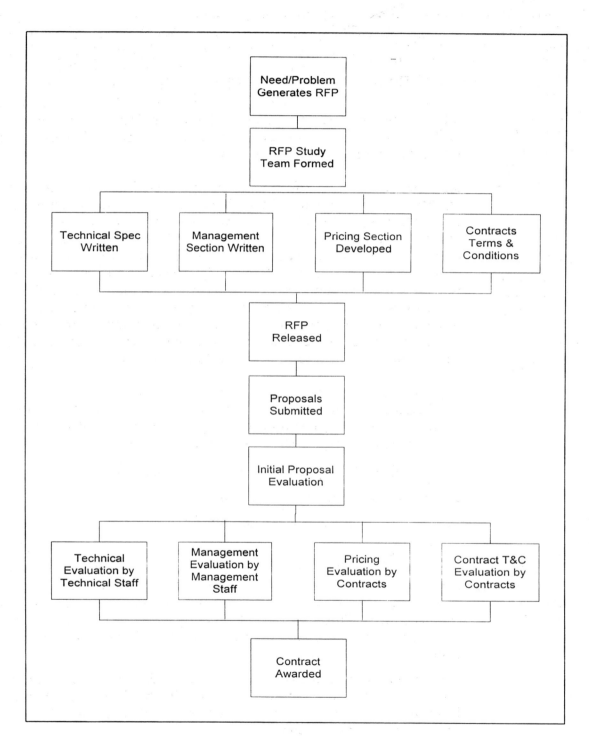

Figure 1-1. *RFI/RFP Development Cycle*

■ PRE-PROPOSAL PREPARATION

RFP Response Cycle

Let's walk through an RFP response cycle and discuss the steps involved in writing a proposal. Appendix A, Pre-proposal Activities, contains a detailed checklist of activities you may consider.

Worst Case Scenario

✎ Time may be lost inside of your company.

The person who will be responsible for responding to an RFP is not always the first person to receive it. At least five working days are usually spent, after receipt of an RFP, determining what product line this RFP is addressing and what department should receive it. So, a short fuse is made shorter and the saying "Time is of the essence" acquires new meaning.

It often begins something like this: Late in the afternoon, just as you are getting ready to leave for the day, your manager appears at your door and says, "Got a minute?" and hands you an RFP that was sent to the Marketing VP who gave it to the Sales VP who gave it to your manager who is now going to give it to you. Your manager actually got it yesterday, but didn't get around to looking at it until this afternoon.

Best Case Scenario

You have been in contact with the customer, know the RFP is going to be released, and your name is on the mailing list. You contact the customer and confirm the RFP was sent to you. The RFP is routed directly to you instead of sitting in receiving while receiving tries to figure out what this document is and who to send it to.

Getting Started

Now that you have the RFP, how do you get started? Figure 1-2 depicts various activities involved in generating a proposal. Keep in mind that for a medium to large proposal, many of the initial activities shown will have to be worked in parallel if a reasonable response is to be generated in the time remaining. Appendix A through H contains a series of checklists that lead you through a proposal from receipt of the RFP to the submission of the proposal. Appendix I is comprised of four proposal status sheets that lead you through "signing in" the RFP to determining why you won or lost the proposal. All of these checklists and status sheets should be used and modified to suit your own company and the type of proposals that you write.

The person responsible for the proposal is generally called the proposal manager. This could be the salesman who asks for and receives the RFP, the VP who takes the project under his wing because of its size, or a proposal specialist whose department has responsibility for managing all proposal activities. Bottom line, however, is that the proposal manager is a worker with responsibility for moving the proposal forward.

Qualify the Opportunity

≈ Qualify the opportunity first.

Perhaps the most important first step in proposal development is qualifying the customer and the RFP. If you receive an RFP without previous account work or knowledge, if you receive an RFP from a customer you never heard of, or even if you have been working the account and know they are writing an RFP, the opportunity must still be qualified.

Proper qualification of an opportunity drives you to research three aspects of the RFP. The first is whether the technology requirements are viable and can be met with existing technology. The second is whether your company has that technology. The third is whether the project has been funded.

≈ RFPs can be misused.

Many customers use the RFP process incorrectly—whether intentional or not. A customer may not do quality research that results in:

- Requests for products that do not exist
- Estimated costs that are below expectation
- Implementation expectation that are overestimated

When this customer receives proposals, and reality hits, the project is usually "taken off the street" and rethought. If the budget is underestimated, the project may be dropped and the money reallocated to a more viable project.

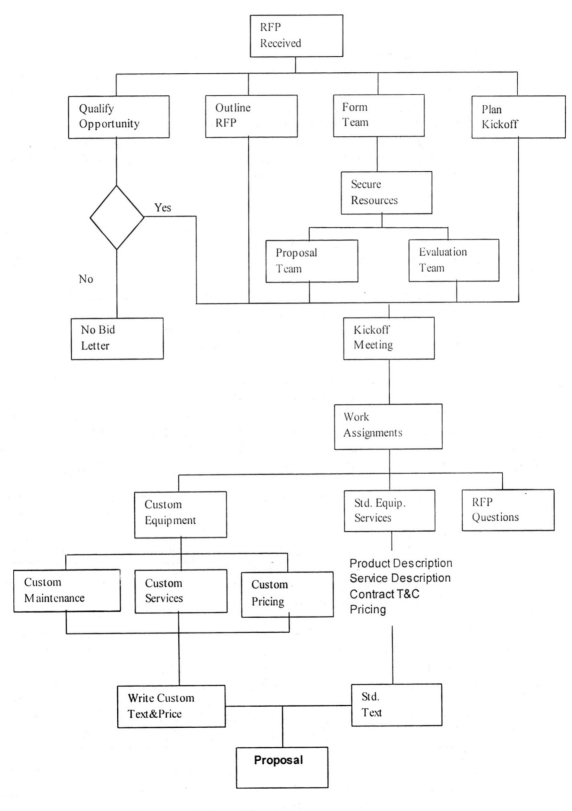

Figure 1-2. *Typical Proposal Flow Chart*

The customer may also try to cut various requirements from the RFP in an effort to reduce prices. This may or may not be done with all of the vendors. The customer may select one or two vendors, who were on the short list, and work with them in an effort to get the prices down to the budget level. This should be a warning sign and you may want to proceed cautiously. The initial cost reductions will allow the customer to spend the money allocated and a vendor will be selected. However, once implemented, the customer may try to regain the lost functionality at the expense of the vendor.

As a vendor in a situation like this, the need to document and sign-off specific agreed upon requirements is critical. If the customer begins with "project creep" requirements, ensure that the additional functionality is first documented, the impact to the project is documented, and the additional functionality is costed. This is then presented to the customer as an addendum to the contract and not started until approved. If not, project creep will begin in earnest and your project will likely fall behind schedule.

✑ Some customers' requirements are not credible and not founded in the appropriate detail.

One of the best ways for a customer to determine what new technology is available in the market is to release an RFP asking for everything in the world but reserving the right to purchase pieces, parts, and separate components. This customer will also reserve the right not to award any contract and is probably not ready, for whatever reasons, to make a major purchase.

The purpose of this type of RFI/RFP is fact finding and obtaining pricing information. This type of opportunity should be listed as a potential high risk and other RFPs should be considered. This type of RFP is called a "fishing expedition" or a "science project" and usually is a waste of time for vendors. Continued effort on this type of RFP should be constantly reevaluated as new information is gathered and the situation is better understood.

Many companies also slant or *wire* an RFP to favor one vendor or technology. This may be an effort to keep an incumbent's equipment or services. It may also be the work of your competition who has convinced the customer to favor their requirements.

So why go to the trouble (and expense) of writing an RFP if you already know what to buy? The reason is that many companies have a policy that requires competitive bids for anything over a certain dollar amount. It stands to reason that if the requesting department is basically happy with the incumbent's equipment or services, they will try to write the RFP in a way that will specify this equipment or service.

✎Some RFPs are wired for a vendor.

When an RFP is wired, the competitive bid process is used to validate to management a decision that has already been made.

Even if an RFP is wired, careful analysis and qualification may indicate that a competitive proposal may win:

- Incumbents frequently have older technology; their response to the RFP would be to upgrade existing technology, which may not be a long-range solution
- Incumbents may write a sloppy proposal, thinking they have already won
- Incumbents may be forced to rescind some features and benefits when these are to be put in writing and attached to the contract

Your proposal will have to demonstrate that new technology has many features and benefits that cannot be had simply by "upgrading." Your selling point may be that it is actually **less** costly to start with a clean slate than to upgrade, rebuild, and carry the previous product's shortcomings along with the new. This is the type of "win strategy" that is developed during the proposal kickoff meeting and carried through your proposal.

✎One choice the customer always has is to not buy.

Determining whether a project has been funded may be more difficult because the amount of money reserved for the project is usually not released for obvious reasons. However, many customers will respond if asked directly whether or not a project has been funded. If it is not a funded project, you should carefully consider whether to spend any further time. Many proposals have been written, expending a massive effort and dollar amount, only to have the procurement placed on hold because of "unanticipated expenses associated with acquiring this technology" or having initial requirements revised "due to changing technology" in the marketplace.

✎Does the customer understand the technology?

For a successful project, the customer must understand the technology involved in addition to financial aspects of acquiring that technology. Part of your job when qualifying the account is to determine whether the customer has:

- Sufficient technical expertise to understand what is being procured
- Sufficient research on the cost and the financial impact that the procurement will have

Perhaps the most important qualifier is "how much pain" the customer is in? This is an apt metaphor because you want to find out why the customer is putting out the RFP. If you can determine that they are losing money, losing clients, or there is a definite negative impact to their business for not implementing the technology, then you can be sure that they will be buying and not tire-kicking.

The reason behind the negative impact may become one of your central selling themes. An example for this "company" may be that they have not implemented a point-of-sale Internet site and are losing business to competitors who are selling through their Internet site. Until they acquire this technology, they will lose sales to the competition, not to mention not being perceived as a "high-tech" operation.

Their "pain" is losing product sales to the competition. Finding out that dollar figure may also play an important role in doing a rough cost justification show a positive return on investment for this opportunity.

Bid/No-Bid Decision

Some basic criteria should be established when making a bid/no-bid decision, such as compatibility with existing products, amount of custom work required, present account relationships, and internal customer politics. (Their IS shop is Blue through and through!) Review Appendix H, Bid No-bid Checklist for some detailed ideas on account qualification and bid/no-bid procedures.

Don't spend $10 to win a $5 contract.

The following points may appear obvious, but very often companies fail to make a thorough assessment of a potential opportunity in terms of what the implications will be if the contract is won. More than once I have heard the phrase, "The worst thing we could do is win that contract." A variation on a theme is, "The good news is we won the contract, the bad news is we won the contract...."

A simple bid/no-bid list might include some of the following:

- Is this a serious request that has been funded?
- Is there and incumbent? And if so, how entrenched is he?
- Is this a new account? Has the sales representative developed an account relationship?
- How has the sales rep qualified the account?
- Which department is responsible for the RFP? Is it the end user, the MIS department, or a special independent study group?
- Is this a request for real equipment or a fishing expedition?
- Can your company afford to win the business? Will your company be spending $10 to win an $8 contract?
- Does your company have the product/service? Or is this an attempt to fit a round peg into a square hole?
- If a new product is developed to win this business, can the new product be productized and the development costs amortized?
- Is this request in line with your future directions?

- Can production meet the order or will it mean adding new people, facilities, and equipment? What will the impact be on existing contracts?
- Who is the competition and what are they going to do? Often we bid, hopelessly overpriced, knowing the competition has the edge.
- Will winning be at the expense of losing an existing account?
- Will winning be at the expense of other product lines and services?
- Is the customer someone you want for a customer? What is the customer's history for paying on time?

When to Bid

Having the right technology and qualifying the customer are the most important criteria for bidding.

Perhaps the most important part of deciding to bid on a project is having the product, service, or technology being requested by the customer. Once you have determined that your product meets, and possibly exceeds the requirements, other impediments such as price can be dealt with and resolved.

If you do not have the product fit, the proposal becomes an effort in fitting a round peg in a square hole. Even if the customer ignorantly requests the wrong product, it will be a tough sell.

When Not to Bid

Knowing when not to bid is a harder decision. The basic decision comes down again to product and price. If you don't have the product, or your price is above the known price range, it may be better to not bid the opportunity. So often companies force a product to fit, win the job, and realize they are going to lose money overall in making the many changes needed to satisfy the customer.

A no-bid letter would be written when you actually cannot comply with the required specifications, and even if they were relaxed or changed you could not provide the equipment or service. This letter is a courtesy to the person and company that released the RFP and would explain why you are not bidding.

A well written no-bid letter is often better than a hastily prepared proposal.

A well-written no-bid letter will accomplish as much, if not more, than a poorly written or hastily prepared proposal, as well as saving time and money. A no-bid letter could have several purposes depending on the situation and your understanding of the account.

A no-bid letter sometimes is written as a last resort to having the specifications changed to allow you to bid on the RFP. The letter would state that you would not bid if the specifications remain as they are and that if changed sufficiently to allow your solution, you would be able to bid. This type of letter can work, as the RFP committee may not have realized that the specifications were too tight and they would really like to see you in the competition. Also, the possibility of a no-bid or several no-bids would lessen the competitive nature of the bid. (Typically, companies like to see a large number of bidders in an effort to make the procurement more competitive. It also allows them to select a "short list" of vendors and play the vendors against each other.)

✍Don't be shy when questioning requirements, you have everything to lose.

However, if you are the only vendor protesting the requirements, it is not likely that the RFP will be changed. Generally it is the combined weight of several vendors that forces the RFP committee to make changes. Therefore, don't be shy!

If you submit a no-bid letter and the result is that specifications are relaxed, care should be taken to ensure that you are not being kept in the competition only for your competitive value. In this situation, the RFP committee is using the competition only to justify a predetermined winner and justification would be harder with fewer companies bidding. See figure 1-3 for an example of a no-bid letter.

On the other hand, there are several reasons why you might want to bid on a job for which you are unlikely to win.

1. First, you want to remain on the bidder's list. It is possible that by not bidding on a job, your name will be taken off the bidder's list and your company will have to requalify for future opportunities.

2. Bidding on a first opportunity may give you a chance on a second job that might be more beneficial. Not bidding on the first eliminates you from the second.

3. By bidding, you establish a better relationship with the customer, allowing you begin the education process on your company and products.

SoftCom Industries
1000 East Industrial Park
Some Town, CA 94000

September 6, 1999

Mr. R.B. Walker
Vice President
Strategic Planning
State Bank Group
Mill Valley, CA 94000

Dear Mr. Walker:

We have received your request for proposal, RFP-12B-3, inviting potential bidders to prepare a proposal for providing contract maintenance services to your facilities. After a careful review of your request, we are confident that we could fulfill your maintenance needs.

However, we feel that at this time that our solution would not be a cost-effective solution for your facilities or our company. A thorough review of your RFP requirements indicates that your basic requirements can be met by companies that specialize in limited contract maintenance. We feel that while SoftCom Industries has the capabilities to provide the functions requested, our full potential would not be realized. Therefore, we are asking you to accept our no-bid to your request. However, we request that we be kept on your list of qualified bidders for future solicitations.

Because we feel that our programs could be effectively used in your industry, we would like to invite your company to a meeting concerning our capabilities in this field. We would be willing to review your RFP and submit a proposal pending changes that would allow us to fully utilize our resources. In addition, we would be pleased to present an overview of our industry and where we, as a company, are strategically heading. SoftCom Industries is making a strong commitment in this direction and would appreciate the opportunity to explore common interest with you.

Sincerely yours,

Figure 1-3. *Sample No-bid Letter*

No-bid Strategy

☜Don't be afraid to no-bid, there may be others.

If you are considering a no-bid situation because requirements are not a good fit with your products, there is a strategy to follow instead of springing the no-bid letter on the customer. As soon as possible, the onerous requirements should be identified and a letter sent to the RFP manager explaining why these requirements are too tight or they are not "consistent" with standard technology. Mention should be made that you consider these serious stumbling blocks to writing a compliant response to their RFP.

If the response to your questions is "no change," you may consider writing the no-bid letter right away. If you hope to reverse the decision, it has to be before the due date to give you enough time to complete the proposal.

An internal decision has to be made at this point: do you keep working on the proposal, anticipating a favorable change, or do you shut down. Shutting down the effort may have serious consequences and may preclude you from gearing up again as key personnel are transferred to other projects or returned to their regular position.

Remember, it is quite possible that the customer did not realize that he was combining specifications in such a manner that no single product could meet those requirements. Your explanation about this may "turn on the light" and the requirements would be changed. You might also wonder why the other vendors have not noticed this and joined you in not bidding. Is it because they have not read the RFP as carefully as you have?

Outline the RFP

Outlining forces you to read the RFP closely.

While you are trying to qualify the account, you also should be carefully reading the RFP and outlining it. This is a first-level outline with the intent of identifying two specific areas of information. The first is what can be considered standard off-the-shelf equipment and services. The second is to identify non-standard equipment and services. Once standard and non-standard items are identified, you will add this input to the bid/no-bid decision. You want to identify the "bad news" as quickly as possible to mitigate any time spent on a poor opportunity.

A simplified version of how the RFP should be broken down from a product and service point of view is illustrated below. As much as possible, all vendors like to bid standard products and services. The first consideration in reviewing an RFP is how much custom work will be needed. If your company is not set up to handle custom work, it may be better to no-bid. Many companies lose money on custom work and services whenever they try to branch out.

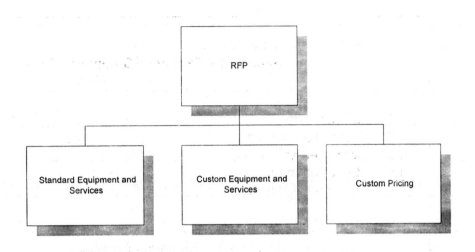

The outline that follows in figure 1-4 is a first cut at the proposal outline. Its purpose is to identify major areas of the proposal and could be taken directly from the Proposal Preparation Instructions (PPI) found in most RFPs. This outline will become the basis for the Table of Contents for your proposal.

A win strategy evolves from a close reading of the RFP.

A second reason to begin outlining the proposal is that it forces you to read the RFP. A careful reading will provide further insight into your strengths as well as providing a list of potential problems. These insights form the basis for your win strategy and will help you communicate the customer's requirements to the rest of the proposal team. An example from an RFP reads:

This subsection describes in detail the required format of the vendor's reply to this RFP. Any deviation from this format will be considered unresponsive. The remainder of this subsection will provide additional descriptions of the desired content of each item in that outline.

Section 1 – Executive Summary

1.1   Introduction
1.2   Technical Summary
1.3   Management Summary
1.4   Cost Summary
1.5   Company Overview

Section 2 – Technical Proposal

2.1   Technical Approach
2.2   Product Description
2.3   Implementation Schedules
2.4   Quality Control and Testing

Section 3 – Management Proposal

3.1   Program Management Summary
3.2   Project Personnel Resumes
3.3   Facilities and Capabilities
3.4   Service and Maintenance
3.5   Education and Training

Section 4 – Pricing

4.1   Introduction to Pricing Methodology
4.2   Equipment Pricing
4.3   Service Pricing
4.4   Totals

Figure 1-4. *Typical Proposal Outline*

■ PROPOSAL PREPARATION

The Proposal Team

✍ Make a case for getting the best resources and people.

It is essential to immediately start identifying a proposal team that will have the strengths and resources needed to generate a successful proposal. The best approach to this depends on the political nature of your company, but one rule holds: **make a strong case for requesting your best people and physical resources, and make it clear that they will be dedicated to the proposal effort for its duration.** The following are typical personnel resources needed to participate in a proposal effort:[1]

1. Technical support
   a. Engineers
   b. Quality control
   c. Testing
   d. Program management
   e. Training and education
   f. Service and maintenance
2. Writing/editing resources
3. Illustration/photography
4. Reproduction services
5. Administrative/clerical
6. Marketing support
7. Competitive analysis
8. Legal resources
9. Financial/costing
10. In-house review and evaluation personnel
11. Management approval and sign-off

As you can see from the above list, a large proposal requires many people. The greater the number of people, the more administrative support will be an absolute necessity. Figure 1-5 illustrates the basic core proposal team that is needed. The core consists of the section leaders (resource managers) who report to the proposal manager. The resources listed below the leaders are on call and will work only as needed and then return to their respective groups (a matrix management program).

---

[1] I recognize that for some companies a proposal team is the sales rep and a systems analyst. While this is a small "team," there are still other corporate and non-corporate resources that can be drawn upon. These resources should be identified as early as possible and use of their time or materials secured for use within the proposal timeframe.

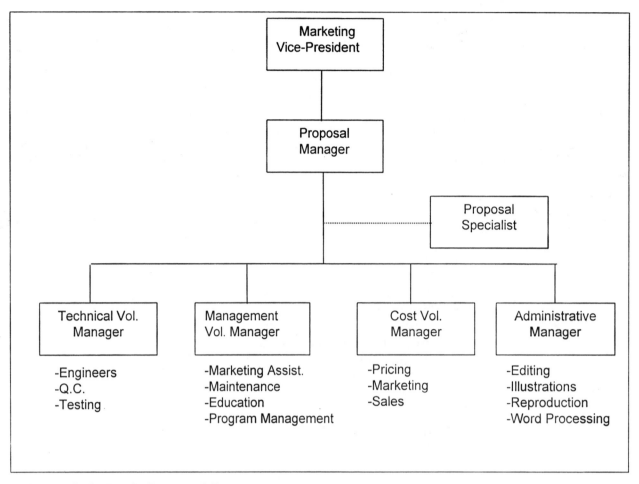

Figure 1-5. *Basic Proposal Team*

Work Space or, The Warroom

Physical resources are also important to consider and often harder to acquire and hold than people. A typical proposal resource effort will initially concentrate on getting the people assigned and **reading the** RFP. Once the proposal is started, someone will realize that there is not enough office space, there are no PCs to write the proposal on for "imported" workers, and other basic necessities are missing. This causes confusion and wastes valuable time as well as subtly telling the team that their proposal is not important enough to have the right equipment and supplies.

Designating a WorkArea

To effectively support a proposal effort, it is important that the personnel resources have a designated place to work other than their own offices or environment. If your personnel remain in their own environment, they will be subjected to the usual daily interruptions and will have difficulty working on your proposal in addition to their normal work. *If possible*, establish a large proposal warroom as a meeting and working area. This room should have ample whiteboard space, chartpacks, wall space, tables, and should be lockable. As close to the warroom as possible, locate a second room or set of rooms where the team members can set up shop. The working room also should have all of the necessities such as PCs, whiteboards, and wall space, and should be lockable. Plan on owning this space for the duration of the proposal.

✍ Commandeer a conference room and hold for the duration of the proposal effort!

Designating a Virtual Warroom

If you cannot collocate the proposal team, it is possible to form a virtual WarRoom. It may be that you will want to have both a physical space for the primary proposal team and a virtual area for the remotely located team members.

✍ Collaborative work over a network can help contain costs.

The virtual warroom would be located on a network accessible server that can be reached via local area or wide area networks or available over the Internet. The virtual warroom should have available copies of the proposal strategy, meeting minutes, and other essential data that remote users will want to read and review. The site should also contain all of the anticipated proposal boilerplate text and illustrations or a reference link to the primary site should provided.

Within the site, it should be divided between informational material, boilerplate, and the proposal sections. Proposal sections, whether completed or in-process, should be posted to the site.

Depending on your company's capabilities, the virtual warroom could be opened to your team members or partners. People outside of your company could access the warroom via an Internet connection and post or ftp files to the site. They would also be able to download current boilerplate or illustrations in addition to current schedules and the latest marketing updates.

In addition to a virtual warroom, proposal writers could use collaborative software links that allow them to collaboratively write and review files on-line. The advantage of this is that concepts and new ideas can be discussed prior to being inserted into the proposal. Collaborative software can track additions and changes in addition to maintaining the original version of the section. The volume or section leader can have access to changes and be able to finalize the section.

On-line meetings allow geographically dispersed people to meet.

Along the lines of the virtual warroom, groups of remote writers can be connected to an electronic whiteboard and be able to participate in real-time in the discussion. A host moderator can lead the discussion and be responsible for taking notes on the whiteboard. These notes are available to all participates and can be saved as files when the session is complete. Other proposal team members, who may have missed the session, can access these "chalk-talk" sessions at a later date.

An example of a virtual conference would be the proposal kickoff meeting described below. This meeting is traditionally held at the headquarters site and the primary personnel are flown in for several days. The meeting itself should be tightly structured, to maximize time, and definite actions are a result of the meeting. This meeting could be held on-line, if proper facilities are available, with great potential savings for the company.

The functionality of this type of virtual warroom will continue to grow and should be used whenever possible. The simple expense of collocating a team can easily be offset by the use of virtual warroom technologies. However, most likely the greatest increase in efficiency will be the ability of remote writers to download files, collaboratively discuss concepts on-line, and upload completed files. If a library management program is employed, potential administrative chaos will be minimized.

Develop the Winning Strategy

Along with developing the mechanics of making the proposal effort successful, it is also important to start early on the proposal strategy and what are called the "win themes." The strategy can be as simple as low-balling (or buying) the opportunity or as complex as positioning your product as a twenty-year solution based on life-cycle modeling.

Along with a strategy, you need to have win themes that are loud and clear messages to the customer. These win themes can be peppered throughout the proposal and can be positioned for different sections. For example, you may develop separate themes for your technical and management solution.

Technical win themes may be your "exclusive" product features, your adherence to standards, your ability to customize without changing core features, or your ability to integrate diverse products as needed to satisfy the requirements.

Management win themes may be your "on-time, on budget" track record, your vast experience and depth of resources, and your "exclusive" project management software.

These strategies and ideas are generally developed in a brainstorming session with people who have read the RFP, know your product, and know the competition. The ideas are presented during the proposal kickoff meeting and attendees are encouraged to add to, question, or come-up with new ideas.

A written list of strategies and themes should be maintained, updated, and given to the proposal team. They should make use of the ideas when writing their sections.

While the basic strategy and win themes should be solid, you should be prepared to modify or add or reprioritize as new information is assimilated. I have found that once the actual writing begins, a whole new set of ideas begin to flow. (I have also found that once the writing begins a whole new set of "issues" and "we can't do this" problems will emerge.)

You should, however, concentrate on one central theme, if possible, and use the lesser themes to bolster your primary strategy. For example, in a competition between software operating systems, one may be a standard not owned by any corporation while the other may be proprietary software owned by a single corporation. If we were bidding the "open" standard product, our central theme may be that the software is open, which means that it is built using agreed upon standards by an international committee. This will prevent the software from ever becoming proprietary or supporting only proprietary applications.

That is the "feature." The benefit is that the customer will not ever be tied to, or constrained by, proprietary technology and will be able to pick and choose the best hardware and application software available at the lowest price.

Competitive analysis would show us that the proprietary solution provider would try to say that his solution is also open, can operate on multiple platforms, and run multiple software applications.

Our marketing strategy, and central theme, is to convince the customer that an open platform is better (a positive) while showing the competition to be not open (a negative) without negative selling.

⟲Features should always be balanced by benefits.

We may develop secondary themes that demonstrate our open products' technical features and compare these features to the competition. Each feature would be paired with a benefit. For example, our solution's security features are much stronger and robust than the competitions. The benefit is far greater control over network access resulting in fewer, or none, break-ins by hackers. Possible second side benefit is lower overall cost because security on the rival system requires more programming, more updates, more oversight, etc., not to mention the cost of a break-in.

These features and benefits discussions should not be held in a vacuum and should not be presented as data sheet material. The discussions should relate directly to the customer and the system being planned. They should be made while discussing how some aspect of the system will be implemented, and the possible consequences of not doing it your way.

⟲Proposals are sales documents.

Remember, your proposal is a selling document competing with other proposals that may not be doing as good a job. If you think your proposal will stand, by itself, on strict technical merits, chances are you will be outsold by a lesser product.

Proposal Kickoff Meeting

Once the decision has been made to bid the RFP, call a kickoff meeting. The kickoff meeting is a combination of a serious working meeting and a pep rally. To prepare for the kickoff meeting, you will need, as a minimum, the materials listed below. Give them to the team as early as possible in order to allow them sufficient time to prepare questions and contribute intelligent comments during the meeting. If you distribute the materials the day of the meeting, team members will be reading instead of listening and will not be prepared to ask relevant questions.

- Copies of the RFP
- One- or two-page overview of the opportunity
- Detailed outline of the RFP by volume and chapter with section leaders' names assigned
- The proposal timeline with milestone dates assigned
- Review and evaluation criteria
- A style sheet
- Competitive information
- Information on the customer such as annual reports, brochures, newspaper articles
- Information on subcontractors and their products

Depending on the size of the proposal, the kickoff meeting could last from a few hours to all day. Be prepared to finish the agenda because it may be your first and only time to assemble the whole team in one place at one time—at least until the end-of-the-proposal party.

The kickoff meeting acts as a pep rally to generate the enthusiasm and energy needed to sustain the proposal effort. Remember, this is not the day-to-day work for most people, and while it may be exciting to help in the design process, it requires 110% effort.[2]

The agenda that appears in figure 1-6 is generic and may not fit your proposal or your purpose. However, the general breakdown of major points can be used for all proposals.

Morning Activities

The agenda is arranged so that the basic and, in some respects, less interesting items are presented in the morning. If you wait until after lunch, chances are you will have a limited audience and attention span.

If the proposal is large and you need to ensure visibility within your company, ask the marketing vice president, or even the company president, to open the meeting and demonstrate his or her commitment to this proposal. This is critical to the proposal effort and for getting the proper support that will be required to obtain the appropriate resources. This introduction will counter the normal reaction to doing proposals ("*Not another fire drill!*") and demonstrate upper management's belief in and commitment to the proposal manager: "And we have given Tom full authority and resources to make this a successful proposal. We feel sure that with Tom's experience and dedication, this proposal will be a winner."

With a lead-in like that, the proposal manager now has to prove himself to the group facing him. His first agenda item is to make a detailed but brief review of the proposal's major deliverables. What will the marketing approach be, what is being proposed, who is the competition, and why is his proposal going to be better? It is the general introduction by the proposal leader that will provide the needed spark of enthusiasm or sound a note of doom.

---

[2] The basic principles for the kickoff meeting should be followed even for a small two-man effort. The kickoff meeting is where it is evident that you have done your homework.

KICKOFF MEETING AGENDA

PC Network Proposal

8:30 – 9:00	Coffee and Introduction
9:00 – 9:15	Management Support
9:15 – 10:00	General Introduction
	RFP Overview
	Major Deliverables
	Marketing Approach
	Technical Approach
	Management Approach
10:00 – 10:30	General Discussion – Questions
10:30 – 10:45	Break
10:45 – 11:15	Evaluation Criteria
11:-15 – 11:30	Proposal Schedule
11:30 – 12:00	Writing, Illustration, Style Sheet Review
12:00 – 12:30	Catered Lunch
12:30 – 1:30	Competitive Analysis
	Known Competition
	Review Competition
	Gather Information from Group
1:30 – 3:00	Assignments

Figure 1-6. *Kickoff Meeting Agenda*

Plan a question and answer (Q&A) period. The Q&A time is essential to a kickoff meeting. It not only allows you to keep on schedule, but gives the participants a definite time to raise objections and get answers to questions. It is important to keep a tight schedule and not get off the track. If someone is really confused, tell that person to wait for the question and answer time or agree to see him during lunch.

Lunch should be served in the meeting room, if possible, or an area that can be set apart for the team. Lunch is an important time for the group members to talk things over, answer some questions, and informally get to know one another.

Afternoon Activities

The time after lunch is devoted to really getting started on the actual proposal assignments. However, putting the competitive analysis section first will get everyone's attention because it is interesting. Some or most of the people involved will not be familiar with a marketing analysis of the competition and will more likely pay attention.

If there is time in the schedule, consider having breakout groups for more detailed discussion of individual sections.

Work Assignments

Getting high-level visibility and approval will be crucial to the success of the proposal. Getting *anybody* to work on a proposal can be a tricky business—acquiring the right people can be difficult, if not impossible. If the proposal is important, start at the top. Once you have completed the proposal outline, go to the senior vice president or head of your division and request authority to recruit the people you need.

Depending on the size of the proposal and how it has been divided and assigned, team members will work either full or part time. This means that people working for you on the proposal will not be working on their assigned jobs and not controlled by their assigned manager.

Management Personnel

The proposal manager has to take overall responsibility for the success of the proposal. The proposal manager must be, above all else, the person who is the most excited and provides the most energy and direction. Without a strong proposal manager who has the respect of the proposal team, the outcome will be marginal at best.

Getting a good team together is going to be hard work, but keeping it together in addition to getting the results you want will be even harder. Managing disagreement among team members will be a primary concern for the proposal manager. One of the best ways to manage a proposal is to have control of all parts. The three status logs described below are tools that you can use to track your proposal from beginning to end. Depending on the size of your proposal, you may choose to use only the first log. If you are faced with a large proposal with many writers, you may choose to use the first and second logs. These are general types of logs; you may wish to create your own to meet your unique needs.

Figure 1-7 presents an overall status report for your proposal that will allow you to see at a glance where you stand and who is authoring a section. This report bundles both art and text so that if the first draft is complete, it means that the art and text are finished. The art log, figure 1-8, is an illustration log used to track the figures that will be part of your proposal. A similar log is used to track tables.

Proposal Style Sheet

✎ The diverse styles of many writers can be controlled with the use of a style sheet.

Pulling a team together to write a proposal means that you will have as many different writing styles as you do people—writing skills and styles vary widely depending on each writer's background.

Section	Title	Leader	Draft 1	Review	Draft 2	Final	Print
1	Ex. Sum	Jones	2/2	Compl.	2/6		
2	Techn.	Meyers	2/6	IP			
3	Manage.	Henry	2/4	Compl.	2/8		
4	Cost	Smith	2/10				
Appd A	An. Rpt						
Appd B	Contract						
Appd C	Data sht						

Figure 1-7. *Proposal Status*

Index Number	Ref. Number	Figure Number	Title	Author	Status Draft	Complete
HW027	1	1-1	H/W Architecture	Bud P-R	6-23	7-3
HW009	2	1-2	Workstation	Bud P-R	6-15	7-3
ED015	3	1-3	Training Schedule	Mike M.	?	??
DI007	4	1-4	Project Org. Chart	Mary E.	6-12	7-3
	5					

Figure 1-8. *Sample Art Log*

Engineers lean toward a highly technical approach while salespeople tend to use marketing buzz words and hard-sell adjectives. Ideally, if your company is large enough to afford it, you would have an editorial staff to meld the various styles so that the proposal has a consistent approach throughout. But many sales proposals are done in the field office with little or no help offered by headquarters. Lacking editorial support, what is your alternative?

✍ *The style sheet should not be overly complex.*

One viable solution is the development of a style guide, often called a style sheet. The main purpose of the style sheet is to make the proposal look like it comes from one company with one consistent message. It should not be so complicated that no one will use it. It should address the overall format of the proposal (such as treatment of section titles, level heads, headers, footers, figure references, etc.); the correct spelling (including use of capital letters) of other companies' names and products (as well as your own); often-used expressions (both English and Latin); and some general guidelines for style in regard to compound words, hyphenation, treatment of numbers and dates, and the like.

This tool can be used by all the writers, regardless of their location with respect to each other. Chapter 2, *Proposal Contents: Overview*, has more information on developing a style guide.

■ PROPOSAL ACTIVITIES

Proposal Leader's Responsibilities

Once the team is formed and the kickoff meeting has taken place, what are the primary steps in keeping the proposal on schedule? Depending on the size of the effort, the proposal leader should at this time be concentrating on outlining the Executive Summary and Cover Letter, and developing the pricing material.

✍An executive summary is a short, concise, and self-contained document.

The Executive Summary is exactly what its name implies: a summary of the proposal, which will be read by a busy top-level executive who will often have time only to read this part of the proposal (and take a look at the pricing.). It follows, then, that the proposal manager should expend a considerable amount of time in summarizing exactly what you can do, how you will do it, how many times you have already done it, and at what cost. This summary usually turns into a living document, reflecting changes as your proposal evolves, and is often the last volume completed, even though it was the first started. More detailed discussion on executive summaries is provided in Section 3.

In addition to writing and costing, the proposal leader will have to be available to answer questions, make critical decisions, settle disputes, and enforce schedule deadlines. Because of these managerial functions, his actual writing duties should be kept to a bare minimum.

Developing RFP Questions

Another ongoing activity will be developing and sending to the customer questions that clarify the RFP. The question and answer activity is very important to the RFP/Proposal process. It allows you "official" interaction with the prospective customer and gives you the potential to develop a relationship with the people associated with the RFP. Questions and answers should be viewed by both sides as a positive means of communication between customer and vendor. During the actual RFP period, communications are restricted and limited, sometimes forced or strained, and always suspect by the customer. Developing a good rapport throughout the Q&A period allows both parties to interact officially and to develop a good working relationship, if one was not established before the RFP was released.

✍Good questions can give you a strategic edge over your competition.

There are strategies for asking questions. One is to let the first round of questions be submitted and answered and hope that your questions will be asked by your competitors. This allows you to keep

✎*Be circumspect when writing questions that will be published.*

your bidding and position somewhat quiet while allowing your competition to expose their position. Good question writing is a balance between giving them enough information to understand the problem, but not giving enough for your competition to understand your strategy.

Generally, all questions submitted are gathered by the customer, answered as a group and all questions and responses returned to all bidders. Published questions usually do not include your company name, but it is usually possible to identify companies because they give away too much information.

There will be some questions that have to be asked before your proposal effort can move forward. One of the first steps in organizing the proposal effort is to get the RFP to the key technical people for their review. If these critical questions are not discovered until near the end of the cycle, *it may be too late*. Questions are usually requested to be submitted several days before the bidders' conference.

Written questions submitted prior to the bidders' conference will be answered first and a printed copy of the answers will be sent to all bidders. Oral questions will be answered as time permits except when a question is deemed too technical to be adequately answered during the conference. All oral and written questions will be responded to in writing

✎*Don't hesitate to question conflicting requirements and standards.*

RFPs are written to satisfy a general need and usually will have conflicting standards or products that do not actually exist in the marketplace. If you allow conflicts to remain unquestioned or try to use these conflicts as a means of justifying a non-compliant bid, there is a reasonable chance that your proposal will be disqualified.

Developing questions to be submitted should be a carefully monitored activity. All federal and state RFPs have this type of statement: "All questions and answers from all bidders will be published and returned to all bidders without identifying the submitters." Many commercial companies are now adding this phrase to their RFPs. This means that all questions should be carefully screened before being sent in order not to compromise your solution. If you need to ask a question that could give your competitors an advantage, first contact the person listed in the RFP as being responsible for all contacts and determine whether your question will be published for all participants. If you are able to submit a question in confidence, list that question separately from all others, submit it in a second envelope, and mark it *Confidential and Proprietary.*

Confidential and Proprietary should also be marked on the page with the question.

How to phrase and ask questions should also be considered. There are generally three types of questions asked:

1. The first identifies a requirement or statement that is possibly incorrect in the RFP and you are seeking clarification. This could be from ignorance or a simple mistake on the part of the RFP writer. For example, a requirement may be for a 32 page-per-minute (ppm) printer when there are no printers on the market that operate at 32 ppm.

2. The second type of question is to ask if your interpretation of a requirement is correct. A question of this type might ask if supplying two 16 page-per-minute printers would satisfy a 32 page-per-minute requirement.

3. The third is to ask (and demonstrate) that a requirement should be revised because it is too limiting, revised because it is not an industry standard, or deleted because technology is not presently available. For example, the requirement is for a UNIX operating system and that eliminates other operating systems that could operate and offer a competitive solution.

Because all questions can be read and reviewed by all participants, questions can become a source of competitive information. If your company is the only one with an XYZ operating system and you identify it in the question, you have possibly given your competition an edge in understanding your position.

✎ *Questions are generally available for all to see. Be cautious in your wording.*

A copy of all questions and answers should be kept with other documents associated with the proposal. As questions are asked and answered, the RFP specifications and requirements may change. These changes may not always be incorporated as an addendum to the RFP and therefore not incorporated into a subsequent contract. If you win the award and are asked to negotiate a contract, ensure that the contract acknowledges all questions and answers as part of the RFP, Proposal, and Questions and Answers.

Generally speaking, if a question causes a requirement to be changed, a formal addendum to the RFP will be published. Answers to questions are not, in the strictest sense, recognized as officially changing requirements unless accompanied by a change addendum.

Below are some sample questions culled from various RFP/proposal efforts. These are meant to give you a flavor for the detail of some questions and the responses by the customers. The fictional company ACME will be used in place of actual company names.

Q. Will ACME be responsible for writing the host side of the system control software interface link?

A. Yes. ACME will provide the host side of the link; however, bidders must provide a specification for the link.

Q. Paragraph 6.4 requires printing of images that have been rotated. This is not possible given the printer specifications. Will you rescind this requirement or change the printer requirement?

A. We rescind the requirement for printing rotated images.

Q. Who performed the needs analysis for this RFP?

A. ACME performed the needs analysis with internal resources.

Q. This requirement requires an effectiveness level of 90%, which appears to be in conflict with paragraph 5.2 that states a 95% effectiveness level is required. Please clarify.

A. You are correct. The requirement will be amended to require 95% effectiveness level.

Q. This vendor requests that the demonstration plan be due two weeks after the initial proposal submission.

A. The requirement remains as stated.

Q. The RFP training price table does not include travel costs. Are we to assume that travel costs for trainers are reimbursable?

A. No. Travel costs will not be separately reimbursable, but should be included in the fixed price for each class.

Q. Please delete the evaluation of performance tests and reviews. This gives an unfair advantage to certain products.

A. The evaluation will be conducted as stated.

It appears that some questions are meant to annoy the customer. It also appears that some questions have been asked because the vendor did not fully read the RFP. Customers will get a sense from these questions which vendors are "for real" and which vendors are not serious. Being labeled as "not serious" will have a potential negative impact on your efforts.

On the other hand, good questions, even aggressive questions, demonstrate to the customer that you are reading the RFP and have given it serious consideration.[3]

■ IN-HOUSE REVIEW

✍ The review team must understand what the customer is asking for, not what is being proposed.

One of the more important jobs to be completed is an in-house review and sign-off of the proposal. The process of assembling your proposal review team starts when you select the proposal team. As early as possible, reviewers should be selected and given copies of the RFP. Their job is to begin reading their section of the RFP to gain an understanding of what the customer is asking for, not necessarily what is going to be proposed. In most cases, it is better not to give the reviewers advance copies or high-level summaries of the proposal so that they may keep their *customer perspective.*

The selection of the reviewers should be based on the subject of the proposal. For example, if the proposal is to design and implement a large data communications network, you would have to have a specialist in network design on the team. However, don't get caught in the "technical-only" trap. This means that each major section of the proposal should be reviewed as closely as the technical section. A non-technical section could deal with customer education or how service and maintenance will be provided.

✍ The Red Team's review simulates the customer's evaluation of the proposal.

This in-house evaluation, normally called a *Red Team Review,* is considered a formal process. The Red Team will use the evaluation criteria in the RFP as a basis for evaluating your proposal. This review is supposed to simulate as closely as possible how the customer will make his evaluation; while it may sometimes get bloody, and should, it is meant to be constructive. The Red Team review should be a milestone on the proposal schedule with adequate time to hold the review and integrate the corrections, comments, and notes that will be its results.

To be effective, the review team should use a copy of the proposal that is very close to being final. This copy should be assembled and printed with all illustrations, photographs, and other artwork just as it would be for the final proposal.

---

[3] Having been on the writing side of RFPs, I can say that there is much discussion among the RFP team as to which vendors are "with it" and which vendors are "clueless." Many vendors hurt their chances by demonstrating their lack of knowledge of the RFP and their industry by their questions.

The Red Team members should be isolated during the review and not allowed to work at their normal locations. This will prevent reviewers from being distracted and interrupted, which would lower the quality of the review. Clerical assistance should be made available when needed to minimize interruptions. If the proposal is short and can be reviewed in one or two days, accommodations such as lunch and dinner should be made in advance.

After all reviews are complete, there should be a debriefing session, if possible, with the proposal team. The purpose of the debriefing is not to nit-pick, but to identify general trends and ideas that will make the proposal stronger. To prevent this from becoming a general bull session without purpose, the proposal leader and Red Team leader should formally direct the debriefing.

The Red Team can write its comments on the proposal itself, or use a special form that allows the reviewer to identify sections and paragraphs and has space for comments and suggestions for correcting the problems. In all cases, make sure that each reviewer signs and returns his copy of the proposal. Large proposals and complicated reviews should be controlled by numbering and assigning each copy to a reviewer.

Be prepared for a difficult time, if you are the proposal leader, from both the reviewers and your own team. It is natural for a certain amount of animosity to be generated during this process. One common complaint from the proposal writers is that "We've worked for weeks developing the XYZ network and some hotshot tears it apart in one day without even knowing what was behind the design." If the Red Team criticism is valid, the customer may have the same problem and ask the same questions. It is the proposal manager's job to maintain an objective attitude toward the criticisms and settle any disputes that might arise.

≥ Keep inevitable conflicts that arise from a Red Team evaluation in proper perspective.

After the review, do you have to incorporate the Red Team's comments? Although some comments will not be valid or relevant to the proposal because of a misunderstanding on the reviewer's part, all comments should be noted with the understanding that if a reviewer from your company, ostensibly familiar with your equipment and services, had a problem, the real customer's reviewer may have the same problem. That is, parts of the proposal can be technically correct but worded so poorly as to cause confusion.

When the review is complete, those review items that will have impact on the proposal should be separated form the general lot. If you are working with a team, the section leaders will receive the comments that are appropriate to his section. The proposal team is responsible for incorporating the changes.

If the changes are so sweeping as to impact the proposal schedule, the appropriate Red Team member(s) should be drafted to help make the changes. For example, a major design change may need extensive work and may depend on the originator of that change to formalize the new specifications.

Virtual Red Team

If you are using technology to develop a virtual warroom, you may also want to develop a virtual Red Team concept. The red team members would not have to be collocated and would be able to provide their reviews as part of an on-line video conference. Comments on proposals could be uploaded to the Internet site and distributed to members of the proposal team. If Red Team members had electronic copies of the proposal, their comments would become red line comments using the red line feature of the word processor. This way, comments could be incorporated directly into the proposal, if appropriate.

The concept is to have the general comments and reviews made as part of the video conference and supporting documentation available through the Internet warroom site.

The cost-benefit of this type of operation would pay back any investment on the first proposal. This assumes a commitment to technology by your company.

■ SCHEDULE

⊗Reverse scheduling gives a true indication of the time required.

Most proposals done in the field office are not adequately reviewed before being sent out because the review is treated as a we'll-do-it-if-there's-time situation. Time in a proposal is more important than anything but is the most often neglected consideration.

The most common mistake in proposal writing is poor scheduling and, therefore, not realizing how many actual working days are available. For example, let's take an RFP that is received on the first of the month and is due in thirty days. The first step is to work backwards from the due date. A more formal schedule should be created that reflects all of the tasks associated with the proposal. If a project management software package is utilized, the software will track much more detail allowing you to drill down to the lowest level task. However, these programs require a fair degree of updating and maintenance, which may begin to impact other time required for writing and reviewing. If the proposal is large enough to warrant the use of this type of program, and you have adequate resources, it will be very helpful.

First, if the proposal is due at 2:00 P.M. and the customer's receiving point is not in your state, you basically have two choices: finish in enough time to mail the proposal or work up to the day before, forcing you to use an overnight service. Either way, two days are lost in transport and delivery. That means you now have twenty-eight days.

Second, if you are having a print shop copy your proposal on a professional machine, they will want at least one full day to do the job. Actually, depending on the size and quality required, a printer will not schedule your job if you can't give him two full working days. Two more days are now lost to printing and packaging the proposal. The twenty-eight days now become twenty-six actual working days. Companies that have their own in-house print shops can probably print and package all but the largest of the proposals in one day.

Third, if the proposal is large enough to warrant visibility at the higher levels, those higher levels will want to review and sign off before you release it to a customer. Plan on one day for the review and sign-off, and one day to make the corrections. This now leaves twenty-four working days. However, one full day is usually consumed in getting ready for the review, so really only twenty-three days are actually available.

Fourth, if the RFP was not addressed to you, you did not receive or start working on the proposal the day it arrived. It is possible that the RFP was sent to the division headquarters vice president because the customer thought it would get more visibility or the VP was at a trade show and talked with the prospect. His secretary, who received the RFP, put it in his "must-read basket" because she didn't know what to do with it. Also, RFPs are often sent to corporate purchasing because the company's purchasing department name is on the qualified bidders' list. In any event, the RFP took two full days to get to you or your boss who said at 5:00, "Got a minute?"

Finally, we are now down to twenty-one actual working days without any work whatsoever having been done on the proposal. Take one more day to thoroughly read the RFP and we have reduced the working time by 33 percent. And, this does not take into account other normal holdups that occur during the proposal writing period, such as getting the RFP printed so that copies can be distributed or waiting for the customer to respond to questions that have stopped the effort until answered.

If a schedule is not developed and followed, it will be almost impossible to complete and submit a reasonable proposal. As with most projects, time spent in planning will more than pay for itself. When developing your proposal schedule, try to plan time as realistically as possible.

✍Anticipate problems and develop solutions.

Don't add an extra day to the Red Team review just because you might need it. On the other hand, suppose you are printing your proposal on your office copy machine and it breaks down, and it is already past closing so getting repairs is out of the question. Look for and plan for problems, anticipate bottlenecks, and develop potential solutions.

If all else fails, ask for an extension to the due date by writing a letter to the customer explaining why you need the extension. This request should be done as soon in the proposal cycle as possible. A request for extension sent the day before the proposal is due indicates poor planning on your part and the request may not be granted. In the letter try to be as factual as possible and point out that you will complete the proposal. Figure 1-9 is an example of a request for extension letter.

■ POST-PROPOSAL ACTIVITIES

When the proposal is finished and turned in, there are still many tasks to be accomplished. After a long proposal-writing period, it is natural to leave the clean-up to administrative personnel, and for the primary participants to move on to the next sales opportunity while proposals are being evaluated. Not completing and paying attention to the post-proposal work is one way to lose control of post-proposal activities. See Appendix G, Post-proposal Activities.

✍Having an audit trail will be invaluable at the completion of the proposal.

First, all associated documentation with the RFP and proposal should be filed in chronological order. This will establish an audit trail for you when you begin negotiations and the customer wants a detailed explanation and justification for your proposal. Establishing the audit trail is most important for non-standard products and pricing, and will allow you to recreate the circumstances and understand why a product was chosen, how it was priced, and what trade-offs were made at that time. Having the audit trail for pricing decisions will be invaluable when you are trying to determine the basis for a greater than normal discount.

SoftCom Industries
1000 East Industrial Park
Some Town, CA 94000

September 6, 1999

Mr. R.B. Walker
Vice President
Strategic Planning
State Bank Group
Mill Valley, CA 94000

Dear Mr. Walker:

We have received your addendum to your request for proposal, RFP-12B-3, and have reviewed the changes to the original requirements. After a careful review of your addendum, we are confident that we could fulfill your maintenance needs and submit a responsive proposal.

However, we feel that in view of the scope of the changes we cannot prepare an adequate response in the time allocated. Therefore, SoftCom is requesting a 10-day extension to your requested completion date of January 30.

With this extension, SoftCom will have the needed time to more fully evaluate the changes and redesign our solution to meet the new requirements. Only after the redesign effort can we begin to develop new pricing. If the extension is not granted, SoftCom feels that we will not have had the appropriate amount of time to develop and write a satisfactory proposal. Without the additional time, we would have to submit a no-bid to your request.

Thank you for your consideration.

Sincerely,

Bud Porter-Roth

Bud Porter-Roth
President

Figure 1-9. *Sample Request for Extension*

⚲Additional post-proposal activities will be required if you make the short list.

Second, when the proposal has been awarded to your company, there will be several requests by internal departments in your company for a complete copy of the proposal. For example, if a project manager has been assigned, he will want a copy of everything to start his project notebook. This will include why product decisions were made and the corresponding documentation that supports that decision. It is also probable that both legal (or contracts) and accounting will require copies of the proposal once the final negotiations are started. Don't forget the Maintenance and Training Department, if they will be involved.

Third, after your proposal is turned in, there are other activities that will generate questions from the customer and responses from you and the proposal team. These documents should be filed with the proposal documents and include any appropriate annotations for future analysis.

⚲The customer will also send you questions to clarify your proposal.

Customer generated questions are a good sign and mean that they are giving your proposal a close reading. Any response that is less than 100% will hurt your effort. Getting a proper answer may mean going back to a team member (who has already returned to his real work) and working with him to understand why something was decided or positioned a certain way.

Fourth, if your proposal makes the *short list* or you become a finalist in the competition, there will be several more steps required of you and your company before the contract is awarded. Typically, customers will weed out proposals that are not compliant in an effort to get down to two or three vendors—the short list. For those who have made the short list, there will potentially be an oral presentation of the proposal followed by a demonstration of the equipment proposed. The customer will visit at least one of your reference sites; the customer may request a headquarters visit and tour of your company (and its books). Finally, there will be a negotiation period once the customer feels that you have the winning proposal.

Negotiations will be in writing (usually) and will potentially cause you to change your proposal and pricing to match the agreement. For example, a customer may decide to have training on-site instead of your facilities (or visa versa) and that changes the price and other contractual incidentals.

■ PROPOSAL DISPOSITION ACTIVITIES

When the customer has made a decision, and the contract is awarded, a win/loss review should be held. The purpose of this review is to help you discover why you won or lost, and how this information can be used by you and your company. See Appendix I, Proposal Disposition, for an example of a proposal debriefing questionnaire.

If you win the proposal, it is good to understand why you won and apply that knowledge to your next proposal and be able to incorporate that knowledge into the corporate proposal database. Being a winner makes it easier because the customer is now your customer and will be happy to tell you why you won and the others lost. Documenting why the other companies lost is part of understanding why you won.

If you lose the proposal, you should be very interested in why your efforts (time, money, resources, and reputation) were not rewarded and how you can improve your next proposal. The information received from the customer should be reviewed with your management and if correctable problems have been identified, a plan should be put into place to make the necessary adjustments.

In either case, you should formally contact the customer and request a debriefing. This should be in person, or at least as a teleconference, and at one-half hour allocated. The customer person should be someone on the proposal team, not a contracts or procurement person. Be prepared to be diligent in asking your questions and getting to some real issues. Most customers are hesitant, if you lose, to get into too much detail and may cite the standard "Your pricing was too high." Of course this may be the reason but high-bidders often win the proposal, so I would not let that be the end of the session.

The real reasons for losing a proposal can be varied and mixed:

- Your proposal didn't really address the requirements, and instead sold what you make, not what was asked for.
- Your proposal may have been total boilerplate with little or no substance to document your effort.
- Your demonstration/site visit may have been ill coordinated and left the customer with a negative impression of your company and management skills.
- Perhaps your proposal was poorly written with many grammar and spelling mistakes.

Responses, like those above, should be brought to management's attention. These are correctable and reflect a company's values, especially in tactical and strategic thinking.

Developing a list or reasons why you won will also help you and your management to reinforce the value of setting up a proposal development program. The cost of the program, compared to previously losing proposals can quickly be cost justified and even more resources can be made available as the win rate increases.

■ ALTERNATE PROPOSALS

Alternate proposals are usually a headache for both you and the potential customer. In most RFPs there is a statement that alternate proposals will be accepted and reviewed subject to the time available. The RFP also will say that, in the event that an alternate proposal is submitted, (most Federal and State governments are firm on this point.) a fully responsive proposal to the original requirements also must be submitted:

Vendors may submit more than one proposal, each of which must satisfy the mandatory requirements of the solicitation in order to be considered. All vendors who wish to submit an alternate proposal must submit a baseline proposal that is fully compliant to all requirements. No alternate proposals will be accepted as stand-alone proposals.

✍ *The solution you bid may meet the requirements but would not be considered responsive.*

From your point of view, since the RFP was written without specifying your technology, the customer either did not do his homework and was not aware of the technology you could provide, or does not believe that a certain technology can solve the problem. You believe that by taking an alternate approach to the problem, using technology not asked for in the RFP, you could more than satisfy the RFP requirements.

It is almost impossible for any customer to keep ahead of today's technology. Because of rapidly changing technology, the high cost of writing RFIs/RFPs, and decreasing time due to intense competition, RFPs may not be as well researched as possible. Also because of personal prejudices and ignorance, some technologies are not considered when an RFP is written. Because of these reasons, the technology you bid may in fact meet the requirements but would not be considered responsive.

For example, an RFP asks for a personal computer system to do desktop publishing and requires the system to run a certain type of software specified by name. This requirement effectively eliminates the software that you would normally propose to satisfy the requirements. If you were to propose your solution only, your proposal would be eliminated. If you were to propose the requested software, and in an alternate proposal provide your software, your proposal would be evaluated.

The hitch in this reasoning is that your company may not represent the "other" technology and therefore you could not actually propose it. See the section above on writing a no-bid letter and the section above about writing questions.

Evaluators will put all alternate proposals on the shelf until the baseline proposals have been evaluated. If there is time and the alternates have potential, they will also be reviewed.

≥Alternate proposals are risky and time consuming.

Most companies have trouble submitting a single responsive proposal by itself, not to mention submitting a complete alternate proposal. There is no simple answer to the alternate proposal trap except to talk to the RFP director before writing the alternate proposal. If your technology is not present in the RFP, and you have to submit an alternate proposal in order to bid your product, you should carefully consider what your chance of winning is and whether you should spend the time writing a proposal.

■ WRITING LEVELS

There are basically three levels of writing in a proposal:

≥There are three levels of writing in a proposal.

- Technical detail. The first level of writing explains how your product works and describes how it meets the requirements. This is straightforward "cut and dried" writing that may use existing boilerplate to provide the technical details.
- Marketing detail. The second level of writing covers marketing themes based on the benefits of using your products: saves space, reduces time, increases productivity, reduces manpower, etc. This is the "features/benefits" pitch and is a combination of exiting standard themes that are tailored to the RFP requirements.
- Business detail. The third level of writing develops a business case for purchasing your equipment by specifically relating the technical and marketing detail to a particular situation. The object of this last type of writing is to develop specific and tangible reasons why and how your equipment will enhance the customer's business. This is fresh writing geared specifically for this RFP.

An example will illustrate how these three levels of writing are applied and the consequences of omitting any of them.

Electronic document management is a technology that allows a company to electronically scan all of its paper records and store those records on optical disk. This requires a customer to buy new computers, optical disk drives, storage machines called *jukeboxes* to house the optical platters, and other associated equipment that may not connect to any other device or computer currently installed.

Because this is a very competitive industry, many companies are selling technology: faster computers, more memory, bigger disk drives, faster communications, etc. They may only concentrate on the first level because they believe bigger, better, and faster is all they need to sell the product. However, unless you proceed to the next level, the benefits, the *customer* will have to determine why your bigger, better, faster is more advantageous than your competition's bigger, better, faster, and the customer's assessment may not be correct.

The second level of writing, for the document management industry, typically includes such benefits as reduced storage space, reclamation of floor space, fewer workers, faster access to documents, and increased productivity. One proposal included the following as a prime benefit of its system:

The workflow facility within our system is aimed at automating the flow of work through the procedural office. No longer is paper-based information 'in the mail' or sitting in an in-box. No clerical staff is required to manage the movement of important files and documents through an organization. This reduces expenses associated with the processing, storage, and retrieval of paper-based information.

In this case, no contract was awarded to any of the competing vendors, even though the above benefits seemed substantial at a first reading, i.e., reduced staff, reduced storage, etc.

Two separate but related reasons conspired to stop the sale:

1. The customer recognized that his company was experiencing increasing costs and diminishing returns due to an increase in paper-based work, but he did not understand how to solve the problem, what he needed to buy, or how to deal with the way his business would be affected by the purchase of new equipment. The customer determined that he could gain more than half of the benefits proposed by all vendors by simply hiring more people and renovating the filing system, thus saving substantial money by upgrading existing equipment and work routines rather than automating. His final conclusion was that computerization not only would not add anything new, but it would cost more to do it.

2. The vendors failed to recognize the customer's fundamental requirements by offering automation and listing the gains without providing him an overall financial analysis of how the system would affect his business. In this case no cost justifications were completed to substantiate the benefits.

In the above example, the last sentence begins, but does not complete, the transition to the third level: "This reduces expenses associated with...." The customer was been left to interpret what those reduced "expenses" actually mean. Not being an expert in this area, and not able to justify the system, the customer **made the safe** decision: don't buy.

What this customer really wanted, and the vendors failed to provide, was a system that would show a return on investment. In any technology purchase, the safe decision to not buy must be overcome. Many customers who want to buy but don't, don't buy simply because vendors did not do their job.

The third level provides the customer with a detailed financial analysis of the proposed benefits. Third-level writing is illustrated in the following excerpt:

Purchasing an optical-based storage system has many advantages in addition to simply adding efficiencies to your operation. Many of our customers have not taken into account the hidden costs associated with paper-based systems. These hidden costs include repair and replacement of filing cabinets and hardware; costs for reproduction including buying and/or replacing reproduction machines, maintenance and service on reproduction machines, and paper costs; time and motion inefficiencies due to physical paper handling; replacement costs for documents that are lost, misplaced, mutilated or simply worn out from use; and customer service delays caused by documents that are not available. While some costs are tangible (such as annual repair and replacement of filing cabinets), others, although somewhat intangible (such as the amount of time it takes to access a paper document in a file as opposed to access electronically), can be analyzed and a value placed on them. The following table is an industry survey that represents approximate costs and savings by adopting imaging technology The second table represents a suggested return on investment analysis based on our understanding of your current situation. We suggest that [our company] be allowed to do a similar study for your specific application in order to determine the actual return on investment period that will serve as a base line for future evaluation of the project.

The last example demonstrates a number of important concepts:

- An in-depth understanding of what is being sold
- An understanding of what the customer's requirements are
- An awareness of the needs of the customer
- A willingness to help the customer make the right decision
- A demonstrated knowledge of the cost benefits

Although the above examples were taken from one type of business, computerized document storage and retrieval, the basic principles hold for other industries and services.

That is, capitol expenditures need to be justified against other projects being considered. A financial analysis of the various projects being considered will determine which projects are going to produce the best return on investment.

Reviewing the three levels again:

1. The first is technical detail that provides the customer with a good foundation

2. The second begins to weave the features and benefits and positions your product against the competition

3. The third provides a financial and business basis for making the decision

■ SUMMARY

A proposal is unique in that it combines an individual's and a team's strengths, weaknesses, and product knowledge, under circumstances not quite controllable, into a document that cannot be duplicated given a similar set of people and requirements. Understanding and duplicating the "winning" proposal process is difficult. Trying to institutionalize and codify the process is an almost, if not outright, impossible task—as if we could understand and re-create at will what is basically a creative and synergistic process. However, as a process, a proposal does have definable and repeatable steps that will help you get closer to winning. That is what this book is about.

⊠ Every proposal is a unique project requiring a creative, synergistic process.

Winning or losing is not based on the proposal or document itself, but on a set of almost controllable variables such as customer knowledge of the technology, pricing, personal contact, sales skills and abilities, and a number of intangibles. One often-heard quote from proposal writers is, "I'll take luck over hard work any day." This is not to say that winning a proposal is sheer luck or that you have no control over the process.

Examining why a proposal was lost can give you valuable insight for the next proposal.

It may be easier to understand why proposals are won by examining why they are lost. An analysis of the following excerpt from an RFP debriefing will demonstrate this principle:

[Many] bid responses were received; however, none of the bidders met the specifications for the computer system. Listed below are the reasons for not meeting the specifications:

- File server not included as specified.
- Specifications called for a landscape-type monitor and bid was for portrait-type monitor.
- Data transmission rate was only 2.5 MBPS and specifications called for 10 MBPS.
- Specifications stipulated enough RAM to store ten documents at the workstation. System bid does not store documents at the workstation.
- Printer stations did not include a controller as specified.
- Bid price did not include cost of training as specified.
- Delivery prices were not included as specified.
- Installation prices were not included as specified.

Therefore, it is recommended that all bids be rejected, specifications be modified and the item be re-bid at a later date.

Some proposals are lost simply because someone didn't follow the rules. A bidder believes his product or service to be superior to that being asked for in the RFP and neglects to meet the requirements as stated, believing his superior proposal will win anyway. Some proposals are lost because of negligence, such as not providing all cost data required. Some bidders do not follow the proposal preparation instructions to the letter, thinking that their technical solution is enough to win.

Everyone is selling.

It is a mistake to think that a proposal will win on its own merits, whether those merits be the best technical solution, the lowest price, or overall compliance to the requirements. Every vendor will have a technically superior solution, be willing to have the lowest price, and be the most compliant or have excellent reasons why they do not need to be compliant. Everyone is selling.

A proposal can be compared in some respects to a person using a resume to get a job. The job seeker will not be hired based solely on resume, but will be interviewed once or several times before a decision is made. However, it was the resume that got the interview, and without the interview there would be no job offer.

⌖A proposal is similar to a resume for your company. First impressions count.

A proposal is similar to the resume in that few, if any, contracts are based solely on the evaluation of the proposal. If the proposal is good, meets all or most of the requirements, and has a reasonable pricing structure, it will get you through the door so that you are on the short list. The short-listed proposals are now given a very thorough evaluation, and detailed questions are usually asked by the customer. The technical level of questions and what area of the proposal is being questioned will give you an indication of what to expect when you are making an oral presentation. Vendors who are on the short list now have a chance to demonstrate their solution, sell that solution at the oral presentation, and re-adjust their strategy, and negotiate pricing, if asked. Also, they now have the face-to-face contact with the customer that is needed in order to win the proposal. Selling the proposal and your company's ability to follow through is what it will take to win the business.

There are certain steps that can be institutionalized in the proposal *development process:*

1. Read the RFP. This is the most important step, the easiest to remember, and yet the one usually not given enough attention. So many RFPs are poorly written with ill-defined requirements that a casual reading of the requirements section will simply not suffice. Remember, inexperienced people are trying to by your product, it is up to you to help them.

2. Qualify the customer. Understanding the background reasons for the RFP, who is involved and at what level, and if the project is funded are key points to qualifying the RFP. A well-written no-bid letter could save you and your company time and money. Know the business reasons behind an RFP will give you additional insight into the customer and help you write a better proposal.

3. Prepare a competitive analysis. Bidding without doing competitive analysis will cause one of two things to happen: you may overprice in an effort not to leave money on the table; or you will under-price and leave money on the table. Competitive analysis also tells you where your products stands vis a' vis the competition and lets you emphasize your strong points, minimize your weak points, and point out possible flaws in your competition.

4. Organize the resources. Only when you understand the magnitude of the effort (by reading the RFP), can you determine

what resources are required. Most inexperienced proposal writers wait too long to get started. When they do get started, it may be too late to solve some internal problems, ask questions, and do competitive analysis.

5. Develop a proposal plan. The success of the proposal will depend entirely on the execution of the proposal plan. The most common error is planning only through the end of the proposal and not including post-proposal activities such as questions and answers, oral presentations, demonstrations, and final negotiations.

6. Get proposal plan approval. Organization, resource allocation, and scheduling will fall short unless the "resource owners" make the resources available. Selling your proposal effort to management is required. (In some cases this will be tougher than selling to the customer.)

Hold a formal bid/no-bid meeting. A bid/no-bid is a formal method of identifying risks, assessing them, addressing them, and getting group consent to continue or stop the process before spending more time. It also allows you to formally identify potential resources needed to "cover the bases."

7. Review the completed proposal Similar to the bid/no-bid situation, you are now getting management approval for how you handled the risks identified in the bid/no-bid meeting.

8. Read the RFP. Once your proposal is complete, a careful re-reading of the RFP will reveal any missing elements in addition to allowing you to checkpoint your selling strategies.

9. Remember, only you are in charge. You will get the credit whether you win or lose. Reward without risk is uncommon, and proposals involve risk.

I have worked with some people who would have missed the deadline because of their fanatical effort to make the proposal perfect. It is essential to strike a balance between getting the job done as well as you can and the time given to do it. A perfect, but late, proposal will accomplish nothing for you or your company.

Although each proposal is unique, there are steps that can be institutionalized. Your company will reap many benefits from an organized, well-planned, and carefully written proposal, in addition to obtaining more business. Once you become proficient and begin developing and preparing more and more successful proposals, you will discover that winning can become a definable and repeatable process.

Your company will also benefit from an organized and efficient proposal development process. Setting down procedures for bidding/not bidding, organizing company information, training people involved in proposal writing, and following up on why you win or lose proposals will increase your win rate.

Overview

Each proposal should be treated as
a unique opportunity.

Overview

■ INTRODUCTION

Although every proposal is unique in content, there are basic sections that are standard to all proposals. The contents of the proposal will be covered in the following chapters:

Chapter 2, *Overview*

Cover requirements, the material that makes up the front matter, and how the proposal as a whole is formatted.

Chapter 3, *Essential Sections*

The Executive Summary, Technical Section, Management Section, Pricing Section, and appendices.

Chapter 4, *Boilerplate Files*

Detailed information on selecting suitable material and creating boilerplate files.

Chapter 5, *Illustrations*

Various types of illustrations and how to use them.

■ PROPOSAL COVER

Many salespeople who develop small proposals in field offices use no formal cover and submit the proposal in a binder or use a report-style cover. However, in most cases, this can be easily upgraded using some simple graphics and a word processor. It adds a degree or professionalism to the proposal when the customer is identified along with the RFP project name.

A standard cover should be developed that reflects your company's product. If your company produces a significant number of proposals, you may want to invest some time and money to have custom artwork designed that can be used for proposal covers as well as for special reports submitted to customers. A master copy of the artwork may be left with a printer who then can print the customer's name, project title, and other information on the cover as needed. The cost of printing covers with pre-prepared artwork is small and the turnaround time is relatively short.

If you are writing a major proposal for an important account, you may consider having a special cover designed with your company name printed or embossed on the front and spine. A unique or custom cover gives your proposal a professional look as well as making it easy to identify.

Think of what best represents your company visually. Care should be taken not to clutter or make the cover too heavy. It should be simple, clean, and have impact. The following are some ideas for the types of illustrations that can be used on the front cover:

- If your company sells computer equipment, use a line drawing or a photograph of your equipment or a person operating it.
- If your company provides a software product such as a spreadsheet, a lightly overprinted copy of the output would be interesting.
- If your product is service, use a line drawing or photograph of people performing the service.

The information that is printed on the cover must include, as a minimum, all of the following (see figures 2-1 and 2-2):

- Your company's name (use your logo, if you have one)
- The name of the customer
- The name of the project
- Volume information (optional)

If there are multiple volumes, the volume number and volume name may be included. For example, Volume 1, in the lower right.

- The date

Always date the proposal cover with the due date that is stated in the RFP or letter of extension. Even if you think you will be submitting it early, you may have a delay and the cover must be printed well in advance.

In summary, a professional looking cover and approach will do much to enhance your image with the customer. When it gets down to being very close in competition, perceptions of your company may be one of the things that tips the balance.

Various types of bindings are discussed in detail in Chapter 8, *Printing the Proposal.* However, it may be mentioned here that three-ring view binders are recommended because of ease of use.

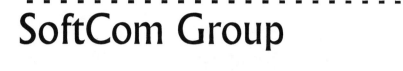

SoftCom Group

Assessment of Digital Technology
Proposal for Digital Communication
Technologies

by
Porter-Roth Associates
1998

Figure 2-1. *Sample Cover Sheet*

SoftCom Group

Assessment of Digital Technology
Proposal for Digital Communication Technologies

June 30, 1998

Prepared by:
Porter-Roth Associates

Figure 2-2. *Sample Cover Sheet with Text Only*

■ PHYSICAL ORGANIZATION OF A PROPOSAL

A proposal is organized around two types of information: that which is constant for all proposals, *front matter,* and material that varies, *body sections* and *appendices.*

Constants

The constants, or front matter, includes everything from the cover letter to the Executive Summary.

- Cover letter. Also called a letter of transmittal, it provides basic information about your proposal such as your proposal number and how long your proposal is valid, and references the RFP number.
- Title page. This is usually a copy of the front cover with additional information.
- Proprietary notice. The proprietary notice cautions the customer about unauthorized disclosure of your proposal.
- Table of contents
- List of abbreviations

Variables

- Section 1 Executive Summary
- Section 2 Technical
- Section 3 Management
- Section 4 Pricing
- Appendices

The first four sections listed above constitute the body of the proposal. In very large proposals, these sections may be separately bound and assigned a volume number dictated by the proposal preparation instructions. For multiple volumes, the cover letter need not be placed in all volumes. It is possible to make one volume the master copy and place all front matter in that copy. If there are appendices, they are treated as a separate section at the end.

■ FRONT MATTER

A careful reading of the RFP is required to determine the order of this front material. If there are no proposal preparation instructions or other guidelines in the RFP, follow the order listed above. There is no *standard for additional material other than that discussed here.* Included below are the basic materials that make up the front matter.

Cover Letter

The cover letter should be bound into the proposal to **prevent** it from being lost. The cover letter is your chance to do something that **is not** as objective as the Executive Summary or the main body of the proposal.

If possible, have the letter written and signed by your CEO or by someone in as high a position as possible. Consider the cover letter as a letter of commitment from your president to the customer's president (see figure 2-3). Some, but not necessarily all, of the key ideas that should be covered are:

- An opening statement or summary sentence that concisely presents your marketing strategy. The opening sentence should be stronger than a "thank you" for the chance to bid; it must be a positive statement about your product or service. This statement is your selling theme and the reason why the customer will award you the contract.
- Any special or unique ideas presented in your proposal that save money and time and that guarantee a risk-free implementation the customer did not expect or ask for in the RFP.
- Special efforts you have undertaken to identify and resolve critical requirements indicated in the RFP. For example, if the customer constantly stresses speed in complying with his requirements and prompt delivery, make a clear statement that you understand his need and have made extraordinary efforts to guarantee shipment on or ahead of schedule.
- The closing statement. The closing statement should include the following: references to the RFP number (if there is one) and project name; how long the proposal is valid (60 days, 90 days); a statement indicating the person signing the proposal is authorized by your company; and the name and address of the person responsible for the proposal.

To summarize, use the cover letter to help sell your proposal by getting the attention of the evaluators and directing them to compelling reasons for buying.

SoftCom Industries
1000 Industrial Road
San Francisco, CA

Dear Mr. Walker:

SoftCom Industries is proposing a complete solution for your Records Management and Storage (RMS) project. SoftCom has the combined resources to ensure the RMS program requirements can be fully realized with mature software that meets and exceeds all technical requirements set forth in your RMS RFP.

SoftCom is proposing our Electronic Records Management System (ERMS) as the basis for your RMS project. The ERMS product is currently installed in over 100 client sites and has been available for five years. We believe that ERMS provides all of the core functions required in the RMS system and database customization will be provided with using standard tools.

Because ERMS meets all of the requirements in your RFP, we believe that your 18-month schedule is not only possible but can be met ahead of schedule. See our project schedule in the Management Section.

Our proposal is valid for the requested 60-day period. Mr. Porter-Roth is an officer of the company who is authorized to make all commitments in this proposal. Future communications should be directed to your account representative, Ms. Anne Smith.

We are looking forward to working with you and your team on the RMS project.

Sincerely,

Bud Porter-Roth

Bud Porter-Roth
President

Figure 2-3. *Sample Cover Letter*

Title Page

The title page contains all the information on the front cover in addition to the following (see figure 2-4):

■ Response to Requirements placed ahead of the project name.
■ The submitted to line. This line should have the name of the person who signed the RFP. Check the RFP for possible instructions that will tell you to whom, where, and how to submit the proposal.

- The submitted by line. In addition to your company name and logo you should include your full address.
- Sequential company proposal number. If you number your proposals, and you should, the number goes here. Concerning the proposal number, it is professional to number your proposal and refer to the number in the cover letter in addition to requesting that the customer refer to the proposal number in any correspondence with you.
- Controlled document number. For a highly sensitive proposal, it is advisable to assign controlled document numbers. This means that if you have ten copies, each copy will be numbered one through ten. A record is then kept of each copy with its number and the name of the person who received that copy.
- Date. Again, this should be the date the proposal is due, not the date you are submitting it.

If you are submitting several copies of your proposal, you may be required to designate one of the copies as the master. The master copy should be the one that contains the original cover letter and signature in ink. It is advisable to have a master copy even if it is not required. The words **MASTER COPY** should be printed on the proposal cover and title page.

Proprietary Notice

This is a statement to the customer that tells him the information you have provided in your proposal is not to be released to anyone other than the people who need it for evaluation purposes and contract information. The proprietary notice basically contains three ideas:

- Although proposal information is proprietary, if parts of the information were public domain before submittal, the customer is under no obligation to withhold such information from the general public.
- If the customer had access to information before the proposal, whether public or not, he is under no obligation to hold that information in confidence unless by prior agreement.
- If the customer receives information from a third party and is not asked to hold that information as proprietary, he is under no obligation to hold such information in confidence.

SoftCom Group

Assessment of Digital Technology
Proposal for Digital Communication Technologies

Submitted To:

SoftCom Group
Mike Roth-Porter
Vice President, Engineering

SoftCom Group RFP 98-7

June 30, 1998

Submitted By:
Porter-Roth Associates (PRA)
PRA Proposal Number 98-7-03
Control Number 2 of 5

Figure 2-4. *Sample Title Page*

If the proposal is being submitted to the government, read the RFP instructions very carefully about how to mark your proposal. You should know that because of the Freedom of Information Act, your competitors can ask for and receive copies of your proposal if it is not protected by the proprietary notice. Contact your legal staff and local government contracting office to make sure you are following the instructions correctly. If you arbitrarily mark every page *Confidential*, even though there is nothing confidential on the page, the government will disregard all confidential markings.

When writing your proprietary notice, get help from your legal department. The example given in figure 2-5 may not be suitable for your proposal or your company.

PROPRIETARY NOTICE

This report contains confidential information of **YOUR COMPANY NAME HERE,** which is provided for the sole purpose of permitting the recipient to evaluate the proposal submitted herewith. In consideration of receipt of this document, the recipient agrees to maintain such information in confidence and to not reproduce or otherwise disclose this information to any person outside the group directly responsible for evaluation of its contents. There is no obligation to maintain the confidentiality of any information which was known to the recipient prior to receipt of such information from **YOUR COMPANY**, or becomes publicly known through no fault of recipient, or is received without obligation of confidentiality from a third party owing no obligation of confidentiality to **YOUR COMPANY.**

Figure 2-5. *Sample Proprietary Notice*

Table of Contents (TOC)

The word processor program that you are using normally generates the table of contents. Typically, you can specify how many levels deep the indexing will go and other variables such as a dotted line from the heading to the number.

It is recommended that you do provide a table of contents with your proposal. It may as simple as the major headings or as deep as three levels down. Three levels down is generally far enough, unless your proposal is unusually long and complex.

The table of contents should be cleanly presented and easy to read. If section numbers are used in the proposal, the table of contents should also have section numbers.

When you have more than one physically separated volume in your proposal, you should combine the TOCs from all of the volumes in the first volume. The second, third, etc., volumes usually contain only the TOC for that individual volume. However, there is nothing wrong in duplicating the complete TOC for each volume.

List of Illustrations

Figure A-1.	Project Management Structure	**A-7**
Figure B-1.	Proposed Software Solution	**B-5**
Figure B-2.	System Configuration Diagram	**B-9**
Figure B-3.	Proposed System Conceptual Process Flow	**B-15**
Figure C-1.	Project Schedule	**C-2**
Figure C-2.	Cost Summary Sheet	**C-7**
Figure C-3.	Bill of Materials	**C-8**
Figure D-1.	Executive Staff Organization	**D-3**

Figure 2.6. *Sample List of Illustrations*

The List of Illustrations (LOI) follows the TOC and should start on a separate page from the TOC. Tables follow on another page as shown in figures 2-6 and 2-7. However, if it is possible to combine both illustrations and tables on one page, it is acceptable to do so.

List of Tables

Table B-1.	Compliance Matrix	**B-4**
Table C-1.	System Configuration Specifications	**C-6**
Table C-2.	Proposed Maintenance Schedule	**C-9**
Table D-1.	Printing from Non-Image-Capable Devices	**D-17**

Figure 2-7. *Sample List of Tables*

Abbreviations List

An abbreviations list should be part of your boilerplate library (see Chapter 4, *Proposal Contents: Boilerplate Files)*; it is not the same as a glossary. The abbreviations list is a key to the acronyms and buzz words that are unique to your company or business (see figure 2-8). It should be placed in the front of *all* the volumes of your proposal, not just the first one. Physical placement is usually after the list of illustrations and/or tables.

■ ADDITIONAL FRONT MATTER

In addition to the regular front matter, there are occasions when other documents will be placed in the front of the proposal, before the text proper. Following are examples and explanations of some of these documents.

Abbreviations/Acronym	Definition
AWM	Advanced Workstation Management. An Ajax designed software management program
AIP	Applications implementation Program. Ajax's collection of developer's tools used to build software applications
ASCII	An acronym for American Standard Code for Information Interchange. The computer codes used to store general computer data (not images)
LAN	Local Area Network
MSA	Maintenance and Support Agreement
PPM	Principal Period of Maintenance
SSRC	Ajax's Software Support Response Center
TSC	Ajax's Technical Support Center

Figure 2-8. *Sample Abbreviations List*

Compliance Matrix

This form is sometimes seen in state or government RFPs and is a request to state whether you are compliant with major requirements and specifications in the RFP (see figure 2-9). As some people try to skirt the issue if they are not compliant, this is an effort to determine what specifications are not being met.

Even if not required, this is something that should be provided as a visible demonstration to the customer that you have met all of the requirements in addition to giving a cross-reference of the RFP paragraphs to your proposal paragraphs.

Compliance Matrix

The following compliance matrix serves as a cross-reference to major paragraphs in your RFP and demonstrates our adherence to the requirements and specifications. Exceptions will be noted as non-compliant and will be fully discussed in Exceptions to the RFP.

RFP Number	Proposal Number	Compliant (Y/N)	Comments
2.1	3.1	Y	See Appd B for additional ref.
2.2	3.2	Y	
2.3	3.3	N	External modem not required
2.4	3.4	Y	
2.5	4.1	N	Extended memory not optional

Figure 2-9. *Compliance Matrix*

Exceptions List

If you do provide a compliance matrix and cannot be compliant in all areas, it is advisable to provide an explanation for each exception. As is sometimes the case, your product may already be capable of doing something that negates the necessity for doing something else required by the customer (see figure 2-10). In addition, the list is highly visible and most likely will be read, providing you with a sales forum few competitors will have.

This section lists all exceptions to the Johnson Corporation Request for Proposal, RFP No. ADH-583-1, dated December 19xx.

1. Paragraph 1.21.3 Contractual Obligation. The contents of the response of the successful Vendor and the provisions stated in this RFP shall be considered as contractual obligations.

Exception: This proposal has been prepared in accordance with accepted techniques for system design and our understanding of your requirements as stated in the RFP. However, it is to be understood that actual results in your operating environment may vary due to variations in volume, environment, personnel, and other factors that we cannot control. Therefore, while the greatest care has been taken to be accurate, we cannot warrant specifications given in this proposal.

2. Paragraph 3.7.12 Compatibility. The proposed software shall remain compatible with the existing applications software, peripherals, computer interfaces and terminal equipment as defined in the Technical Section 2 paragraph 2.1 -2.21 of this RFP.

Exception: Our software will not be compatible with the existing software and cannot be converted. We propose to use the software described in the Software Section of this response. Full specifications and costs are given with a description of the software and why it cannot remain compatible with existing software.

Figure 2-10. *Exceptions List*

Bonds

Some RFPs require that a bond be established at the time of proposal submission. The bond request will be in the RFP and will be explained in the instructions. Be careful in not pricing the cost of the bond in

---

with the pricing section since some RFPs specifically state that they are not responsible for the cost of the bond.

Buy USA Statement

This is a form that you are required to sign. Basically it says that you will buy a certain percentage of your equipment that is manufactured in the United States. Careful reading will explain its full intent.

Minority, Small, Women-owned, and Veteran Business Enterprise (MSWVBE) Requirements

Most government RFPs require bidders to fill in a MSWVBE form. The form applies to two basic categories.

The first is if your company is a MSWVBE. If so, you may have to provide official status or registration from the State. If you are a MSWVBE, you will be eligible for additional point consideration on the evaluation. This means that you will be given, for example, 5% add-on to your final point value in the evaluation. The percentage and method will vary from State to State. It is important that you correctly list your business and fill in the forms completely and accurately. If you want to apply for MSWVBE status, don't wait until the proposal is due.

The second is if your business will employ a MSWVBE, as a subcontractor, for a percentage of your work. As above, if you qualify, you will receive additional consideration.

If employing a MSWVBE subcontractor, the requirements may be complex and require that you competitively procure the services of a MSWVBE. This means that your company is responsible for writing an RFP for the services and sending it to at least three MSWVBE companies and advertising the RFP in an MSWVBE or public newspaper. This takes time, effort, and makes for additional work in the proposal.

Be prepared and review this section ASAP!

Proposal Road Map

This is sometimes required or desirable when a proposal is so complicated that the logic of your response is not easily followed. The road map can be similar to a preface in a book, or it is sometimes graphically illustrated as shown in figure 2-11. This is somewhat similar to the compliance matrix and should easily be generated from your proposal writing outline.

Proposal Road Map

The following road map serves as a cross-reference to major paragraphs in your RFP and our proposal.

RFP Number	Proposal Number	Comments
2.1	1.1	Executive Summary
3.1	2.1	Technical Section
3.2	2.2	
3.3	2.3	
4.1	4.1	Management Section

Figure 2-11. *Proposal Road Map*

■ PROPOSAL ORGANIZATION

Some of the larger RFPs will require that a specified format be followed for ease of evaluation. However, sometimes these formats are an unorganized collection of information due to lack of experience or lack of understanding on the part of the RFP writers about the intended project. Therefore, it is your responsibility to ensure that your proposal is organized and formatted to best demonstrate your product's features and benefits within the guidelines presented in the RFP.

The following are instructions from an RFP as an example.

Vendor Proposal Format

A total of five (5) exact copies of your proposal must be submitted. One copy must be marked ORIGINAL MASTER and others marked COPY on the Title Page. Use a three-ring binder for each copy. The proposal must be divided into sections and tabbed as follows:

Section 1	RFP Response Requirements (refer to Section 2 of this RFP)
Section 2	Insurance (refer to Section 3 of this RFP)
Section 3	References (refer to Section 4 of this RFP)
Section 4	Qualification of Respondents (refer to Section 5 of this RFP)
Section 5	General Contract Requirements (refer to Section 6 of this RFP)
Section 6	Executive Summary
Section 7	Proposed System Operations (refer to Section 8 of this RFP)
Section 8	Proposed System Configuration (refer to Section 9 of this RFP)
Section 9	Project Plan and Maintenance (refer to Section 10 of this RFP)
Section 10	Vendor's Section (refer to Section 11 of this RFP)
Section 11	Pricing (refer to Section 12 of this RFP)
Appendix A	Terms and Conditions of Purchase. (Refer to RFP Appendix A)
Appendix B	Business Information Form. (Form XZY01, Refer to RFP Appendix B)
Appendix C	Respondent's Certification Sheet. (Refer to RFP Appendix C)
Appendix D	Optional for Vendor's Attachments

Vendors may add as many Appendices as necessary to complete their proposal.

■ PROPOSAL FORMAT

Style Sheet

If no proposal format is specified by the RFP (paragraph numbering guidelines), a style sheet developed and used in the early phases of the proposal will save you considerable time and work, especially if you are working out of a small office with only a few people developing and typing the proposal. Otherwise you will see inconsistencies in such things as paragraph indentation and spacing, treatment of headings, margins, and illustration styles. If you have word processing operators or typists, you will save hours of time, effort, and frustration by providing them with a style sheet for the draft preparation.

The following are some items that can be standardized:

- Indentation of paragraphs (if any), and by how much
- Headings/subheadings
- Bullets
- Pagination (placement, spacing, section number, etc.)
- Margins
- Trademark names and logos
- Abbreviations
- Buzz words
- Basic spelling (e.g., disc/disk)
- Dates
- Illustration formats and callouts (see Chapter 5, Proposal Contents: Illustrations)
- Footnotes

The key to a successful style sheet is to be realistic. You cannot expect a large non-homogeneous group to read a 20-page style manual before they begin writing. If, however, during the kickoff meeting some discussion is spent on the style sheet explaining why and how it will save time, most writers will make an effort to follow it. The best style sheet is a simple one that can be given to your writers and typists to follow when preparing the manuscript. There are several ways style sheets can be prepared. One may be simply a list of instructions with examples (see figure 2-12).

Since PC word processors are commonly available, it is most efficient to provide the writer with a template style sheet built with the word processing program to be used. The template can be an existing one that is pre-built and comes with the word processor or custom built for proposals. This can be passed out on a disk or made available over the network. Each writer must be advised to install the template and **NOT TO CHANGE IT**.

During the kickoff meeting, the writers should be advised on the basics of using the template. Some formatting is not template available, such as the placement of graphics, so that written guidelines should be established for these.

Abbreviations and Acronyms		
Abbreviation/Acronym	**Definition**	**Style**
AWM	Advanced workstation Management. An Ajax-designed software management program.	
AIP	Applications Implementation Program	Ajax's collection of developer's tools used to build software applications
dpi	Dots per inch	All lowercase, one space after the numeric value. **Example:** 300 dpi
gigabyte (GB)	One billion (1024 x 106) characters	No space between the numeric value and the abbreviation. Example: 2GB
LAN	Local area network	
MSA	Maintenance and support agreement	
NCSC	Ajax's National customer Support center	
OCR	Optical character recognition. A technique used to convert text contained in images to ASCII data that is suitable for use by word processing programs	
PPM	Principal Period of Maintenance	

Figure 2-12. *Sample Style Guide for Abbreviations and Acronyms*

Style Sheet

1.   **Heads and Subheads**

Level 1 major heads are typed with 5 spaces from text above and 2 spaces to text **below.**

Level 1 heads: all caps, bold, no indent

Level 2 heads: upper and lower case, **bold,** indent 5 spaces

Level 3 heads: cap first word only, bold, indent 10 spaces

Level 4 heads: cap first word only, normal, indent 15 spaces

Example:

LEVEL 1 MAJOR HEAD

    Level 2 Subhead

        Level 3 subhead

           Level 4 subhead

2. **Bullets**

Bullets are indicated with a small **"0"** and are indented 5 spaces in from the head or subhead under which they fall. Allow 2 spaces between the bullet and the text following it.

Example:

MAJOR HEAD

- Bullet item 1
- Bullet item 2

3.   **Dates**

a. A full date is set off by commas.

The meeting was held September 1,1988, at the corporate headquarters.

b. When only the month and year are given there is no comma after the month.

The company was founded March 22, 1997.

c. The year may be abbreviated......etc.

Figure 2-13. *Sample Style Sheet*

If a graphics program is to be used for illustrations (see Chapter 5), standards for graphics should also be established. This usually requires that all writers use the same graphics program so that the pre-built illustrations are consistent with each other. For example, a "computer workstation" illustration is different from program to program and even within programs, they may have variations on a server graphic. As a worst case example, one writer uses a workstation that is positioned on the floor and is designated as a "tower" case. Within the same section, another writer illustrates the same workstation as a "desktop" case with the monitor sitting on top of the case. Abbreviations and acronyms lend themselves to a list with their meanings as well as style (see figure 2-13).

Notes

Essential Sections

Knowing there are essential sections will help you to organize your proposal.

Essential Sections

■ INTRODUCTION

≈Although each proposal written will be unique, there are basic sections that are standard to all proposals.

Although each proposal written will be unique, there are basic sections that are standard to all proposals:

- Executive Summary
- Technical Section
- Management Section
- Pricing Section
- Appendix

These sections in turn have elements common to all proposals. For example, an Executive Summary generally contains an introduction, a statement of the problem, a review of the major sections of the proposal, and information about the company writing the proposal. The technical section provides a description of the product or service offered while the management section explains how the product or service will be implemented. The pricing section provides a breakdown of the prices of equipment, maintenance, and training. Appendices are generally reserved for information too detailed for inclusion in the main proposal or information that may assist the evaluator that is not specifically asked for in the RFP.

≈Some modules may be pre-written, but most must be custom-tailored to the customers' requirements.

These basic proposal elements can be thought of as modules. Viewed as modules, some of these modules can be pre-written as standard boilerplate files, such as a description of the hardware or a list of the training classes. Some modules, however, *must be written fresh each time*, such as a discussion of how your product will meet the customer's requirements.

This chapter will cover the purpose of each section, who reads them, how to develop each section, what material can be standardized and used for all proposals, and what material must be custom-written for each proposal. (Chapter 4 provides a detailed review of "boilerplate" material.) These section reviews also contain examples of effective responses to RFPs, in addition to guidelines for formatting standardized material.

■ THE EXECUTIVE SUMMARY

The Executive Summary is an abstract of your proposal. It presents a summarized view of each major section, reviews any unusual features and benefits contained in your proposal, delivers the major selling points, and provides any pertinent information not requested in the RFP.

✑ The Executive Summary is a real workhorse for your proposal.

The Executive Summary is a real workhorse for your proposal. It not only summarizes the proposal, but it educates people not familiar with your products and company; it produces the first impression of your company; it translates complex technical concepts into understandable benefits; and it sells those benefits to the reader. To be effective, the Executive Summary must do the following:

- Tell the reader what he/she is buying in simple understandable terminology
- Explain complex technical concepts in terms that will be grasped by non-technical readers
- Convert complex technical concepts and features into understandable benefits
- Sell the reader on the benefits of the proposed solution
- Sell your solution over the competition's solution, features, and (perceived) benefits

One RFP provided the following instructions for an Executive Summary:

An Executive Summary is a short, concise and self-contained document that will focus on the key issues of the RFP....

Who Reads the Executive Summary?

✑ The primary reader is the high-level decision-maker.

Although read by a variety of people, the primary audience for the Executive Summary is the high-level decision-maker. The executive reads the Executive Summary to gain a working knowledge of all proposals submitted in order to understand the primary differences between the proposed solutions and to determine relative values of products versus price. This person is interested in *what* results will be achieved by your product, not so much *how* they will be achieved.

✑ The Executive Summary provides the evaluator with a capsule view of the solution.

The Executive Summary is also read by the evaluation staff who wants to read a summary of the proposal before going straight into the detailed technical sections. The Executive Summary provides the evaluator with a capsule view of the solution so that as he/she begins to read the technical details, he/she is able to read them with greater understanding. Providing the evaluation staff with the Executive Summary exposes them to the features and benefits of your proposal from a business point of view, rather than a strictly technical point of view.

Remember that evaluators are going to read three to six (or more) proposals that will be variations on the same topic. The executive summary gives you a chance to let the executive and the evaluation team understand what makes your proposal (solution) different from the pack. If the executive summary is done correctly, your technical section will be more easily understood and grasped by those who make decisions.

Development of the Executive Summary

☙Few RFPs provide guidance as to how the executive summary should be prepared.

As important as it is to your proposal, few RFPs provide specific guidance for the development and content of an executive summary. The following four examples taken from recent RFPs demonstrate how ambiguous the guidelines can be:

1. *The Executive Summary should consist of a concise description of how the proposed system will address the needs spelled out in this RFP. Excessive technical detail should be avoided in this section. After reading this section, the reader should have a clear conceptual understanding of the approach recommended by the bidder.*

2. *This section should be limited to a brief narrative which outlines the bidder's proposal. The management summary section should contain little technical jargon and be oriented for the non-technical executive. Pricing information should not be contained in this section.*

3. *This section provides an overview and summary of the proposed system and its major components. It should contain a general system description, major functions or capabilities as they apply to future requirements, and any areas of concern that need to be addressed. It should be written at an appropriate technical level for senior management review.*

4. *The management summary section must provide an overview of the vendor's overall approach and include at least the following information:*

- *A discussion of the proposed approach for meeting the requirements of this RFP*
- *An overview of the proposed technical solution*
- *A discussion of the vendor's organization and relevant experience*
- *A discussion of the costs required by this RFP*
- *A summary discussion of anticipated problems and proposed solutions*
- *A discussion of assumptions made by the vendor for the proposed solution*

As can be seen from the above examples, there does not seem to be any consistent or well-defined approach to writing an Executive Summary. In the first three examples, basically the same request is made—summarize the proposal—but the writer is left to interpret what *summarize* and *outline* mean.

✍ Bidders often are required to list potential problems as well as solutions.

The third example contains a statement that most proposal writers do not notice or would like to avoid, "...any areas of concern which need to be addressed." This statement is vague, but in general, the company issuing the RFP is asking you, the company writing the proposal, to list problem areas, how they will be addressed, and the risks associated with those problems. Many writers hesitate to openly list areas of concern, problems, and exceptions to requirements for fear the competition will not have the same problems. However, this type of statement in an RFP serves three purposes:

- It asks potential bidders to think through their solution and list weaknesses and remedies
- It demonstrates to the executive and evaluator reading the proposals which companies understand the problems and are willing to address them
- The "weakness" may be in the RFP requirements and you are pointing out to the reader areas in which the requirements were not fully thought through

✍ Sell at the executive level.

Being able to address potential areas of concern will also allow you to position yourself against your competition, and, perhaps make the reader question the competition. For example, perhaps an "area of concern" is overall projected communications bandwidth needed versus the customer's current capacity. You know your competition can't achieve the throughput needed, given the bandwidth constraints, but your product can "grow incrementally to meet the needs"... Therefore, you have cast a shadow on the competition while highlighting one of your features. That is good selling, especially at the executive level.

The fourth example provides the most information, but is also vague when it states the summary must include "at least the following information." The last statement suggests the information requested is not enough and the author may include almost anything else that may be of interest.

✍ At a minimum, the Executive Summary should introduce the proposed solution, and state what it is and who is providing it.

At a minimum, an Executive Summary should contain an introduction to the proposed solution, state what the solution is, and identify who is providing that solution. Below is a possible outline for an Executive Summary. This outline is generic but does mirror the basic sections of a complete proposal. It is possible that some proposals would not include items 2, 4, 5, and 6, for example, as they may not apply to your company, service, or product.

1. Introduction
2. Design Concept

3. Technical Approach
4. Project Management
5. Maintenance
6. Education
7. Pricing Structure
8. Corporate Profile
9. Future Products
10. Areas of Concern

Introduction

✍ The first paragraph of your proposal should begin selling your solution.

The first paragraph of your proposal should begin selling your solution. Many proposal introductions begin by thanking the company for the chance to bid on this project and then proceed to go into great detail about their own company, how great their products are, and their extensive qualifications. It may be several pages before the RFP, its requirements, and the proposed solution are first mentioned. Often, in this style of executive summary writing, stress is placed on company image and the product's strengths become of secondary importance. This results in a confusing message to the customer because what "solution" is being sold is not clearly stated, and the reader is left to answer the question: Which is really more important — the company or the product?

Very few "trust me" proposals make it to the top of the short list. As an example, in the old days, the saying was, "You can't get fired by buying IBM!" This is a "trust me" proposal line and large companies, not necessarily IBM, traded on their name. Today's buyers are more sophisticated and technically astute and would not respond to a poorly written trust-me proposal from a big-name-company.

This is not to say that a company's name does not have value: it still does. Buyers respond to equally good technical solutions whether they are from a big-name-company or a startup. If you were the startup, how would you position yourself? The final decision may be based on the safety of a large, established company if the alternate is a startup with no track record.

✍ If you know your product is strong, focus your attention on where you are weak.

Your proposal strategy may not necessarily focus on the product, but on the company's reputation and strengths. For example, if you are the small company and you know your product is equal to or better than the competition, you must focus on why buying from a smaller company will benefit the customer. For example, because you are smaller, your development team can react faster to on-the-spot-changes instead of going through a monolithic established development team, which may take weeks for the approval. If you know your product is strong, focus your attention on your strengths, but don't ignore your weaknesses.

Generally, the larger the procurement (in dollars and business importance), the more important it is to sell the company itself — reputation, depth of resources, knowledge of the market, number of years in the business — than to sell the product itself. At a certain level, which will differ from industry to industry, it is assumed that the product will work properly; therefore, the issue becomes the ability of the company to execute the project, i.e., implement, install, maintain, and educate. Big, established companies know this and exploit it whenever possible. Small companies bidding on a large project must effectively counter the "big company selling process," e.g., "If you buy from two guys in a garage, you'll get what you pay for."

✑ The larger the contract the more important it is to sell your company.

Below are two examples of introductions taken from actual proposals. The first is an excerpt from a winning proposal:

[This customer's] stated goal of growth by acquisition or expansion requires a computer system that can grow with it. The RFP states that the computer system should allow growth by expansion, not replacement of hardware, software, application packages, and personnel.

Our solution will provide you with that incremental growth.

It is our intention to prove this statement through our proposal and by demonstrating our corporate commitment to a broad compatible product line. A product line that allows you to grow incrementally, not by replacing, adding only as much capacity as needed to the existing platform.

This is a very strong opening and in a few short lines establishes these points:

✑ A winning introduction states that the requirements are understood and can be met, and recognizes the real selling themes.

The opening statement restates the customer's primary goal and sets the tone for the proposal: we understand your requirements and we are willing to work with you to meet those requirements.

The proposal not only recognizes the customer's goal, but it promises to meet it.

The third paragraph establishes the proposal theme: system growth through compatible product lines. This topic becomes a selling theme and is reinforced throughout the proposal. For example, in the section on training, the proposal states that overall training time and costs are reduced over the life of the project because the hardware and software upgrades are incremental and do not require new training since it is the same equipment and software.

This theme also counters the competition by suggesting that the competition can't grow incrementally and therefore the customer may be forced to buy more capacity than is needed. In addition, if the customer has to move up to the next level of computer, there may be additional training required. Thus, expenses will be repeated each time that the customer outgrows current capacity.

The second example is the opening paragraph from a losing proposal:

[This company's] systems meet the needs for highly reliable, general-purpose computer systems for users with heavy volume processing. For such customers, computer system failures, damage to the database, or interruptions of computer service can result in serious financial loss. Our hardware and software minimizes the risk of system failures and protects the information stored in the database. [Company] has the long-term stability and industry knowledge to provide superior products and services.

This opening paragraph has several problems:

A losing introduction is too general, is weak, and uses negative selling.

1. The opening sentence is so general almost any computer manufacturer today would fit that description. It is similar to a car manufacturer stating "our cars have four tires, an engine, and are suitable for transportation on roads."

2. The second sentence is negative; instead of explaining the advantages of a highly reliable system, it points out what could happen if a system were to fail. Selling from a negative point of view is never as successful or powerful as selling positive features. Also, this statement has negligible impact because it is true for any company using computers for day-to-day business operations.

3. The third sentence continues the negative selling by implying this manufacturer is the only one who can protect you from system failures.

The opening statement of your proposal must be powerful, draw the reader into your proposal, and promise a solution other vendors will have a difficult time matching. The introduction will set the tone for the entire proposal. The most effective executive summary leaves the reader with a clear concept of what is being proposed, why your solution is better than other solutions, what is different about your solution, and most important, why he/she should make a decision to buy your solution.

Of course we realize that these statements must be backed up with a strong and believable technical and management section. But the executive will depend on his technical staff to verify the claims made in the executive summary.

Design Concept

> ✍ *The design concept section states how and why you arrived at your proposed solution.*

The second section of the Executive Summary states how and why you arrived at your particular solution. In this section, the discussion should center on relating the design to the solution and what factors influenced your decision. For example, an RFP may require personal computers to provide a number of functions including word processing, accounting, desktop publishing, and office productivity tools, in addition to being on an intranet with e-mail.

In this particular case there could be many solutions; specifically, the solution could be based on an Intel/Microsoft architecture, an Apple architecture, or one of the many high-powered UNIX workstation vendors. The job for the design section is to explain why one hardware/software platform was chosen and how the customer will benefit from that choice.

> ✍ *Rephrasing requirements helps the reader when evaluating complex technical proposals.*

The best approach is to rephrase the customer's requirements and demonstrate you not only understand what is being requested, but you also understand the problems that relate to proposing different solutions. This involves understanding the customer's requirements and then matching those requirements to your products.

If time, knowledge, and resources permit, this is an excellent place to include what are termed "trade-off studies." If, for example, you were selling UNIX-based workstations, you would list three solutions: PCs, Apples, and UNIX machines. Each competing solution would be briefly explored and reasons given why they were rejected. For example, a UNIX workstation may be better at multi-tasking or running several programs at the same time than the other two, but there are not as many software business applications available. Apple equipment may have a better graphical interface than the other machines but is not the primary computer in many companies and therefore a company will have to support two operating systems. That means buying application software twice in addition to training and service redundancies.

This type of "object trade-off analysis" allows you to speak to the differences in solutions without being overtly negative. It may also cause the reader to compare your analysis to the competitor's proposals to substantiate your reasoning.

Technical Approach

Once you have explained why a particular approach was taken, the next section should provide details of that approach. The following example is taken from a winning proposal and is the lead-in paragraph to the technical section:

The purpose to be served by the [customer's system] *is to provide an integrated information system that is acceptable and usable for a wide range of applications within the municipality. These applications will enable City employees to access comprehensive databases maintained on the server in addition to using local PCs and applications for data manipulation.*

Based on these considerations, [this company] *recommends a system composed of a central processing complex located in the computer center linked to facilities located in other metropolitan areas by means of a high-speed data communications network. Remote office site equipment is to consist solely of remote PCs, and printers connected via the communications network to the central processing site.*

☙ *The technical section provides details of the chosen approach to the solution.*

The first paragraph restates the requirements in general terms and introduces the reader to the key concept of centralized databases accessed by remote terminals. The second paragraph provides more detail and begins to draw the reader into a non-technical description of the solution. As this example continues, in the original proposal, it adds more detail about the communications network, the database and data server, and the types of software programs that are available for the remote PCs. This also sets up the reader for a key argument in the proposal, centralized versus decentralized databases because this company knows the competition is proposing a decentralized database.

After reading this portion of the Executive Summary, the reader should have a reasonably good grasp of the solution and be able to intelligently determine if it meets the general requirements in the RFP.

Project Management

Project management is becoming more important as equipment, systems, and projects become progressively more complex. Although many RFPs do not require a project management section, a thorough and detailed project plan provides a clear understanding of responsibilities, milestone dates, and relationships between you and the customer. The following paragraph taken from an Executive Summary provides an example of the level of detail needed in this section:

≥ *Project management is becoming more important as equipment, systems, and projects become more complex.*

The City stated non-technical requirements are essential to a successful implementation of the system. Our approach provides a detailed project plan for implementation, applications development, system training, system maintenance, and also considers that the City will be required to take an active role in the overall project. Figure 1-3 is our first cut at a complete project plan with dates, activities, and assignments.

This section continues with a brief outline of the proposed project team, proposed schedule, and how the two companies will interface once the project is started.

In many cases, there may not be enough data to accurately project dates on a project timeline. In this case, it is best to let the reader know that these dates are an estimate, subject to negotiation and the final contract. But the point is, you have taken the initiative and have laid out the key milestones for the project, which give the reader insight into how the project will unfold. Compare this type of schedule to your competition's lack of schedule or a proposal that states, "… project scheduling will be developed as part of the detailed design."

Maintenance

≥ *Often, the cost of maintenance will exceed the value of the contract over time.*

If your proposal is for a product that requires maintenance and support, it will be important to convince and sell the executive on your company's ability to meet those maintenance requirements. As equipment becomes more complex, becomes an integral part of doing business, and in some cases becomes the basis for profitability in a business, the executive begins to understand, for example, that a computer system that is not operational may be costing his company thousands of dollars in lost revenue for each hour or day that it is not functioning. Many companies are beginning to include penalty clauses that require cash penalties for each hour a system is down beyond an agreed-to limit. This example was taken from an RFP to purchase approximately $1.5 million of hardware and software:

Contracts resulting from proposals will contain a penalty provision for excessive system down time, equipment failure, or failure by the bidder to meet response times for repair requests.

The demand for quality maintenance programs is becoming more prevalent for a number of reasons:

1. Vendors bidding on projects are growing so fast they cannot adequately train service personnel

2. Vendors may bid and win a job in an area where they do not currently have maintenance personnel

3. Vendors are the subjects of mergers or acquisitions, often leaving the customer without maintenance support

4. Vendors bid products that have not been fully tested resulting in the customers unknowingly becoming "beta" test sites

A secondary factor in determining the return on investment is the overall cost of maintenance for the life of the project. In a growing number of cases, the cost of maintenance for a major computer system over a seven-year projected life cycle will equal or exceed the purchase price. For budgeting purposes, maintenance costs become a significant number and potential customers are beginning to give the maintenance section a higher evaluation factor.

Education

Education can provide long-term benefits by reducing costs.

Just as it is important for the executive to feel confident that your company can provide adequate maintenance, it is also important for him to know that you are able to provide high-quality training. As with companies that bid products that sometimes are not ready for release, these same companies often are behind in their development of training classes and materials.

To be effective, this section of the Executive Summary should contain an overview of your education department, the types of instructors employed (All instructors have a minimum of 5 years...), the type of instruction available (lecture, video, self-paced), how classrooms are equipped, and if instruction is available at the customer's site.

Often, a comprehensive, documented training section will convey to the executive reader that your solution takes into account all aspects of a successful project. A well-written overview of your education department may also convince an evaluator and executive that your company is well established and is fully able to support a large contract.

Pricing Structure

Pricing information in the Executive Summary provides the customer with an overview of how you arrived at your total price.

The pricing section of the executive summary often does double duty. First, it is the proper place for your price. Second, it is often the place where contract terms and conditions are reviewed. Including pricing and contract information in the Executive Summary is optional if the RFP instructions are not specific.

The reason for its inclusion is to provide the customer an overview and summary of your total price and any noteworthy additions, exceptions, or special conditions that relate to your overall pricing. Before including any pricing information, read the proposal preparation instructions as some RFPs specifically state that pricing information is to be provided only in the separate pricing section.

There are many reasons for including pricing information in the Executive Summary:

- Demonstrate your price/performance advantages
- Justify pricing for an optional product not requested
- Clarify why you took an exception to a requirement
- Explain the basis for a discount
- Acknowledge special terms and conditions in the RFP

Often, there is no other place in a proposal to explain how you arrived at your price, what special terms and conditions are being offered the customer, or why you have elected not to bid on a portion of the RFP. For example, if you were offering the customer what is sometimes called a showcase discount, you would need to explain why this is mutually beneficial. (A showcase discount is an offer to discount your price in return for your company being able to use that site and installation as a customer reference site and allowing you to use the installation for tours when needed.) A second example would be to explain additional pricing for products or services not requested in the RFP such as a project manager and related staff. A third example would be to justify additional money to meet an aggressive installation schedule. Customers will sometimes provide optional installation schedules and additional evaluation points will be awarded to those companies offering the shortest installation time.

The price summary section may be a difficult section to write because:

- Pricing cannot be completed until the technical solution is finalized
- Pricing is usually one section that requires management review, which means additional decision-making time
- Discounts cannot be fixed until total price is determined
- Discounts normally require management approval
- How much discount to be offered is often subject to debate
- Additional time is required to write this section after all discussions are complete

The price summary section may also be one of the most powerful and meaningful sections that the executive will read. Pricing will always be a consideration when a customer is making a decision to purchase. Prices higher than those quoted by the competition will not eliminate your proposal necessarily; however, higher prices that cannot be justified may be cause for elimination from the competition.

No matter where it appears, pricing will be the first section

Pricing that is uncommon, whether too high or too low, will draw the attention of a reader. If, for example, four proposals are priced at $850,000 and one is priced at $400,000, there is most probably something wrong with the low price proposal. Pricing is where strong competitive analysis will certainly pay off. Also, proposal evaluators like to see prices grouped within 10% to 20% of each other because it indicates that they have done their homework in getting roughly equal vendors to bid on the project and therefore the group is likely to be very competitive.

Corporate Profile

A corporate profile enables you to sell your company and possibly provide some little-known facts about it.

Providing a corporate profile enables you to sell your corporation and any special qualities that would differentiate it from other companies. It also allows you to provide some pertinent facts about your company that may not be commonly known or recognized. For example, many companies are growing at such a rapid rate that it is possible an evaluator may remember a much smaller, less capable company unless told otherwise. A corporate profile should include at least the following:

- Date company was founded and primary objective/mission
- Types of equipment and/or services provided
- Special characteristics of the company or management style
- Basic company organization
- Number of people employed
- Primary locations or locations of major divisions
- Features and benefits of corporate organization

It is also helpful to include an organization chart of management—company president, vice presidents, directors. This enables the executive to determine how your company is organized and where his/her project will be placed.

Future Products

This is an optional section for your Executive Summary. The purpose of this section is to provide the reader with a sense of your company's direction and to demonstrate that your company is concerned with staying abreast of, or ahead of, current technology. Insight into future technology may also convince the potential customer that he is buying a solution that will allow him to grow and change with technology instead of having to request bids every time technology makes an advance. Providing the customer with insight into your future products indicates your company has technological and

⊠ Describing future products tells the customer your company is concerned with staying on the leading edge of technology.

financial strengths that may not otherwise be obvious in your proposal.

This is also a chance to show the customer that you have future products that your competition may not have planned. This not only makes your products more attractive but also makes the competition less attractive without negative selling.

Summary

As one of the most important sections to your proposal, the writing should be clear, concise, and relevant to the issues at hand. If there are directions in the RFP, follow them. If not, use the above examples to guide your writing.

The executive summary should also make use of strong illustrations and graphics whenever possible. Diagrams, photos, and spreadsheets will help you to convey your message graphically and break up the text. It will also make your page visually appealing so that the reader may spend more time reviewing and considering your sales points. Whenever possible, a feature should be compared to a benefit. Features and benefits go well together, but are often overused, overstated, or not compared correctly. A feature without a benefit is nothing more than a chest-thumping generality that will quickly try the reader's patience.

Above all, the executive summary is meant to sell by capturing the readers' interest with good writing and strong selling themes.

■ TECHNICAL SECTION

⊠ The technical section serves as the cornerstone for all other parts of the proposal: it is the product that is being sold.

The technical section serves as the cornerstone for all other parts of the proposal. In one sense, the technical section is the product that is being sold. The Executive Summary has explained why something should be purchased; the technical section explains what is being purchased, and provides sufficient evidence that the claims made can be verified. It also provides the basis for the management volume that usually follows, and explains how the product will be installed, tested, serviced, and managed.

The primary purpose of the technical section is to define the product against the requirements in the RFP. A thorough understanding of the requirements must be demonstrated first in order to convince the customer that your solution is based on his needs. This understanding of the requirements and needs expressed in the RFP becomes the basis for the technical section.

Depending on the product or service being proposed, the technical section can become quite detailed and often vendors have to determine just how much technical data they should provide before they have given too much information. It must always be considered possible that if you lose, the competitor who wins will be able to get a copy of your proposal and have access to proprietary information, pricing, and selling strategies. Generally, companies provide proprietary information only under what is commonly called a *nondisclosure statement.* This is a signed agreement between the two companies stating that the receiving company will not disclose any of the information learned to anyone not directly related to the project in question and not to any person or persons outside of the company.

A second method for handling sensitive material is to invite the customer to your company for a technical briefing and demonstration. One computer company states in its cover letter, "Because of the high degree of advanced technology involved in this proposal, we would welcome the opportunity to make a personal presentation to your technical staff. At that time we would be able to answer any questions that relate to confidential and proprietary information."

In addition to providing a detailed description of the solution and the products that make up that solution, the technical section must demonstrate your knowledge of the industry.

Who Reads the Technical Section

The technical section is read by the people who developed the RFP and who will be responsible for the project. This group is composed primarily of technical people, and although they may read other sections, they will approach this section from a technical point of view rather than from a marketing and sales or pricing perspective. This is not to say they will not understand marketing-generated benefits or a five-year pricing model.

≥ The technical section should make no assumptions concerning the evaluators' knowledge and acceptance of your technology.

Although the technical section evaluators are generally competent in their individual areas of expertise, they may not be familiar with your technology and industry. Therefore, your technical section should make no assumptions on the part of the evaluators concerning their knowledge and acceptance of your technology. The technical section should be written on a level that is consistent with the audience, but care should be taken to explain industry-specific concepts and, especially, concepts that are unique to your technology and company.

Development of the Technical Section

Introduce the section by demonstrating you understand the problem and how to deal with it.

As with other sections, the RFP may provide specific instructions for the technical section or it may be very unstructured with little or no guidance. Whether the RFP instructions are specific or very loose, they are written as generalized guidelines and may reflect several authors' opinions, biases, and ignorance. This means that unless you completely wire the RFP, i.e., to favor one vendor or technology, the technical section guidelines probably will not be completely suitable for your company and its product. It is your responsibility to ensure that your story is properly presented, that you establish the forum needed to tell your story, and that this is done in a manner consistent with the spirit of the RFP. It will not be beneficial for you or the customer to ignore the RFP instructions and guidelines because you think you have a better idea and method for presenting your material.

The basic technical volume should contain the following:

- Section Overview. The overview provides a short explanation of how the section is organized and may provide some additional information.
- Introduction. The introduction contains a technical discussion of the problem. This is a statement of your interpretation of the RFP requirements.
- Technical solution. How you propose to solve the problem.
- Product descriptions
- Installation and implementation
- Project organization and key project personnel
- Assumptions

Some of the items above may not be applicable, e.g., you may not be proposing computer equipment, or any equipment for that matter. However, whether you are bidding software products, engineering services, or maintenance services, the basic rules apply for a technical section just as they do for the Executive Summary and management sections. You must introduce your section by demonstrating that you understand the problem; you must provide your solution, tell the customer how you intend to implement the solution, and how long that will take.

The following discussion of the section topics mentioned above is intended to supplement any proposal instructions you might have and provide you with examples. These examples will help you get started if the RFP contains little or no guidance.

Section Overview

The section overview is a one- or two-paragraph introduction containing a brief statement concerning any issues that have been discussed outside of the RFP, and a statement addressing any issues concerning the RFP requirements. The overview can be used even if there are proposal instructions that outline the technical sections. It is possible to include a paragraph head, such as *Overview,* at the beginning of the section. This overview may state that several paragraphs have been added to the format to clarify your proposal. The following is a brief example of a section overview:

> *Section 2 of our proposal follows the proposal instructions. In addition, we have repeated verbatim, in italics, the requirement from the RFP that is being responded to before the response. Our response is based upon your RFP, information that was released during the bidders' conference, and two subsequent site visits and discussions. Reference to information obtained outside of the RFP is specifically referred to when it differs with the RFP or is in addition to the RFP.*

> *This section is fully compliant with all requirements. We have made a general assumption concerning the difference between the normal input rates and peak input rates. This assumption is documented in paragraph 3.5. We have also, based on this assumption, provided an alternate solution to the peak load requirements by proposing a split workshift.*

Introduction

This paragraph should be as concise as possible in restating the key issues driving the RFP. If the RFP is for a computer office automation system, the key issues will revolve around worker productivity, greater office efficiencies, lower expenses, better customer service, and how these improvements will increase the customer's profit margin whether it be by reducing expenses or increasing volume without increasing expenses.

The introduction reveals your *insight* into the issues and provides you with the initial forum to establish your solution, or as discussed in Chapter 1, the third level of writing in which you develop a business case for your solution.

And finally, after you have demonstrated your understanding of the requirements and shown how resolution of those requirements will increase profitability, you should provide a technical summary of the solution. For example, one proposal for office automation equipment began:

The overview section briefly discusses any previously addressed outside issues and RFP requirements.

The introduction reveals your insight into issues and how you can develop a business case for your solution.

The technical solution is based on an open and adaptable architecture with a demonstrated commitment to industry standards. Workstations are PC compatible running standard software and are connected together using your existing Ethernet. Scanners and printers are standard industry models and may be dedicated to individual personal computers or become multi-use.

Technical Solution

✎ This section is a direct response to the requirements listed in the technical section of the RFP.

In this section of your proposal you will be required to explain in detail your solution and how it meets all requirements that are in the RFP. Generally, this section is a direct response to the requirements listed in the technical section of the RFP and you will be requested in the instructions to follow the format of that section. For example, in an RFP to purchase an office automation system, the technical section will list and describe specific functions the equipment must perform; what type of communications capabilities are needed based on the amount of traffic over the network; what is expected of the data server in terms of number of people connected to it; how much data storage is anticipated; what the response time should be; and what type of work is to be performed at the workstations such as word processing, desktop publishing, spreadsheets and accounting, electronic mail, etc. An excellent method for responding to this type of request is to repeat the requirement from the RFP and then respond to that requirement directly below it, as shown in figure 3-1.

Responses to requirements should be brief, but provide enough information to satisfy the reader. If more detailed information needs to be presented, it can be included in an appendix, as discussed below.

Product Descriptions

In a proposal, product descriptions are generally taken from the product data sheets, product manuals, and other available information. If the RFP does not provide you with enough guidance as to how detailed the response must be, you will have to make your own determination. Past experience with the customer can help you decide how much technical detail must be in your response.

Many RFPs require product descriptions in the technical section, but this may create a problem. These descriptions can be very long, technical, and difficult to read. Although these descriptions relate to what is being bid, they do not lend themselves to supporting the proposal themes and story. In many cases, the product description section interrupts a strong theme in your proposal.

> ### 3.4.1 System Security
>
> RFP Requirement
>
> The system must provide the capability to detect false log-ons and lock a workstation in which three efforts to log on have failed. Upon three failed attempts, the data server will lock the workstation, record the time and date, identify the workstation, and alert the system operator.
>
> Response
>
> The AJAX system is capable of detecting false log-on attempts, locking that workstation, recording the attempt in the system log, and notifying the system operator. The AJAX security system is user-programmable with lockout periods assigned by the system operator. Lockout periods are defined at the time of system initiation and may be changed as a group or individually thereafter. The AJAX system will also allow the system operator to define the number of log-on attempts before a terminal is locked. See Appendix E, Operating System Security, for a detailed explanation of the security system features and options.

Figure 3-1. *Requirement/Response Format*

✎Use short summarized product descriptions in the body of the text and include more details in an appendix.

It is possible to satisfy all requirements by using short, summarized versions of the product descriptions for the product section and placing the complete product description in an appendix. This approach has several benefits for both you and the reader. It allows you to tailor the short versions to the specific proposal being written by including pertinent, but not highly technical information about the proposed project, the customer, and your proposal themes. In addition, it saves the reader from having to read or skip over pages of material he may not be interested in and that interrupt his train of thought. If the reader requires more information, the full product description is available in the appendix.

By following this approach, you will be able to include more information in the product description than originally intended. Quite often proposal writers condense the normal product description in order to include it in the required proposal section. Because this description is sometimes not complete enough, the reader must make an assumption about the product, or he is forced to submit a question to you and wait for the answer. Either way, you are not controlling the reader's expectations and this lessens the overall impact of this section. By having the full version in the appendix, the product description can be expanded by including material from

Long product descriptions are suitable for the boilerplate library and should be placed in an appendix.

manuals and may potentially be updated periodically by the product manager. Since this information is usually used *as is,* it is easily turned into a boilerplate file that can be kept and maintained as a company standard for that product.

Assumptions

Often, RFPs do not include sufficient information, whether due to oversight or lack of experience in the field on the part of the authors, leaving you with many unanswered questions. However, it is possible the customer will not know all the answers and will ask you to make assumptions to fill in the information you need. Also, it is possible that, due to time constraints and unforeseen issues, you are unable to ask questions and receive the information needed in time to finish your proposal. Making assumptions is a standard method for continuing to work on your proposal when all of the information is not complete.

When making an assumption, ensure the reader understands what it is based on.

Assumptions should be based on your expertise in the subject area, and be carefully documented and supported in your proposal by providing the reader with as much information as needed to clarify why you had to make an assumption and what information the assumption is based on.

Figure 3-2 is an example taken from an RFP that allowed assumptions based on two conditions:

- Assumptions made due to a lack of information about the project and the application
- Assumptions made due to a choice between two methodologies
- The first condition indicates the customer is not a technical expert (as is often the case) and is depending on the vendors to provide the best solution. Your solution may involve technology the customer is not familiar with, or your approach to the application design may be different from what the customer anticipated.

The second condition may be a result of the technology being bid. If, for example, an RFP requests personal computers capable of providing desktop publishing, accounting, word processing, and general office automation, there are at least three types of computers that could fulfill these requirements: PC-type personal computers, Apple computers, and UNIX-based personal computers.

This section of the proposal will provide a detailed description of the system solution proposed by the vendor. The section should include the following subsections:

A. Understanding the Problem. Each vendor will show that they have fully understood the problems addressed in this RFP and the site visits. Each vendor must demonstrate a clear understanding of this industry, our needs in relation to this industry, and the needs of our customers. The vendor must also demonstrate that they have examined the present system volumes, the projected system volumes, and can discuss the potential problems to be overcome and what tradeoffs must be made—if any. Any assumptions made in making the overall system design should be stated and clarified. Clarification falls into two categories:
   1. Assumptions made due to a lack of information about the project and the application
   2. Assumptions made due to a choice between two methodologies

B. Technical Solution. This subsection will provide a complete definition of the vendor's proposed system solution. The proposal must address all phases of the proposed vendor-client relationship as follows:

   - Detailed system design
   - System development
   - System integration
   - initial installation

The technical solution will be reviewed for scope and completeness. All areas detailed in Section 3 of the RFP must be addressed. The vendor will demonstrate how he will meet the business requirements of the proposed system.

Figure 3-2. *Assumptions*

If this were the case for your proposal, you would explore the three alternatives and then make your recommendation. This recommendation will be based on your knowledge of the customer, several assumptions about the long-term requirements, and the product fit.

⊗ Making assumptions can be risky if your knowledge is inadequate or incorrect.

Making assumptions can be risky; however, if your knowledge of the customer or products involved is inadequate or incorrect in regard to what you believe the customer wants. Basing a solution on a wrong assumption can contribute to losing the proposal. For example, one computer company based its solution on using equipment that was installed at the customer's site. The assumption was that because this equipment was fairly new and was supposed to be well-engineered, the customer wanted to retain this equipment. Several proposal themes were developed to show how cost-effective the proposed solution would be, in addition to demonstrating technical ability to interface with the existing equipment. This proposal lost because the customer was looking for a solution that would replace existing equipment.

Summary

The technical section has three main goals:

1. The primary goal of the technical section is to demonstrate your product's ability to meet the requirements set forth in the RFP. The demonstrated solution must be presented in such a manner that it is clear to people not familiar with your products and that it is superior to the competition's proposals. (Remember, the RFP is evaluating many proposals whose technology they may not be familiar with.)

2. The second goal of the technical section is to demonstrate your understanding of the customer's requirements and your ability to anticipate problems, resolve those problems, complete the design, and provide a workable solution.

3. The third goal of the technical section is to demonstrate your ability to actually perform the work required.

✍ Without a technical solution, there is no chance of winning.

Although there are aspects to winning a proposal that are clearly outside of the RFP, such as account knowledge and direction, insider relationships and information, and company politics, you must have a basis for winning the proposal and that basis is the technical solution. If your solution is clearly superior to other solutions, you can overcome objections that relate to non-technical aspects such as maintenance, training, company history, and a smaller installed base than your competitors are offering. Without a solid and technically correct solution, your ability to negotiate with the customer is diminished.

The technical section of your proposal can become an unusually difficult section to structure and write. While it contains the very heart of your proposal, it generally is not given as much attention as the executive summary or pricing section because fewer people understand the product on this level. Because fewer people are available to write it, and it is one of the larger sections of most proposals, this section often will take longer than planned to complete. The time factor becomes even more critical because other sections cannot be finished until the technical section is complete.

These potential problems are compounded by circumstances that are outside of the proposal effort but directly influence the project. For example, the technical section of a proposal for a computer system is generally written by a systems analyst who is responsible for customer accounts, presales calls, and other sales activities. This person is also responsible for customer account management including loading new software, troubleshooting, and managing problems. These duties may require the analyst to be at a customer's site instead of writing a proposal. As these problems cannot be foreseen, it is wise to start the technical section as early as possible with the goal of having a rough draft well before the deadline. Once the rough draft is complete, it is possible for others to help fine tune, edit, and make corrections as needed.

✑Add graphics to this section!

The technical section must also make liberal use of illustrations, graphics, charts, and other means of communicating what the product looks like, what it does, the technical tradeoffs made (that your competition didn't make), and other visual means of presenting your story. This is especially important because technical data tends to be densely written and dry. The illustrations will help break up the text while adding value to the text itself.

✑K.I.S.S. Keep it short and simple.

Because this section of the proposal is very technical and difficult for the reader, it is important to continue to repeat your selling themes, benefits, and product superiority in this section. Also, a consistent style and method for responding to the requirements facilitates the reading of this section. Finally, don't overwrite the technical section by throwing in every datasheet and other technical documentation. It won't be read, and will frustrate the reader who is looking for an cogent answer.

One truth still holds for proposal writing, "I'm sorry this letter is so long. I didn't have time to write a short one." George Bernard Shaw.

■ MANAGEMENT SECTION

✑The management section provides insight into what physical resources will be required and who is responsible for supplying those resources.

The management section is written to assure the potential customer that you do have the experience, facilities, and ability to carry through with what has been proposed. The management section also demonstrates your understanding of complex issues such as site preparation, installation of equipment, test procedures, and education of users.

The management section describes what personnel are required from both companies, what their relationship is to each other, and who has responsibility for which requirements, and defines how the work will be accomplished. In addition to the people required for the project, the management section also provides insight into what physical resources will be required and who is responsible for supplying those resources.

This section is as important as the technical solution. If you are not able to install and service your equipment, the customer may pick another solution. This is true especially when proposing a solution that will be part of a company line-of-business operation. If your product is not working, it may be the cause of lost business.

Who Reads the Management Section?

✎ *When competing head to head with similar technologies, project management may be the deciding factor.*

Generally speaking, the management section is read and evaluated by the same people who read the technical section but personnel concerned with training and maintenance may also be reviewers. Once you have convinced the evaluators that your proposed solution is the correct solution, the next step is to convince them that you can install and maintain the system. The people reading the management section are now interested in *how* you are going to deliver, install, and test the solution. In this regard, the technical and management sections must work together in order to have a consistent theme.

For example, in one proposal by a major computer company, the technical volume stressed ease of installation, no requirements for a special computer room for cooling and cable runs, and some basic functionality once the system was running and tested. However, the management section stressed the need for a large and involved project team to oversee installation and test of this equipment. The complexity of the management plan was not consistent with the technical volume's theme of simple installation. As a result, the vendor lost points on the evaluation.

Development of the Management Section

✎ *Even if not required, you should consider including a project management section.*

Many RFPs do not require a management section, but simply ask for information about your company. RFPs that do require a management section often make it a part of the technical section. The following examples are taken from RFPs that were for multimillion-dollar projects:

Management. This section should include a description of the bidding firm, including age of company, number of years in business, number of employees, sales for most recent year, and a description of at least three currently installed systems of similar size.

This first example requests information about the vendors' management and company but does not request any information about installation, testing, and acceptance.

Management Support and Experience. This section should describe how the vendor proposes to meet those requirements dealing with vendor requirements found in the technical section of this RFP. Vendor must provide five reference sites that have similar applications and equipment.

In the second example, the vendor requirements that are referred to relate to service and maintenance, not to installation, testing, and acceptance. In both examples, the system proposed was well over a million dollars and required a considerable amount of coordination between the vendor, one subcontractor, and the customer.

The following example is taken from an RFP for a very large system that required over a year of work before it was brought on-line:

The vendor must demonstrate in this subsection their approach to the design, development, and installation phases of the project. A description of each task proposed by the vendor to meet the requirements of this RFP must be included. The proposal must also include a summary and detailed schedule indicating task start and completion dates, total time to complete the task and the vendor resources required for the tasks. For each task identified, the total vendor days estimated to complete the task must be listed.

This example provides a simple and clear outline for a management section by asking for basic information about design, development, and installation phases. The vendor is being forced to think through his solution and plan for setbacks, delays, and conflicts, in addition to addressing the project down to a task level. This level of detail requires vendors to have an established project management group that is familiar with project planning. Vendors who do not have this expertise will be quickly disqualified.

Below is a possible outline for a management section. This outline is generic but does mirror the basic sections of a complete management section. At a minimum, the management section should contain an introduction to the proposed management plan, what your capabilities are, who is responsible for installation and acceptance, and what the customer's responsibilities are. It is also possible to place descriptions of the service and maintenance plan, training classes, and corporate profile in this section.

- Introduction
- Project Management Approach
- Project Organization and Responsibilities
- Management of Subcontractors
- Project Schedules
- Acceptance Testing and Sign-off
- Corporate Capabilities and Facilities
- Maintenance Program
- Education Program
- Personnel Resumes
- Corporate Reference Accounts
- Corporate History

Using Proposal Boilerplate Material

See Chapter 4 on developing boilerplate files.

The management volume is a good place to make use of boilerplate files. Many management modules can be developed, standardized, and incorporated in a boilerplate library. Since these modules are in a standard format, they can be used as complete drop-ins for RFPs that do not request a certain format. For RFPs that do require a specific format, the modules can be used separately to satisfy other requirements. The following is a list of modules that can be developed as boilerplate files and kept readily available:

Resumes. Complete resumes should be kept on key company officers. Resumes also should be kept on account executives, project managers, lead engineers, and product developers who may be part of projects. You should also have available resumes for senior management: president, vice-presidents (CEO, COO, CIO).

Corporate profile. A standard company description should be written, including such information as history, company goals, personnel, manufacturing locations, and major product lines.

Service department. Normally, there are standard policies and contracts that state how a company maintains its products. These policies and contracts can be rewritten to provide a general description of your maintenance department and the services that are provided.

Education department. If your products require training, there will be a training department with class descriptions and dates. An overview of your training department should be written to include such information as your training philosophy, description of classes, descriptions of instructors (i.e., what types and how much experience) and how classes are developed by professional course designers.

Education is also an important area for selling. If your company has developed specialized training, such as computer-based training (CBT), video-based training (VBT), or other unique methods of training, these should be promoted—especially if your competition is behind in this area.

Reference accounts. Most RFPs require you to provide at least three reference accounts. These references will be used to verify your product works as stated, your company's performance in such areas as installation and service, and your overall performance as a company. This type of material includes information such as a very brief history of the referenced companies, why your company was chosen, and what equipment or service is currently in place at the customer's facility in addition to a designated contact with name, title, phone number, and address.

The reference accounts should be chosen to match the business application being proposed. For example, if you are bidding on a personnel computer system, you would try to have references to similar personnel applications that your company has provided.

Project management. Many companies who have project management departments develop a standard methodology over a period of time. Based on a standard organization and method, this file would contain a statement of work, the project plan, and a schedule.

Chapter 4, *Proposal Contents: Boilerplate Files,* discusses suitable subject matter for pre-written material and includes samples of a resume, corporate profile, maintenance schedule, class description, reference account, and organization charts.

Having boilerplate files on standard business areas will save you enormous amounts of time. Imagine having to create from scratch three reference accounts or tailoring the education department offerings by re-keying information from a brochure. This time can be better spent developing the "solution" or working on the "pricing," which typically don't receive enough attention.

Installation and Implementation

Installation and implementation are closely related activities and are generally tied together in an RFP. Installation refers specifically to when the equipment will be installed, what work is required before it can be installed, and what is needed during the installation. Implementation refers to the project in general and how such items as application development, training, bringing the system on-line, etc., will be achieved.

If your proposal requires installation of equipment, and prior to installation certain prerequisites must be met, an installation plan should be developed and submitted to the customer. This plan should be a schedule including an explanation of each step in the schedule. For example, if you are proposing a computer system that requires a special computer room, a controlled environment, filtered power lines, communication lines, and myriad other details, an installation schedule will be required if the system is to be installed on time. Generally, computer companies do not install computer rooms, which means that the customer is responsible for ensuring that the computer facilities are adequate for the system being purchased. However, it is your responsibility to provide the customer with the specifications for your equipment.

Many companies have an installation guide that outlines the exact operating specifications and all other requirements for their equipment. This guide is usually sent with the proposal as an appendix and referred to when writing the installation section.

Implementation is a broader view of the project schedule. It is concerned with identifying all of the project tasks and listing those tasks in a complete project schedule. Although the actual scheduled dates may change, the task list should not unless the project itself changes during final negotiations. The purpose of the implementation plan is to identify and break down the overall program into smaller, hence more manageable, pieces. Once all of the tasks have been identified, they can be organized by related groups, interdependencies can be established, schedules developed, and work assignments made.

It is important for a customer to know which work is his and when it needs to be completed.

For example, if you were bidding on installing a computer system, the implementation plan would be divided into major tasks, which are then subdivided into subtasks required to complete that piece of work. This task list and schedule will help you establish what tasks need to be performed before other tasks can be performed (interdependencies) and what tasks can be performed in parallel. Figure 3-3 is a simplified task list and schedule for a computer project.

This plan has be "collapsed" to just the major tasks and some of the subtasks, as you can see from the numbering. It is possible that your company can develop a "standard" project task list and this can be customized for each project. The proposal would include the standard list customized as much as possible for the proposal.

Project Organization and Key Project Personnel

RFPs for large complex systems often require an organization chart and resumes for the personnel who will be involved in the project. The organization chart identifies the project leader and defines the structure of the program; it also identifies key personnel by name and position. In addition, the RFP may also request resumes of all personnel who will be assigned to the project.

The organizational relationship should be presented in two charts. The first identifies where the proposed project resides within your organization and the second is the organization of the project. The customer is usually very interested in where the project resides within your organization and how close or far away it is from upper management. Even a simple diagram, as shown below, provides the customer with some sense of the project organization.

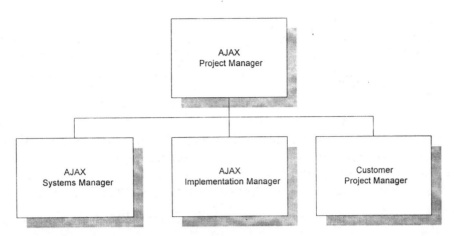

Resumes should be written in a standard format and generally be consistent in content (i.e., the depth of information provided) and in format. Project personnel resumes are written to emphasize that your staff has the skills needed for the current project. A standard format may include:

- Name
- Title
- Education
- Experience

Information concerning experience should begin with the last job completed and then describe this person's role in the current project. This type of resume is not the same as a resume that is used by a job applicant. Chapter 4, *Proposal Contents: Boilerplate Files,* discusses in detail formats for organization charts and resumes, including examples.

Summary

✎ *Planning is a key indicator to the customer of your capabilities.*

Having a strong management volume can be a deciding factor in the evaluation of your proposal. Often, a technical evaluation staff recommends at least two companies whose solutions meet all requirements. If the prices are also similar, the evaluation may focus on the management volume. Such requirements as project management, experience with similar applications, maintenance, education, references, or your company's financial profile may be stronger than the competition's and give you the extra points required to win. Also, there may be other intangible benefits derived from a strong management section. For example, providing a project plan complete with the names of the personnel involved, their positions and duties, and their resumes can be a strong indicator to the customer that your company is well organized, with the ability to execute your plan.

■ PRICING SECTION

Rounding out the basic proposal format is the pricing section. This section is perhaps the most misunderstood, has the most misconceptions about it, and generates the most debate when talked about after a long day of writing. Its value and worth should not be underestimated.

Who Reads the Pricing Section

Generally, this section is read and analyzed by an accounting group; however, everyone associated with the RFP will, sooner or later, look at this section. For larger, more formal and structured companies that release RFPs, the pricing evaluation is a formal process. This group will have comparative numbers for pricing hardware and also be able to use your competition's proposals for comparisons. The evaluation team will summarize each proposal's pricing section and score it, if required.

✑ For most companies receiving proposals, this is the first section to be looked at. It will influence the review or other sections.

This group will not, though, be able to relate functionality or other attributes to price. For example, many companies today purchase personal computer (PC) clones from various manufacturers and then add proprietary hardware and software to the unit. This practice will often double or triple the "street" price of a PC. Accounting personnel begin to have trouble understanding why a PC that they can buy for $4000 (street priced) is now priced at $12,000. Of course they may not understand that the addition of a special plug-in board is $1000 and the software to run it is $1000.

In one particular instance, a customer asked a vendor to develop and price an "upgrade" kit for the vendor's proprietary add-ons. This allowed the customer to buy PCs from their regular supplier at a lower price than the vendor could buy them. Once this practice was established, the upgrade kit became a standard offering from this vendor and even became a perceived selling point. This vendor also used the upgrade kit as a way of selling upgrades for existing PCs so those customers could minimize purchase of new units.

ID	Task Name
1	**PROJECT INITIATION & CONTROL**
2	**Organize Project**
19	**Project Control**
25	**Hardware Ordering and Acquisition**
29	**Software Ordering and Acquisition**
34	**Site Configuration and Site Survey**
35	Schedule Site Survey
36	Obtain Facilities Layout
37	Obtain Detailed Writing Schematics
42	**Installation Plan**
43	Site Preparation Plan
44	Site Equipment List
45	Installation Schedule
46	**Phase One - Backfile Conversion Muni and Superior Courts**
47	**Functional Design Stage**
48	Conduct High-level Application Analysis
60	Review Reporting Requirements
72	Finalize Workflow Application Requirements Definition
78	System Requirements Analysis
89	Technical Design Stage
103	Establish Security Rules
107	Develop Application
112	Application Interface Development
117	**Hardware Installation/Platform Services**
118	Receive HW for Internal Testing
119	Install HW for Internal Testing
120	Test Hardware
121	Verify Hardware Configuration
122	Ship HW to Marin Installation
123	Prepare Site for Hardware Installation
124	Verify Site Preparation
125	Install HW at Marin Site
126	Configure Hardware at Marin Site
127	Load All Third-party Software
128	Exercise and Tune all SW and Peripherals
129	Review/Accept HW Installation
130	**Software Installation at Marin Site**
131	Test and Verify Network Connectivity
132	Install Software
133	Establish Interface Terminal Emulation Connectivity
134	Full System Testing
135	**System Acceptance and Test Plan**
136	Prepare Draft of Acceptance Test Plan
141	Submit Final Test Plan to Marin
142	Perform System Acceptance Tests
143	System Acceptance
144	Sign Ready-for-Use
145	Backfile Conversion
148	Production Cutover
150	**Develop Custom Reports**
151	Review technical report specifications
152	Present custom design for approval
153	Develop and test reports
154	Verify test specifications
155	Document custom reports
156	Deliver custom reports
157	**Develop Procedures and Documentation**
158	Prepare System Administration Documentation
162	Deliver System Admin Documentation
163	Develop End User Documentation
168	Deliver End-user Documentation
169	Develop Users Manual
170	**Training**
171	Schedule System Admin Training
172	Deliver System Admin Training at Marin
173	Schedule End-user Training
174	Deliver End-user Training at Marin
175	Provide Training

Figure 3-3. *Sample Project Management Schedule*

In smaller, less formal companies that issue RFPs, the pricing evaluation process is often completed by the technical evaluation group. This group may be less skilled in pricing analysis and value projections and therefore their analysis may relate more directly to the established budget and comparative pricing.

If you can determine who will be reviewing your pricing section, it could influence the amount of information you provide and the method for organizing and presenting the pricing information.

Development of the Pricing Section

The content of the pricing section will vary widely. It may be as simple as an equipment list with prices, or so detailed as to include your cost estimating techniques. Many proposals are delivered with standard unit pricing and extended pricing that is taken from the established price book. Even large multimillion dollar proposals prepared for state or federal governments use prices directly from their established price guides.

Guidelines for pricing vary widely. Be prepared to be creative.

If the RFP provides instructions for setting up the section, these instructions should be followed. They should also be read and understood well before the proposals are because they may cause you to do work you had not anticipated. Also, often the pricing instructions are mixed together with contract instructions and these may require that you review the contract and provide feedback on any items that you may question.

The pricing section is a complex section that may require considerable calculation to arrive at a price. For example, if the project is for developing a computer system that requires custom code, the effort to price this code may take several weeks of time and involve personnel from engineering, project management, contracts, and pricing. Pricing is also difficult because it is often the case that you can't price the item until "programming" has been estimated and the programming estimation may only come after the proposal team decides exactly what is to be build.

Generally speaking, companies that have established products with part numbers and commercially available established prices are not asked to break products into component parts and then justify how the costs for individual parts were determined. This type of pricing is requested only in RFPs that require the vendor to build unique one-time-only products. For example, when pricing a PC, the vendor would not normally be asked to price the monitor, modem, SCSI card, etc., separately.

If you are bidding for state or federal contracts, the pricing may be based on the General Services Administration (GSA) price list. A GSA price list is used by the federal government to establish your lowest price for each product. Once you have established pricing for the GSA, you must be very cautious when bidding prices lower than those established whether to a commercial customer or to another federal customer.

A careful reading and understanding of the GSA contract should be required for anyone writing proposals. If you have a GSA contract but do not completely understand it, you should ask for an appointment with your local federal contracting office.

Organization of the Pricing Section

The pricing section generally contains:

- Equipment and license price breakdown
- Services and education
- Totals
- Shipping schedules
- Payment schedules
- Standard terms and conditions

✍ *Review and follow the RFP instructions.*

If your proposal is sufficiently detailed to warrant an in-depth pricing section, but the RFP does not ask for detailed responses, you can use the pricing outline in figure 3-4 as a guide. This outline is taken from an RFP that was released to procure a very large computer system. One frequently encountered problem results when bidding computer systems that require custom applications to be designed and coded: there is no place in most pricing models to show these prices. Similarly, if your proposals include project management, acceptance testing, and other tasks that you normally charge for, it is difficult to find a place in the RFP's pricing model for these prices. The pricing model you build for your proposal must meet, as a minimum, the model requested in the RFP. The outline in figure 3-4 is an example of a well-organized pricing section, and may provide you with additional ideas to include in your proposal's pricing section.

Remember that it is also a good idea to provide the customer with a physically separate price volume so the people who evaluate the proposal are not influenced by the price. It is wise, even if not asked, to create a separately bound price volume, mark it as such and, if possible, give it to the purchasing agent. Make only one copy and mark it *CONFIDENTIAL and PROPRIETARY.*

It is also possible and *sometimes* allowed to turn in the cost volume one or two weeks after the main proposal is due. This is because costing a large proposal often cannot be completed until the configuration, equipment lists, and personnel requirements are finalized. These may not be ready far enough in advance to allow the cost volume to be complete in parallel with the main technical sections. Discuss this possibility with the purchasing agent designated in the RFP.

The cost study must be presented in the following format:

A.　　Cost Total
1. Total all hardware costs.
2. Total all software costs.
3. Total all maintenance costs.
4. Total all project management costs.
5. Total all education costs.
6. Total all delivery/administration costs.
7. Total discounts available and where applicable.

B.　　Detailed Cost Schedules

The detailed cost schedules attached must be completed by all vendors submitting a response to the RFP. Unit pricing must be filled in, including hourly rates when applicable. A similar representation of this form will be accepted; however, any modification to the form must be highlighted and explained in detail.

Pricing must be submitted for the following categories:

• Hardware, all components

• Software, all components

• Software license fees

• Shipping and freight

• Taxes

• Implementation, includes project management, installation, development, customization, program testing, and system testing before as well as after the system is placed in production.

• Maintenance, regular maintenance as needed for normal operation of the image system; this category includes on-site, off-site, and upgrade costs.

• System support, for unexpected problems in which the vendor's organization must participate in order to be resolved.

• Supplies, as needed for ongoing production operations; required weekly, monthly, or annually.

• Training, must include training at the vendor's facilities as well as the cost for on-site training. Basic rates for customization of course material must also be included.

• Consultation, for post-installation projects to be costed on a time-and-materials basis.

Figure 3-4. *Pricing Outline*

Government RFPs, whether state or federal, sometimes will provide you with a series of forms that constitute the cost volume. These are fill-in-the-blanks forms and you have no other choice but to comply. A sample pricing for PCs is below.

Item	Quantity	Unit Price	Extended Price	Maintenance Price/Year
PC	5	3000.00	15,000.00	150.00
Monitor				
SCSI				
Hard Drive				
Ethernet				

Pricing Strategies

Generally speaking, most vendors have only a vague idea of how much the customer will spend and how much the competition will propose. Most often, the sales representative is asked "What's the price? What do we have to come in at to be competitive?" Using his "insider" knowledge, the sales representative will determine a figure and that becomes the target or "bogey" in proposal-ese.

This gets us back to qualifying the opportunity when the RFP is released. In one example, the customer put out an RFP for consulting services. Proposals came in around $45,000 to $55,000, which is not too bad for a price spread for 6 vendors (considering the poorly written RFP.) No contract was awarded! The customer had budgeted $10,000 for a $50,000 job. The delta was so great that even with reducing the requirements vendors could not get below $20,000.

Estimated pricing is estimating what the customer thinks the budget will be.

While it may not matter in some respects, the customer may have totally misjudged the amount of money they needed for a project. (The misjudgment is rarely on the plus side!) So, the vendors may come in within 10% of each other, but be 50% off from what has been budgeted by the customer. Thus, it is as important to understand how the customer derived the "bogey" as well as the competition.

Then, a certain amount of gamesmanship is played before completing the pricing section. The sales representative will want to have full list price for those items that he receives commission on and a healthy discount on those items that he does not receive commission on; and he will want to provide a number of things free, such as an extra training class, a no-charge project review, or an extra set of manuals.

These no-charge items, of course, come directly out of the training department's budget, or groups such as project management or manuals, which are considered profit centers. These groups are not willing to give their products away or even discount them because the margin made is often very small, relative to the margin made on the primary products that the company makes and sells, such as hardware and software.

Creative thinking is often called for to achieve the target.

If the proposed price is too far out of range of the target, a price reduction has to occur, if your proposal is to be considered competitive. Creative thinking is often called for to achieve the target price.

Discounting should not be the first option; it should be used last to arrive at the final target price only after all other "fat" has been trimmed from the proposal price. The first place to look is the basic product that is being proposed. Using a computer system as an example, a thorough review of the hardware and software configuration frequently will show up excess equipment to "cover the base." This excess is sometimes proposed to cover up a poor design or to provide an extra margin for specifications that are not completely understood. Sometimes excess equipment is proposed to dress up the system and add functionality that has not been requested and is not in the specifications.

High pricing often covers our lack of understanding of the RFP.

After this excess equipment is taken out, the next place to look is in the preliminary design for the project. Can the number of programmers be reduced without significant impact on the design itself or the delivery date? Sometimes, this can be achieved by rethinking the design schedule. Often, the application effort is overestimated because the RFP was not clear and a certain margin was built in to cover "project creep."

Revisit the RFP requirements that are suspect or not clear. Make an assumption, which is included in your proposal, and base your pricing on the assumption. This way, you can lower the price, but leave it open to negotiate if the customer disagrees with your assumption. Also, the idea of "Options" may help to reduce your costs by breaking big cost items into component parts that the customer may select. Be careful with options because they may confuse the customer.

If the price is still high according to the estimate, and as much excess as can be comfortably trimmed has been removed, then further price reductions can come from discounting.

✎*Discounting has no rules.*

Discounting has no common rules. The most frequent questions asked are: Do we just add a discount and not say anything? Do we attempt to explain it? What if the customer wants to know why? Several tactics seem to be in use:

Large quantity discount You explain that the customer qualifies for a quantity discount because he is buying more than X amount (usually 10).

New account discount. This discount is applied "one time only" and only applies to new accounts.

Old account discount. This discount applies to "favored" customers who have demonstrated that they consistently spend a large amount every year.

Showcase discount. If the customer allows you to use the completed installation as a reference site for customer tours and verification of equipment operation, you will give them a discount.

Partnership development discount. This applies if you can convince the customer to allow you to beta test a product or build a product that is somewhat unique to your product line and you "need customer input."

Try and buy discount. If the customer is willing to give your product a chance for X amount of time, you will discount the basic product.

Straight discount. You explain that this discount is used to get the business so you can meet your quota. The customer and salesman win. Company may or may not win.

A note of caution: What is termed *selling discounts* instead of product can have long-range effects. A discount should have a reason and should be effective for a single purchase only. Discounting sets a precedent that is hard to overcome once established and can affect future relationships with a customer who comes to "expect" a lower price.

Summary

Because the pricing section is perhaps the most volatile portion of the proposal, this section requires more time and work than is normally expected-and at a time when everyone on the proposal team is close to exhaustion or mayhem. This combination of factors can lead to a poorly priced, written, and explained pricing section. On top of these problems, the pricing section is often the only one that gets management's attention (both yours and theirs). Frequently, management will want a review of the pricing section with detailed information about any deviations or discounts. Being bottom-line oriented, most managers take a critical look at the pricing section and usually they are able to justify changing something. This change will further impact your ability to complete the section on time.

The only possible answer to these difficulties is proper planning, strict adherence to a schedule, and the ability to persevere.

- Plan. Having the pricing materials available and in place at the start of the proposal will help. If your company does not have any formal methodologies, at least collect several recently submitted proposals and copy what is applicable for your proposal.
- Schedule. Not only is strict adherence needed, but the schedule must be functional and include time for management reviews.
- Persevere. Being in charge of a proposal is not always a popular task. Fellow workers stay clear of you, managers can get very busy on other projects, people in other departments often drift away because you do not directly control them. If you have planned correctly, kept to your schedule, and know this proposal is a winner, it is up to you to simply outlast everyone else to get what is needed.

Be prepared to modify your pricing.

Finally, after you submit your proposal and make the short list, you must anticipate and be prepared for customer changes. These changes can take several forms: frequently a customer will want to add or subtract equipment; he will want to reduce functionality to reduce the price; or he may make totally unexpected requests that force you back to the drawing board. But in whatever form these changes occur, they will affect the pricing schedule. This last stage may be a good opportunity for you to win, if you outlast your competition and continue to provide quality and professional answers.

■ APPENDIX

An appendix may provide more detailed information.

An appendix is a separate section of your proposal that contains supplemental information. Generally, this information is considered of value to an evaluator, but may be too detailed to include in the main body of the proposal. For example, you may be writing about your software development methodology, but would not insert the "manual" in the body of the proposal. If the manual is brief or a summary is available, you may refer the reader to "Appendix A,

Summary of AJAX Software Development Methodology, for more complete details."

Some RFPs will require an appendix and will outline what material goes into the appendix. Most RFPs, however, do not require an appendix and therefore its use is optional. Like other sections in your proposal, the appendix should be organized early to minimize confusion.

Appendices are named by letter, not number:

Appendix A - Product Data Sheets

Appendix B - Sample Contracts

Appendix C - Training Schedule

Appendix D - Maintenance Schedule

Appendix E - Annual Report

✍ Set up your appendix contents early to avoid confusion. The appendix section should be set up in the beginning stages of the proposal effort and a copy of its contents distributed with the proposal table of contents. If established early, writers will be able to refer to the appropriate appendix as they write and need to make a reference. If not established in sufficient time, writers might create their own appendix, which may conflict with other appendices, and this problem may not be recognized until the final version of the proposal is being read.

Any additional appendices should be added to the end of the list and not inserted ahead of other letters. When an additional appendix is added ahead of other letters after the list has been established, there is the chance that some writers will have already referred to the original list. Any writers who have not received the changed list will make incorrect references. Again, this may not be caught, if at all, until the proposal is being given a final review

The appendix can be used for providing any information that may be of value to your proposal. It can include separate binders with technical manuals or non-technical material such as:

- Annual and financial reports
- Company brochures and data sheets
- Reprints of articles about the company or product
- Industry surveys
- Industry analysts' reports
- Sample contracts
- Sample training class outlines

- Training schedules with places and dates
- Personnel policies and guidelines
- Unusual policies and procedures
- White papers on your industry or company

✍Appendices should not be used as dumping grounds for excess material. Material should be relevant and accessible.

Although the appendix will help you organize material for your proposal, it should not contain material that is not directly related to your proposal. Each appendix should be referenced in the proposal and provide information that enhances or supplements the topic being discussed. Sometimes an appendix is used to provide unrelated material and this will lessen the impact of any material that has value.

Unless requested in the RFP, material in an appendix may not be considered or read by the evaluators. Therefore, any material that is needed to satisfy a requirement in the RFP should be in the main body of the proposal. You should not depend on material in an appendix to satisfy requirements in an RFP.

■ SUMMARY

We covered a lot of ground in this section. The proposal you submit should be well organized, information should flow naturally from one subject to the next, and the "sales pitch" should be understandable and supportable. Self-inflated claims such as "...the industry leader..." have little relevance and may do more harm than good.

✍Use features and benefits that sell.

The sales message should be centered on features and benefits first, and comparisons to the competition second. Negative selling is never a good option, but fair comparisons and assessments between products have value. Remember that many product comparisons are meaningless unless the comparison treats the products equally on a feature by feature basis.

The proposal you write will be one of several being read by evaluators. Evaluators like proposals that make their job easy, which means, if your proposal follows the RFP instructions it will be looked upon favorably. The more time an evaluator has to "find" the answer to a requirement, the less time may be given to understanding whether the response is compliant or not.

If there are few or no proposal guidelines, use the general guidelines suggested in this section. When in doubt about this, always ask a question to get clarification from the customer. When in doubt about the amount of writing needed, error on the light side. Too often proposals are so bloated that the real story never gets through.

Boilerplate Files

Standard files, in the form of boilerplate,
will help you maintain consistent information
to all users.

Boilerplate Files

■ INTRODUCTION

The term *boilerplate* originally described standard contract terms and conditions (T&C). For example, payment terms such as *NET 30* or *FO.B. Destination* are part of the usual T&C. In recent years, boilerplate has evolved to mean anything, whether text or illustrations, that is standard material representing your products or contracts. For example, an account of a past successful project that demonstrates your company's ability to perform on a similar contract is a boilerplate reference.

✑ Boilerplate files should be an important part of your proposal development effort.

Boilerplate files can become an important part of your sales program and one of the more useful tools provided by marketing. Be prepared, however, for resistance to preparing boilerplate files as some people see them as being "canned" text that avoids addressing the real issues. This argument has some merit, in that boilerplate can be "overused" and fresh "solution oriented" proposal writing is not completed. It is up to the individual proposal manager or writer to ensure that boilerplate is used properly.

If set up correctly, maintained, and supported, boilerplate files can help in many ways:

■ Having at least 50 percent of a proposal pre-written allows the sales team more time to keep in contact with the customer.

■ Boilerplate files give headquarters some margin of control over, and ensure consistency of, information being sent to customers.

■ Boilerplate files enable you to respond more efficiently to an RFP, in addition to producing a better more complete document.

■ They visually demonstrate to the customer that your company can produce a major effort in a short amount of time.

There are some potential problems in using boilerplate files, however. Pre-written material can be as dangerous as it is helpful if not kept current. Since most proposals become an attachment to a successful contract, obsolete or incorrect information also will become part of the contract.

Keep in mind that the purpose of a proposal is to tell a potential customer you understand his requirements, you have a solution to those requirements, and you are able to address all the issues in our proposal; it is a written personal commitment to meeting his unique needs. Using boilerplate files exclusively in generating a proposal achieves no more than stapling a few data sheets together and attaching a cover letter. Think of a proposal in terms of modules of information with the pre-written boilerplate files as completed modules ready to be inserted at the appropriate places.

✍ Using boilerplate files exclusively in generating a proposal achieves no more than stapling a few data sheets together.

The purpose of this section is to help you develop ready-to-use materials about your company, products, and services; how to use them to your best advantage; how to organize and index them; how to get them to the people who will be using them; and how to maintain the files to ensure they are always current. Two types of boilerplate files are considered: written text that is stored on-line or in reproducible masters, and artwork in the form of illustrations, tables, and photographs.

This section will also discuss how the Internet/intranets and collaborative/groupware software can be effectively used for distributing proposal information and collaborative working on proposals.

See also, later in this section, the discussion on developing, distributing, and maintaining the boilerplate files. If done properly, your corporation will have a department responsible for ensuring the boilerplate files are accurate and current. *Having old or out-dated information is worse than no information.*

■ TEXT BOILERPLATE FILES

One way to gain control of the proposal process is to have as much material as possible already written. The following is a list of standard material that can be written, formatted, and ready for use when preparing a proposal. A common question or concern is how much or how little should be written. It is advisable to always provide as much information as possible since it is easier to delete something if not needed than to write something new at the last minute.

It is a total waste of time to have someone rekey a data sheet or training class description instead of having that already prepared.

Descriptions of Products or Services

If your company sells such products as equipment, machinery, or computer systems or hardware, existing data sheets for your products can be edited, reformatted, and used as boilerplate material. If your product is software, you may be able to develop the boilerplate files from sales literature, technical data sheets, or manuals. If the product is a service, such as Internet development, boilerplate can be developed from existing product sheets.

✑A common question is how much or how little needs to be written.

Although marketing material seems easy and straightforward to use, some of it may not be suitable for proposals and will need to be extensively edited. The problem is that marketing literature tends to be of an advertising nature whereas proposals are more technical and conservative. Be aware of inconsistencies in style, presentation, and amount of information that may result from combining sales literature modules with technical material taken from manuals or data sheets.

If your company provides services, use existing profiles of the services offered and how those services are carried out. This may include a description of the service itself, the personnel profiles, and any unique products used to perform the service. In this case, service is the product offered. If there is no literature already written suitable for boilerplate files, have a marketing writer prepare new material as part of the boilerplate files.

✑RFPs may be a series of questions causing you to cut and paste your boilerplate responses.

RFP requirements are not written such that you are able to drop a whole section into a response requirement. For example, your boilerplate on a personal computer may include everything from the monitor specifications to the floppy-drive specifications. In the example below, the RFP requirements call out each component of the personal computer as unique requirements. It would be inappropriate for you to drop a complete data sheet in as a response and force the evaluator to find the information.

In the example in figure 4-1, you would have to "cut and paste" the data sheet into the appropriate response section. While this may cause you more work, it helps the evaluation and ensures that all of your correct features and benefits are found.

The RFP requirements may call out each component separately such as:

1) Our system requirements for monitors are as follows:

   a) Color monitor

   b) Resolution 1600x1200

   c) 21" monitor

2) The CPU should be 300 MHz or better

3) The hard drive must be 10 gigabytes

4) Floppy disk drive must be 120 megabytes

5) The Ethernet card must handle 100 Mb/s

Figure 4-1. *Example RFP Specifications*

If you were to just "dump" your workstation data sheet into this RFP section, chances are you would lose points for not following the RFP guidelines even if your equipment met the specs. If you practice "dumping" throughout the proposal, evaluators may find you non-responsive.

Company Services Provided

Services vary, of course, from company to company. However, the following two are common to most companies and lend themselves well to boilerplate files. The numbered items can be written in detail. stored as separate files, and combined during the proposal effort.

1. Introduction and overview of organization
2. Service hours
   -Normal hours
   -Outside of normal hours
3. Response time to repair
   -Normal response time
   -Faster than normal response time
3. Location of repair depots
4. Location of spare parts depots
5. Need for spare parts on site
6. Ability to meet special requests
7. Normal repair procedures
8. Preventive maintenance program

9. Normal inspection visits

10. Special services offered

Maintenance and Hours of Service

The first and perhaps most important is how the product will be serviced after purchase. This section should be more detailed than the information outlined in the contract T&C. Tables, such as the one in figure 4-2, are very useful, easily maintained, and provide information that can be used in a variety of places.

Table B-1. Extended-hour Maintenance Coverage		
Day	*Coverage Time*	*Charge*
Saturday or Sunday	8 hours	Add 5.0% to BMMC*
Saturday or Sunday	12 hours	Add 10.0% to BMMC*
Monday-Friday	16 hours	Add 25.0% to BMMC
Monday-Friday	24 hours	Add 40.0% to BMMC
Monday-Friday	12 hours	Add 15.0% to BMMC
		*Basic Monthly Maintenance Charge

Figure 4-2. *Sample Table for Maintenance Response Time*

Education

The second is education. Most companies offer some type of training program that customers will pay for. Therefore, this service needs to be discussed in detail. If your company has standard classes and training facilities, describe all classes (see figure 4-3) and the facilities. If your company provides training through other companies or self-paced tutorials, describe each one.

■ Introduction and overview of organization

■ Description of training philosophy

■ Description of training facilities
  -classroom atmosphere
  -monitor screens available
  -internal facilities
  -lunchroom, etc.
  -workshops available
  -laboratories

- Resume of typical instructor
- Location of training facilities
- Possible on-site training
- Materials supplied
- Descriptions of all classes
- Ability to provide unique training
- Ability to respond to special requirements

Corporate Descriptions

✍ Corporate descriptions are provided to allay any fears that your company is too small to handle the project.

Often, an RFP requires a description of your corporation, who will be in charge of the project, what type of project management you follow, and who are the senior people involved in the project. Relationships are easily depicted and revised by developing a hierarchical organization chart. This is also a very good place to describe any unique equipment or facilities that will differentiate your company from other companies. A corporate description can be taken from annual reports.

Corporate Profile

The corporate profile should include the following information:

- Date company was founded and primary objective/mission
- Major product line and any other equipment and services offered
- Number of people employed
- Personnel functions as a percentage (sales 20%, service 40%, R&D 20%, management 20%)
- Description of special laboratories, equipment, and processes
- Primary locations of manufacturing plants, repair depots, sales offices, service offices, and other significant locations
- Basic company organization and organization charts
- What countries you are located in
- What the reporting relationships are if you are owned by another company

Administration Training

Course Title: Ajax workstation Administration

Duration: 5 days

Instructional
Materials: 1. Workstation Administration Student Guide
2. Book, "Workstation Administration," by Jones and Wiley
3. System command Summary

COURSE DESCRIPTION:

This course is designed for persons assuming total responsibility for the administration of an Ajax workstation system. It is an advanced course which focuses on the fundamental skills required to maintain the Ajax workstation system environment.

It includes information on management of the database and management of the workstations.

Topics are presented using a problem-solving approach. Guided by the instructor, students are expected to refer to the manuals to determine the steps necessary to accomplish administrative tasks.

Maximum students per session is ten. Additional courses may be scheduled at prevailing rates.

COURSE OUTLINE:

1. Editor use
2. Documentation
3. System Startup and Shutdown
4. File System Management
5. user Setup and control
6. Backups
7. Device Configuration
8. Workstation Operations
9. Database Operations
10. Preventive Maintenance Procedures

Figure 4-3. *Sample Class Description*

Project Management

✍In a tight
competition, a
well-written
Project
Management
plan may be
the difference
between
winning and
losing.

Project management may or may not be a factor in your proposal depending on the size and type of business you are bidding. If, however, you do bid on large jobs that require project management, try to collect old proposals and talk to current project managers to get the information. This is usually a sensitive area and care must be taken not to overstate your abilities. These files in particular should be an outline of possibilities and should be reviewed and revised for each new proposal by the designated project manager.

A project management file should include the following:

- Project management approach
- General project principles employed
- Project team organization
- Project staffing and duties
- Project leader and duties
- Project plan
- Project deliverables
- Vendor's responsibilities
- Customer's responsibilities

The project plan should be your first attempt at putting together what you perceive to be the major steps of a project plan. While this plan may not be accurate or even close to the final plan, it gives the customer something to review and consider. There is also a fair chance that your competition will be too lazy to do this and will only talk about putting together a plan "...after contracts have been signed...."

Figure 4-4 is an example of a project plan. It is important to emphasize that putting a plan together, even for the smallest project, will help you to:

1) Think through the steps involved—for your own benefit
2) Provide the customer with a "better than a guess" idea of what is involved in installing and maintaining your equipment
3) Provide the customer with a subject in your proposal in which he may ask questions and begin a dialogue with you about the project

ID	❶	Task Name	Duration	Start	Finish	May 30, '99
						T | W | T | F | S | S | M
2		**AJAX Proposal**	**984 hrs**	**Tue 6/1/99**	**Thu 11/18/99**	
3		**PreRFP Activities**	376 hrs	Tue 6/1/99	Wed 8/4/99	
4		**Prepare Survey**	216 hrs	Tue 6/1/99	Wed 7/7/99	
5		Discuss market	2 wks	Tue 6/1/99	Mon 6/14/99	
6		Determine survey objectives	3 days	Tue 6/15/99	Thu 6/17/99	
7		Draft of survey	1 wk	Fri 6/18/99	Thu 6/24/99	
8		Testing	1 wk	Fri 6/25/99	Thu 7/1/99	
9		Final copy of survey	4 days	Fri 7/2/99	Wed 7/7/99	
10		**Survey**	160 hrs	Thu 7/8/99	Wed 8/4/99	
11		Conduct survey	2 wks	Thu 7/8/99	Wed 7/21/99	
12		Analyze results	2 days	Thu 7/22/99	Fri 7/23/99	
13		Create summary report	3 days	Mon 7/26/99	Wed 7/28/99	
14		Prepare presentation	5 days	Thu 7/29/99	Wed 8/4/99	
15		**Present results**	**0 days**	**Wed 8/4/99**	**Wed 8/4/99**	
16		**Marketing Plan**	608 hrs	Thu 8/5/99	Thu 11/18/99	
17		**Conceptualize**	112 hrs	Thu 8/5/99	Tue 8/24/99	
18		Brainstorm	3 days	Thu 8/5/99	Mon 8/9/99	
19		Create strategy	8 days	Tue 8/10/99	Thu 8/19/99	
20		Forecast sales	2 days	Fri 8/20/99	Mon 8/23/99	
21		Determine advertising budget	1 day	Tue 8/24/99	Tue 8/24/99	
22		**Write Plan**	136 hrs	Wed 8/25/99	Thu 9/16/99	
23		Draft of plan	1 wk	Wed 8/25/99	Tue 8/31/99	
24		Review plan	2 wks	Wed 9/1/99	Tue 9/14/99	
25		Prepare final plan	2 days	Wed 9/15/99	Thu 9/16/99	
26		**Present marketing plan**	**0 days**	**Thu 9/16/99**	Thu 9/16/99	
27		**Advertising Campaign**	360 hrs	Fri 9/17/99	Thu 11/18/99	
28		**Input**	56 hrs	Fri 9/17/99	Mon 9/27/99	
29		Prepare product brief	2 days	Fri 9/17/99	Mon 9/20/99	
30		Prepare creative brief	1 wk	Tue 9/21/99	Mon 9/27/99	
31		**Kick-off meeting**	**0 days**	Mon 9/27/99	Mon 9/27/99	

Figure 4-4. *Sample Project Plan*

Personnel

Other corporate descriptions that can be pre-written are resumes of leading company officers as well as lead engineers and product developers who may be part of projects (see figure 4-5). Once the format is decided upon, it will be faster to develop **resumes for** everyone involved in the project. Many RFPs require resumes for the project personnel.

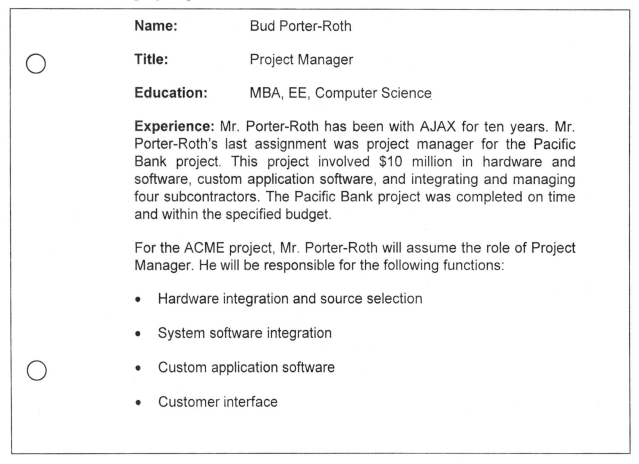

Name: Bud Porter-Roth

Title: Project Manager

Education: MBA, EE, Computer Science

Experience: Mr. Porter-Roth has been with AJAX for ten years. Mr. Porter-Roth's last assignment was project manager for the Pacific Bank project. This project involved $10 million in hardware and software, custom application software, and integrating and managing four subcontractors. The Pacific Bank project was completed on time and within the specified budget.

For the ACME project, Mr. Porter-Roth will assume the role of Project Manager. He will be responsible for the following functions:

- Hardware integration and source selection

- System software integration

- Custom application software

- Customer interface

Figure 4-5. *Sample Resume*

Reference Account Descriptions

An important boilerplate file that can be developed is a description of past projects or customers that are successfully using your product and can be used as references in the proposal. The reference account file should include at least the following information:

- Name and address of company
- Type of business or industry
- Contact name, address, and telephone number
- Contract number
- Length of contract or performance period
- Dollar amount of contract
- Description of project or application
- Description of equipment installed

✍ Ensure that your reference accounts are current and still in good standing.

This type of boilerplate file is very useful, but is also very sensitive. The most powerful type of reference account description is one in which you can actually name the account and a person within the account to contact. It is also impressive to be able to visit that account if a site visit is requested in the RFP. On the other hand, few sales representatives feel comfortable with potential customers calling existing customers directly if there is a chance that the reference account has experienced any problems. Figure 4-6 is a sample reference account description.

Another problem with reference accounts is they tend to change—not only from good to bad, but from one level of equipment or service to another. It is especially important that reference account files are kept current as changes occur.

The actual types of reference accounts that should be in the boilerplate files depend on your business. For example, a large software company might have several markets for its business, such as banking, communications networking, retail point-of-sale, and perhaps a library system. In this case, the software company would have one or more references for each type of business. If your business is service-related, the references would be two or three of the largest and best-run accounts.

The actual format for writing a reference account could be as follows:

- Introduction and description of service performed
- Situation at account before your company
- Situation that led to the change
- Situation after your service
- Description of services performed
- List of equipment used to perform the job
- Amount of work being performed by the above equipment
- Appropriate high-level customer quotation

Name: ACME Bank

Location: St. Louis, MO

Project
Leader: Joan Crawford
            1919 State Street
            St. Louis, MO
            (312) 555-1212

Contract: FP091765

Type: Fixed Price

Performance
Period: 1/4/85 - 1/4/92

Description: AJAX was responsible for supplying a turnkey computer system to automate ACME Bank's automated teller machine (ATM) system. This system is fully installed and is currently handling 500 transactions per hour per branch. There are a total of ten branches with two ATMs per branch.

Ajax provided all system hardware, system software, peripheral devices, the communications network, and the ATM. Ajax also provided, through a subcontractor, the applications software. The application involved working with ACME customers in the design of each screen, the acceptable response time, and additional functions.

Ajax also was responsible for the system training, end-user training, and system maintenance. This system has met and exceeded all requirements and has increased bank activity by 42%.

Current plans require installation of new branch sites, upgrading the current computer to the next performance model, and developing new services based around current installations.

ACME currently has the following installed equipment:

4 ea. Bonus Computer Systems, model 11-21
4 ea. interface modules
20 ea. Alpine ATMs, model 50
10 ea. X.25 gateways and communications peripherals

Figure 4-6. *Sample Reference Account*

A reference account is most useful if the work being performed is similar to the type being proposed so the potential customer can see your work and relate that work to his job. Customer references with demonstrable products that are installed and working, not future or intended products still on the drawing board, lend more credibility to your proposal.

Reference accounts should be cross-indexed by the application, or work being accomplished, the name of the account, and the size of the account (whether in dollars, workstations, lines of code, etc). Most customers like to read about jobs similar to their own for a number of reasons:

- They like to know that you, the vendor, speak their language. There is nothing worse than paying a vendor and having to teach them "the business..."

- Many customers don't want to be the "beta" site for your first stab at developing a new application.

- A second or third generation customer is going to benefit from your previous experience—especially in fast moving technology fields.

Capabilities and Facilities

✍ Providing capabilities and facilities information will distinguish your company from the competition.

A capabilities and facilities section reinforces your ability to handle a contract by demonstrating you have the resources needed and they are available. These resources will vary according to the type of company, but typically would include:

- Description of corporate facilities including number of personnel employed and total square footage available

- Description of facilities, factories, assembly areas, warehouses, parts and re-manufacturing depots

- Descriptions of unique equipment or custom-built facilities such as a custom design microchip manufacturing plant, a special satellite acoustic test area, or a wind tunnel

- Capabilities of facilities to perform work, e.g., microchips per hour, total build capacity

- Ability to meet or exceed increasing demands or peak work abilities

- Ability to build new facilities or increase capacity of existing facilities

✍ New and smaller companies must prove themselves.

Providing this type of information, whether required or not, may help distinguish your company and proposal from the competition.

For example, a new service company bidding on a large contract must demonstrate to the potential customer that it does, in fact, have the resources to handle the contract. Perhaps it is a large landscaping project for a city park and your company is a new landscaping business. For a large job, the city (who wrote the RFP) knows that to meet the time requirement, the winner will have to move so many cubic yards of earth per hour and in order to do that, they will have to demonstrate the appropriate number and type of earth movers.

If your company owned the equipment and had available all required resources, it would put your proposal in a better position than a company that has to rent or lease more equipment and hire additional resources in order to complete the contract.

Previous Proposals

✍ Previous proposals are a good source of material but it must be scrubbed before use.

In addition to the basic material collected from headquarters' sources, there are also proposals written in the field that may yield some excellent material for proposal boilerplate. Many good proposals are written in the field and there is a good chance that parts of the proposals can be cannibalized and turned into boilerplate. Below are some examples and ideas:

- Application specific executive summary. Often an executive summary is written by an industry expert, whether it be the sales rep or a consultant brought in to help. It is a good idea to warehouse proposals that deal with vertical industry applications such as transportation, pharmaceutical, insurance, etc. These executive summaries can be "scrubbed" by the proposal boilerplate team (for lack of a better term) to eliminate customer references but keep industry specific insights.

- Product specific write-ups. As discussed in previous sections, an RFP can be made up of a list of questions to be answered. It is a safe assumption that if one customer asks a question, it will be asked again in the future. This is similar, in a sense to the Internet FAQ (frequently asked questions) file. Most companies know from experience that there are certain questions that are asked over and over. Having ready-made answers to these questions and available help on-line will greatly enhance the proposal effort, and potentially provide more accurate answers.

- Product comparisons. Often, an RFP wants you to compare two products, such as two databases, and explain why you would choose one over the other. For example, you give the customer a choice between Oracle and SQL Server and they want to know the differences and trade-offs.

- Third party or partner proposals. Depending on how you operate as a business, you may team or subcontract to a system integrator or value-added reseller. Third parties often specialize in vertical market area, such as insurance, and their proposals may provide a wealth of detail that you would not normally have access to. Careful review of final third-party proposals, and permission to "copy," should be a regular exercise for the boilerplate team.

These are some of the subject areas that will enhance your boilerplate files. One major computer company, for example, maintained executive summary outlines for all of the vertical markets they covered. The above areas should not limit your thinking but provide a starting point.

■ GRAPHICS BOILERPLATE FILES

✎Illustrations of all types play a vital role in a proposal.

Illustrations should play a vital role in any proposal; however, because they are even more difficult and time consuming than writing text, illustrations often are not used to advantage or used at all. Like boilerplate text, illustrations that are common to your company can be prepared beforehand, indexed, filed, and be available for use in any proposal. These illustrations can serve all field offices and provide the same benefits as boilerplate text. Incorporating illustrations in proposals is discussed in detail in Chapter 5, *Proposal Contents: Illustrations.*

Remember that illustrations, like text files, can become out-of-date and using old illustrations may "technologically" date your proposal in addition to providing inaccurate data.

Following are descriptions of the types of illustrations that should be in the files. Most illustrations can be found in existing company literature. Review product brochures, training files, and product manuals for sources of illustrations. If not available, new illustrations should be drawn or photographs taken.

✎Your graphics program may already have boilerplate drawings.

Many illustrations are electronically generated and may already be available over the corporate network. With the ability of word processor programs to handle illustrations, and the number of illustration software packages, it has never been easier to put illustrations into a proposal. Many illustration software programs come with extensive clip art resources that can be used to generate diagrams of computer systems, computer networks, architectural layouts and designs, and many other business applications.

These "clip-art" figures can also be enhanced with drawings made specifically for your company by skilled graphic illustrators. In addition to drawings, other forms of artwork can be incorporated electronically such as digital photographs and scanned images. Digital photographs allow you to take a picture of a facility and insert into your proposal without the support of the art department or other group. A scanner can digitally copy almost any image—from photographs to drawings—and allow you to insert the digital image into your proposal. This means that even if there is a detailed representation in a manual and you don't have access to the original, it is possible to scan and insert that drawing.

A wide-range of software tools will help you to illustrate your proposal.

There are also other "electronic" tools available that will enhance your proposal by providing graphics or illustrations. A list includes, but is not limited to, the following:

- Drawing Software. This type of software ranges from simple to extremely complex. The most useful programs are those with predrawn illustrations for computers, networks, office furniture, buildings, high-technology objects such as satellites, etc. These predrawn illustrations can usually be linked with arrows, circles, network clouds, and many other connectors. The average user no longer has to be an artist to put together a reasonably good diagram.

- Organization Software. These programs generally are designed to build organization charts and other charts that show placement of personnel within a company.

- Workflow Software. Workflow may be specialized for certain industries, but in general the software shows how a work process moves from one step to another. The workflow diagrams can be cut and pasted into a proposal.

- Project Management Software. This allows the user to develop and build a project. The completed project task list can be shown as a written task list or a chart with tasks connected. The completed project, whether written or drawn, can be inserted into the proposal.

- Screen Capture Software. Screen capture software allows you to take a picture of what is on your computer monitor and save it. The saved image can be pasted into the proposal at the appropriate place. A screen shot may be taken to show proposed screens or work that has been competed for other customers.

- Spreadsheet Software. Spreadsheet programs can provide everything from simple tables to graphical charts and illustrations. These illustrations of numbers will provide users with different views of the same data.

- Internet. While this is not a software package, many types of illustrations, charts, photographs, and others can be downloaded from Internet sites. Care should be taken to properly recognize copyrighted material or original authors.

Products or Equipment

✎ Product illustrations can be found in many areas of the company.

Manuals are a good place to start in developing the boilerplate files. If your company has a graphics or technical art department, the original illustrations from manuals will be kept there. The idea for the project should be discussed with the manager of the illustrations department and a plan for obtaining the required illustrations should be formed before any work is started. This plan should include the sizing requirements for the art.

After obtaining a complete set of manuals for the products you will be writing proposals for, start searching for illustrations, making notes of the manual and page numbers. When a complete manual is thoroughly searched, copy the marked pages on a photocopier and write the manual number and page on the back of the copy. The art department or printers who produced the manuals will need this information when they begin to search their files for the illustrations you are requesting.

Possible illustrations for products or equipment are:

- Screen-shots of product designs
- Screen-shots of products used
- Photographs of products
- Line drawings of products
- Wiring diagrams and schematics
- Cross-section and cutaway drawings
- Parts breakouts
- Unique features diagrams

Figure 4-7 is an example of a stock boilerplate illustration that can be used to support text descriptions of products.

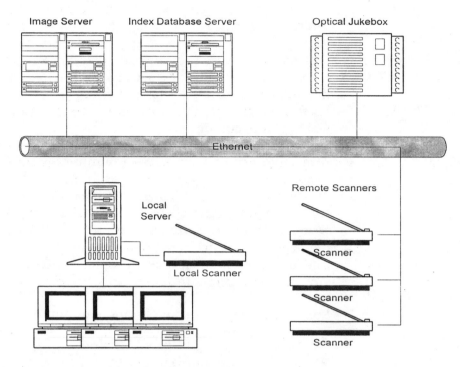

Figure 4-7. *Typical Boilerplate Illustration*

Facilities

In proposals, facilities are often described but not illustrated in any manner. For example, if your company is in the aerospace business and you have a special vacuum chamber, a photograph of the facility it is housed in and several photographs of the chamber add credibility to the text.

Types of facilities are:

- Headquarters buildings
- Typical training classroom
- Research laboratories
- Personnel at workstations
- Special equipment
- Special tools designed and used
- Manufacturing buildings
- Manufacturing assembly areas
- Quality control areas
- Clean room areas

■ Unique transportation facilities

✎Photographs add credibility.

Photographs have more credibility and should be used instead of line drawings or architectural renderings for facilities with working equipment or special features. These illustrations should be placed as close to the text as possible for maximum impact. Photographs are difficult to use in a proposal and usually require special treatment and handling.

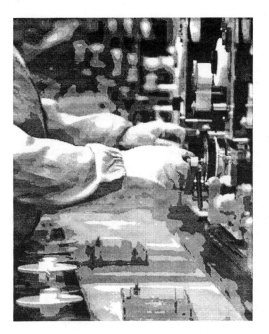

However, a picture of a clean-room adds credibility to your proposal and gives the reader some assurance that you have experience in this area.

Headquarters Organization and Personnel

✎Organization charts visually show the customer how a project will be managed.

In a proposal that requires a management section to demonstrate how a program will be implemented, the RFP will ask for a management organization chart and resumes of key personnel. Organization charts can be done several ways and kept in the boilerplate library. The first might illustrate how your company or division fits into a larger holding company, if that is applicable. Or, as shown by the chart in figure 4-8, start with the top management of your company and chart down to the vice president's level. Next, start with the vice president responsible for your division or group and branch down to the line managers who will be working on this particular program.

This sequential breakdown of management organization allows you to use all of the charts or just the one closest to the project. It also complements the text if your company is large and the relationships are complicated. The primary purpose of an organization chart is to show the potential customer how close his project will be to top management.

As part of a management plan, the RFP also may ask for the resumes of key personnel on the project. These would be kept in the text boilerplate files, but photographs of the people for whom the resumes are written would be kept in the illustration files.

Also, as part of the management plan, the RFP will request schedule charts and implementation flow diagrams. These charts can be kept in basic form and then filled in by the proposal team.

These type of organizational charts are easily developed with current software packages. The software to build an org chart is even available in most word processing packages and can be handled by almost anyone on the proposal team.

If you are in charge of providing these org charts but haven't the resources, it is possible to hand-draw the chart and give/send/fax to an administrative aide to have the chart produced. Once completed, the chart(s) can be inserted into the text at the appropriate place in your proposal.

Reference Accounts

Many RFPs request reference account descriptions be provided in the proposal. Depending on your product or service, the text for these accounts can be enhanced by providing photographs of working installations or of your product or service being used by a customer. This will reinforce to the evaluator that your company has its products actually in the field in operation as opposed to a company that may still be in the design stage and not have a working product or reference.

AJAX Corporation

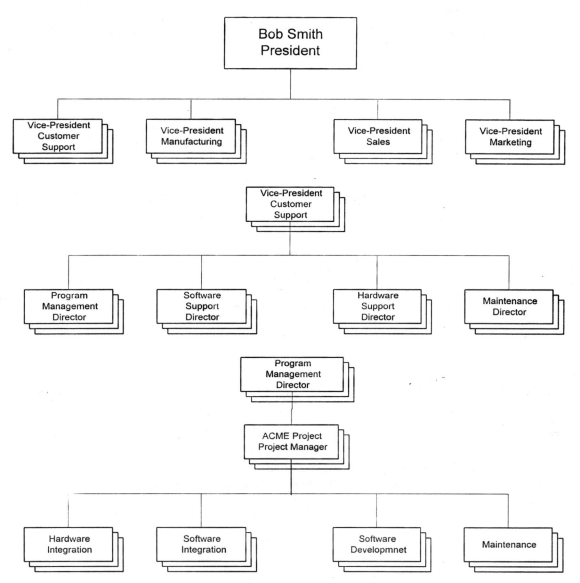

Figure 4-8. *Management Organization Charts*

These illustrations will logically be placed with the text write-up. Illustrations can range from digital photographs of installations to "screen shots" of completed software designs. Below is a screen shot of a database program that provides indexing for criminal case documents. This type of software can be very effective when illustrating computer programs or development.

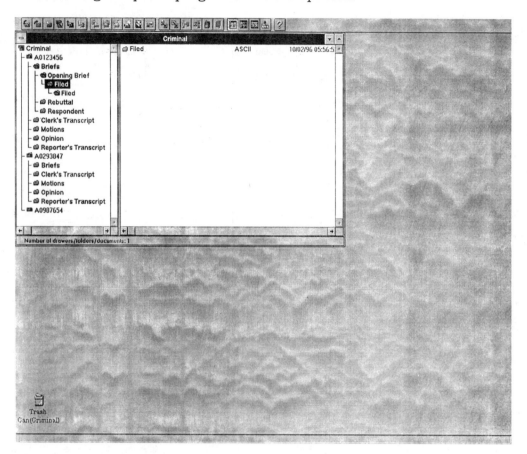

Cost/Pricing Information

✍Use standard forms if available; otherwise develop a spreadsheet.

Depending on your company, you may have standard forms for pricing equipment in a proposal. These forms also may contain standard costing breakdowns for direct, indirect, or overhead information. This type of breakdown and form can be requested in the RFP. If available as boilerplate material, the finance group at headquarters will be better able to control the information than if this information is generated in the field.

However, if you use a basic spreadsheet program for pricing, the output can easily be cut and pasted into the proposal. When describing certain parts of your pricing, such as development costs, the spreadsheet model can be inserted into the text as part of discussion.

In addition, if the RFP requests that diagrams be developed to show such things as return on investment periods, spreadsheet graphic charts can easily be used to illustrate the numbers.

Cover Artwork and Illustrations

✎ Cover art adds a sense of professionalism to your proposal.

Given professional resources, a company can develop specialized covers to be used for proposals. The covers may reflect the application or the vertical industry for which the proposal is being written. Examples of applications are:

- Accounts Payable
- Human Resources
- Purchasing
- Corporate Correspondence

Examples of vertical industries are:

- Banking
- Insurance
- Healthcare
- Transportation

Covers can be designed by professional graphic illustrators and may reflect your company's overall look and feel. If your company's logo and graphics are ultramodern, the covers should have the same look and feel to them.

With modern networks and communications, the covers can become part of the boilerplate files. The cover would come with an instruction page that specifies how to set up what will be typed on the cover, such as, "AJAX SEEP Program" along with the date of the proposal.

Covers can even be designed in color and prepared for printing on local color printers or the completed cover file (illustration and insert type) taken or transmitted to a color copy vendor.

■ USING BOILERPLATE FILES

A proposal should be as personal to your customer and his requirements as it can be. This leads the customer to believe you really spent time thinking about his needs and problems and have arrived at a unique solution. The boilerplate files allow you and the sales team to spend more time in being creative because the bulk of the work has been done beforehand in the form of boilerplate material.

There is, however, one pitfall to be aware of. Don't think that because you have boilerplate files handy, you do not have to start as soon as you would have without them. It's easy to procrastinate when you know you have ready-to-use materials at hand. You may think you have plenty of time, and then realize too late that the proposal is more complex than you thought, or you discover you need to have approval and pricing for some special service requirements. Don't be lulled into a sense of false security; the end result of this kind of proposal effort can be as bad or worse than any achieved without boilerplate material.

⚒ Boilerplate files are best used as a skeleton to be fleshed out.

Pre-typed boilerplate material is usually placed in an appendix because of differences in typeface, style, and organization. For example, in the program management section of a proposal, the resumes of key people may be referred to in an appendix. Sometimes an RFP will ask for technical product descriptions to be placed in an appendix, not in the proposal proper. Another example would be reprints of printed articles about your company. These would most properly be placed in an appendix.

Boilerplate files are best used as a skeleton to be fleshed out. The boilerplate material provides all or nearly all of the core information, but it is up to you and the sales team to bring the files together as a cohesive whole. This means custom introductions to sections must be written, bridges must be provided between boilerplate facts and the customer's needs, and in general, the boilerplate material must be tailored and personalized as much as possible.

⚒ Break boilerplate into small units if possible.

If possible, boilerplate should be broken down into small units that reflect a whole product. In the previous example with the personal computer, the requirements often force you to describe a PC component by component instead of as a whole unit. Therefore, if your boilerplate topic was AJAX Personal Computer, the subtopics to the file may be:

- Monitors
- CPU types
- Harddrive options
- Communications options
- Keyboard/point device options
- Etc.

With this type of componentization, the files will be easier to use and will be easier to update.

■ INDEXING FILES

✍A well thought out index is important to establishing a boilerplate file system.

In order for you and others to readily access your boilerplate files, you need to develop a method for indexing them. There are **three key** considerations:

- ■ The indexing/numbering system must be understandable and easy to use.
- ■ The system should allow for new files to be inserted with minimal work and effort.
- ■ The index number should indicate whether or not the files are current with the latest product revisions.

Written Files

The first step in developing an index system for text files is establishing categories such as products, services, education, corporate history and organization, account references, and other general files.

One very simple method is to have the index number composed of eight characters in two parts: the first part signifies the year the file was released (designated by an R) and the second the sequential number of the file (designated by an S). For example, R98S063 indicates the year of release was 1998 and the file is number 63.

After assigning the numbers, file the material alphabetically by category. A typical index might look like this:

Corporate

History	R98S001
Organization	R98S002

Maintenance

System maintenance	R98S021
System operation	R98S014

This method permits you to insert a new file in front of others without having to renumber the files from the new file forward. In addition, it helps you to determine if the file is up-to-date. If a product was updated in 1997 and the release date in the index number is 1996, the user will know the file is not current.

Illustrations

Assigning categories to illustrations is similar to categorizing text files. Depending on the type of product or services your company offers, illustrations could be separated into categories such as equipment, facilities, organization charts, reference accounts, cost charts and graphs, diagrams, and system configurations.

There are many types of illustrations:

- Line art. Line drawings may be created with pen and ink, pencil, or computer-generated. They can depict anything from a piece of equipment to a wiring schematic.
- Photographs. File photographs may be original glossy photographs or prescreened photos ready for reproduction.
- Screen Shots. Screen shots are images of what is on a computer screen.
- Computer-generated illustrations. These may range from workflow diagrams to spreadsheet charts.

You can number the files just like the text files, but add a *P* or *D* or *C* to indicate whether an illustration is a photograph or drawing or computer generated. The illustrations can then be filed alphabetically by category such as products, corporate organization, facilities, etc.

Once established, the index can be kept on-line on a computer, if one is available, accessible to all users, or a copy of the index could be sent out to the field offices and updated as needed. Users would then cite the reference number when requesting illustrations.

However, with today's communications capabilites, the Internet, intranets, and private networks, it is most convenient to provide the proposal boilerplate files on-line 7-days a week and 24-hours a day. Proposal writers and teams are apt to be working around the clock. Having immediate access to the files at any time will facilitate their work and make it easier on the personnel who maintain the proposal database. Imagine having to request a file you need at 10:30 P.M. from a person?

Communication networks and universal access, with proper security of course, will provide a tremendous productivity increase to your company's proposal writing efforts and success.

■ DEVELOPING BOILERPLATE FILES

✎ *Boilerplate files must be maintained.*

Undertaking the development of a boilerplate library is a sizeable task. It should not be undertaken unless it is to become a standard business operation at your company. The problems of not keeping the files current and accurate are more severe than not having the files in the first place.

Why have boilerplate, other than the convenience? If you are a company with distributed or centralized offices, and have to respond to many RFPs to win business, there is a reasonable chance that your proposal writers are:

1. Retyping company data and information each time
2. Using past proposals as a basis for new proposals
3. Using data sheets/information that are out-of-date
4. Not responding well to certain sections of the RFP due to lack of comprehensive information

Without adequate controls, your company may be losing proposals because they are not well written and not representative of your true product capabilities. Also, if a proposal is won, it may have been based on obsolete or out-of-date products, which now forces you to upgrade or provide products at no charge or reduced charges, according to current price schedules.

Product and service boilerplate allows your corporation the ability to centrally control the information that is used in a proposal and therefore ensure that the product information is current.

Having good boilerplate files allow the sales and technical personnel to concentrate on defining and developing the solution by taking the "burden of searching for and typing" information that already exists.

Having good boilerplate allows the proposal team to concentrate on putting together an attractive and appealing proposal that is interesting to read.

✎ *Make sure you scrub boilerplate taken from an old proposal.*

How is a proposal written today in your company? Chances are that without any formal proposal support proposal material is taken from data sheets, press releases, old "successful" proposals, and other information gleaned from the corporate databanks. With regard to old proposals, this is one of the most common practices in that the office administrator may have the last proposal written in hardcopy or electronic versions. This copy is taken by the sales rep and cannibalized as needed for the new proposal. Because this old proposal may in fact be a second or third generation from the original proposal written a year ago, it is very likely that basic information is no longer correct.

While you would expect a sales rep to catch mistakes, it is almost impossible to catch all the mistakes or outdated information. Thus a proposal is submitted with wrong product names, or worse yet, names of the last customer are left in because a global search/replace for Bank of America didn't catch BankAmerica or some other variation of the name.

✎ Old proposals may contain outdated data.

Old proposals may also contain products that have been superseded or have become obsolete. Product specifications may have changed from 10 megabytes per second to 100 megabytes per second, and new features, benefits, and selling themes may not be included. Even for a well-run office, these problems occur.

Returning to the original theme for this paragraph, who or how are proposal boilerplate files created and maintained? Most typically, the job of creating and maintaining the files should be part of the marketing organization. Marketing is generally responsible for creation of sales collateral and the basic sales themes that are published. They support sales. However, some of the boilerplate needs go beyond marketing material and, therefore, marketing must have access to documentation in training, maintenance, and engineering. It would be too much to expect each of these organizations to maintain their own files for the following reasons:

1. It is not generally in their charter
2. The files will not be consistent in writing and appearance
3. The collection will be distributed which makes it harder to access and to choose files from a central database
4. Along with the files, there is a need to provide assistance when new products or sales themes are being generated. The field should have a consistent set of people to work with.

The other side of the coin is to have sales support the proposal files since they are the ones who use them. This is possible if the sales department has the appropriately skilled people and can obtain the resources necessary to maintain the files. Sales would also have, perhaps, better access to recent proposals and could adapt parts of them as boilerplate such as an excellent executive summary, or a section on why your product xyz is better than the competition.

Establishing the boilerplate files also give your company a chance to develop a proposal writing style and proposal format style. This is important in that proposal from XYZ Company will always have a professional look and feel to them that many companies simply do not have. Many people writing proposals may be competent in their professional position, but not everyone is a competent writer. Few people are also good a setting up an effective page layout and design that complements the writing, which adds value to a proposal.

Using professional writers and graphics people in the initial setup and design of the boilerplate files will allow you to develop a consistent, professional, and appealing look to your proposal. Once established, with perhaps a sample formatted page or two in the boilerplate, many writers will be able to adopt the style in their own writing.

■ DISSEMINATION OF MATERIAL

After text and illustrations are indexed and ready for use, the most important consideration is how to make the material available to the users. If you are working out of a single office and developing the files for your own office, it remains fairly simple to keep the files available on a local server or PC. However, if you are at headquarters and the boilerplate library is being developed for multiple field offices, the problem of distribution needs to be considered.

The best approach to keeping boilerplate text files available for users, as well as for updating them, is to keep them on a network server. This also applies to any computer-generated art. If the boilerplate files are available on-line, they should be on a network-accessible server that has 24-hour connection service. This allows users to have independent access at any time.

The reason for this type of access, besides being useful, is that you may want to prevent users from downloading the database to their own servers. If users have the database locally, they may not remember to update it periodically and will not have the most current information. If the information and product specifications change and they are using old data, it is very possible they will turn in a proposal that commits you to an incorrect product.

It would be possible, depending on your company's capabilities, to periodically disseminate a copy of the database to all field offices via the company network. This provides the field office with the latest version of the files and provides local access which will reduce traffic on the network, if that is a concern. It is also possible to update individual files via network download to ensure the latest product boilerplate is correct. If this is your method, don't forget to also update the index file. All of this should be transparent to the user.

✎ Security is a primary concern with boilerplate.

In terms of security, it may be better having the files on a central server with greater control of access. Field offices may not exercise

---

the same control over the files. It may be impossible to prevent anyone from leaving with a copy of the data; however, good security would prevent them from logging on to the network after they have left the company. Security should be considered and reviewed with the appropriate personnel.

As mentioned before, it is essential for the boilerplate material to be kept current and accessible to the people who need it the most; if not, they simply will ignore it and go back to using old proposals and outdated material. In essence, the boilerplate files must be easy to use, easily accessible, and easily changed to fit unique needs.

Keeping the files current will ensure success of the proposal boilerplate database.

■ MAINTENANCE OF THE BOILERPLATE LIBRARY

Maintenance falls into several categories: adding new files as new products are developed or new material is written, drawn, or photographed; determining the category for new material and assigning index numbers; updating existing files; filing the material itself; and informing all interested parties of changes made to the boilerplate library or its index.

New products, whether major or minor, need to be researched and added to the library. If not maintained and up-to-date, the field users of the boilerplate files will find a way to get the information on their own. This begins a cycle of duplicated effort in which the keepers of the boilerplate library will become frustrated and ineffective. The boilerplate team must be proactive instead of reactive.

The proposal boilerplate should be updated with the regular product updates.

The boilerplate team must be linked into various parts of the company such as education, training, engineering, etc., to ensure that they are part of the release schedule for new products. The proposal files should be updated on the day the new product is released. It is very probable that proposals will be written based on unreleased products and therefore the request for this material will be made by the field.

The boilerplate team should also have access to, or be aware of, major proposals being written by the field. These proposals can become a tremendous source for new boilerplate material in areas that may not be covered by normal product literature.

The boilerplate team should also be receptive to suggestions for additions to the boilerplate and/or changes to the boilerplate. It must be remembered that the field personnel are using these files 24 hours a day, 7 days a week and if something is missing or doesn't work, they should have an open channel to the boilerplate team.

By keeping the boilerplate files modular, by subject and file, the files can be updated individually, or new files added, without renumbering existing files or having to update the whole database with each new release. This also means that the database will not have to be taken off-line for updates and users will always have the most current files when they access the database.

It is also effective to indicate in the boilerplate index the most recent update date and file(s). This way, proposal teams can periodically log on to the boilerplate database and see if new usable files have been added. Otherwise, they would somehow have to search the database or index and try to determine if a new file has been added. Think of how manuals are updated with a list of changes and change pages described in a general cover letter.

If you have company e-mail, it may be possible to sent out a notice each time the files have been updated. Sales generally keeps an email list of sales reps and administrative personnel who would receive the update notice.

Developing and maintaining boilerplate material is a demanding, time-consuming task; but you will find establishing and supporting a usable, current library of well-written text files and good quality illustrations is not only well worth the effort, but it will contribute to winning more contracts.

■ SUMMARY

Having a current, standardized boilerplate library will save the proposal team members hundreds of hours of work in addition to providing more accurate information than they could develop on their own. These files can make the proposals look more professional and perhaps provide that little extra that is needed to win. Keep in mind that color photographs and lots of bells and whistles will not be why a customer selects your company; it is the content that counts. However, also keep in mind that a proposal, which is unorganized, hastily written with poor grammar and spelling, may be rejected for these reasons.

Boilerplate can be extracted from data sheets, manuals, training materials, marketing literature, and even from field-written proposals. A company usually has a wealth of material to mine when gathering material. The material can be creatively used to make response files that range from general product descriptions to files that respond to individual technical questions.

Given proper maintenance and dedicated resources, the boilerplate files can help standardize the information content and format. The more that can be standardized, the less sales has to do low-level writing while more high-level thinking can be achieved.

Illustrations

Illustrations are essential for conveying
information and clarifying text.

Illustrations

■ INTRODUCTION

✍ Through graphic representation, products take on reality and complex concepts become more meaningful.

The value of incorporating illustrations into a proposal cannot be overemphasized. Through graphic representation, products take on reality and complex concepts become more meaningful. Text that is devoid of illustrations, especially in technical documents, is difficult to understand without the benefit of visual assistance.

In a proposal, illustrations can be a powerful tool for conveying information. They provide the reader with a visual anchor or point of reference for product descriptions, giving the product offering an authenticity not possible from a written description alone. In addition, illustrations enable the mind to better assimilate the message when it is presented in two complementary mediums, by providing visual relief for the eye—especially when the reader is faced with several hundred pages of complex technical descriptions and jargon. And remember, your proposal is not the only one being evaluated.

✍ All illustrations should directly relate to and clarify the subject matter.

However, like the writing they support, illustrations are subject to misuse and abuse. All illustrations in a proposal should directly relate to and clarify the subject matter. Illustrations used merely as embellishments or gimmicks will lessen the overall impact of the proposal by creating confusion and distracting the reader. A misleading or irrelevant illustration may cause the reader to misunderstand your product's capabilities or the services you are selling, and therefore lessen your chances of winning the contract.

On the other hand, a meaningfully illustrated proposal not only helps describe your products and services, it reflects well on you and your company by demonstrating that you have a clear grasp of the problem and can illustrate a viable solution. Because your proposal may be the first communication from your company read by an evaluator, it is imperative that the first impression be positive or there may not be a second chance. In one sense, your proposal is the first "product" the customer is given, and how this product is received will set the stage for all communications to follow.

The purpose of this chapter is to provide you with a guide for distinguishing between different types of graphics; suggestions for some sources of ready-to-use art; some tools, techniques, and standards you will need to be familiar with; and how to organize it all.

This section will focus on electronic graphics that can be electronically generated and inserted into a proposal. The prevalence and quality of these programs almost guarantees the user with high-quality illustrations.

■ THE ART OF ILLUSTRATIONS

The term illustration refers to a variety of graphics such as line drawings, paintings, or photographs of such things as system configurations, equipment, places, or people. Illustrations may also be charts, graphs, or maps. In a proposal, illustrations are referred to as figures. However, illustrations need not be confined to figures; a good drawing or photograph can be used to make an appealing cover that helps to arouse the interest of your reader, or may be inserted facing the title page to introduce your product. Statistical material is presented in tables, which are not strictly illustrations. However, for simplicity's sake, both tables and figures are referred to as illustrations in this book.

Types of Illustrations

Line Art

✐ *Line art represents a product or service.*

Line art is the basic figure drawn to resemble the actual product. Line art can be anything that you draw such as your computer workstation, a satellite antenna, or a workflow diagram describing how a business process is being reengineered.

Line art is generally called a "Figure" in the proposal and is labeled with a figure number and caption at the bottom of the figure. The figure number may be a simple sequential number as in Figure 1,2,3...or it may be numbered with the section number preceding the sequential number as in Figure 5-1, 5-2, etc. The figure caption should be short and descriptive.

The caption should not be long and is not used as a descriptive paragraph. The figure itself should illustrate and complement the subject of the text. The caption is located at the bottom of the figure and should be flush left with the margin. The word "Figure" and the number appear in bold while the caption appears in italic. The caption should be in initial caps. See figure 5-1 below for an example of line art and the placement of the figure caption. The word "figure" when used in the text to reference the figure to the reader is not capitalized and the figure number should be part of the reference instead of "See the figure below..."

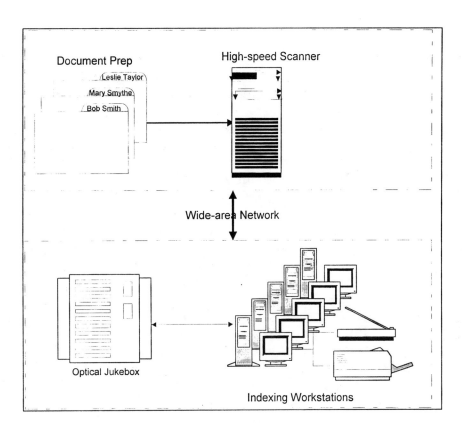

Figure 5-1. *Placement of Figure Title and Caption*

Photographs

Without giving a short course in photography, it is sufficient to say that photographs are harder to work with in the average small office, but they provide a more precise image of a product than a drawing. Photographs give the reader more assurance that your product is real and finished. A line drawing, as in figure 5-1, may represent only the concept, not the actual product.

✎Photographs can be effective but are more difficult to work with.

Photographs may be taken specifically for a proposal and project but may also be taken from company files. General photographs are typically located in marketing, but specific photographs may be located in engineering, education, or service. In order to receive a photograph, you will have to properly identify the photograph and give the source where you saw it, if there is no general index. Also, don't make this a last minute request, in the best of all worlds it will take a least a week if not longer to receive your print.

✎Photographs require more time to work with – writer beware!

Photographs in proposals are usually black and white. To reproduce correctly, a photograph must be made into a halftone. A halftone is made by shooting a photograph through a line screen that separates the image into black dots and clear areas. The more lines (or dots per square inch), the finer the texture of the halftone. A very coarse screen is used in newspaper printing. If you look at any newspaper photograph carefully, you can see the dots that make up the image.

If you use photographs that are film based (not digital), a professional print shop should be consulted. The print shop will be able to convert the photograph to a halftone for printing. The print shop will also be able to size the photograph to fit into the page or space provided. The print shop can reduce, or enlarge, the photograph to meet your needs so be sure to measure the space for your photograph when you take it to the print shop. Make sure you're organized and do not make these requests at the last minute. Print shops may take several days to produce a half-tone.

It is also possible to scan the photograph on a scanner and turn the photograph into a scanned photograph that can be electronically inserted into the page or space provided. Once scanned, the photograph can remain on your hard drive but not inserted into the proposal until the final review and printing. Otherwise a section may become difficult to manipulate because of the file size.

The third possibility are photographs taken with a digital camera. If possible, photographs should be taken by a professional photographer to ensure that the photograph being displayed in your proposal is high quality with proper lighting. Photographs that are dark or amateurish may have a negative effect on the overall proposal.

Once taken, all of the photographs can be reviewed and the best selected for inclusion. Like a scanned photograph, the file size of the digital image is large (even when compressed) and should be withheld from the proposal text file until final printing.

For both scanned or digital, it is best to name the file with a sequential number, if you keep an art log, or name the photograph file with the figure number that applies to your photograph. The art log is discussed later in this section. (The problem with naming the photo with the figure caption number is that these numbers may change as figures are added or subtracted, therefore having a neutral number helps in maintaining the placement and order.

If you use an art log and assign a sequential number, that number should be placed on an empty line above the figure caption, shown below:

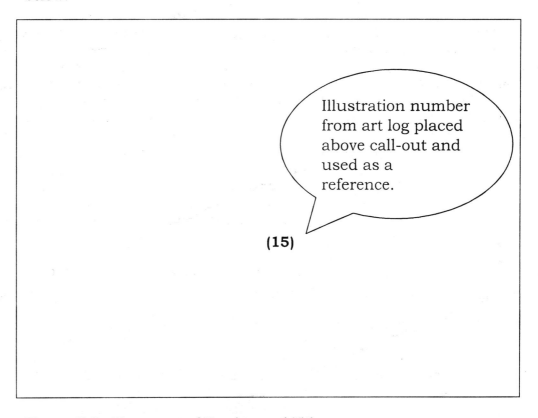

Figure 5-2. *Placement of Number and Title*

✍ Color art is not usually necessary.

Color photography usually is not necessary but, if included, will require considerably more time and money. If color photographs are to be printed, they must be sent to the printer for screening and color separation—a very expensive process. Or, you can manually insert individual color prints in the proposal. Usually, using color photographs does not warrant the extra time and expense.

It is also possible to use a color digital camera or scanned color photograph that can be inserted digitally into your proposal. If you are using color photographs or other color work, the proposal page(s) will have to be printed on a color printer. To ensure printing consistency, it may be best to have the complete proposal printed on the same printer. Copies can be made using the printer or a color photocopy machine may be used.

✍ Be careful when printing on two types of printers.

Note that if you print only the color pages on a color printer and the rest of the proposal on an office laser printer, the print density, type, and page format of the two printers may not match. Review the two pages closely and determine whether the match is close enough to be of good quality. If not, review your options and either print the whole proposal on one printer, or reassess whether the color usage is warranted. You may also consider placing the color page(s) in an appendix so that the difference in the print quality is not as noticeable.

Remember, many RFPs admonish you not to include excessively elaborate materials and use of color is discouraged.

Note of Caution

While photographs do enhance your proposal and can be more effective than a line drawing, they are awkward and cumbersome to use. If the photograph is a half-tone, it will have to be manually pasted into the blank space left, or page, and special care needs to be taken during the reproduction process. This can be time-consuming, when you don't need it, and the results may not equal the effort if less than professionally done.

If the photograph is digital, this makes the work much easier since the work is done electronically and the printing can be done on a laser printer. However, large photographs or sections with many photographs can become difficult because they make the size of the word processor file very large—perhaps on the order of many megabytes. This can make the file cumbersome to work with during the proposal writing period and difficult to transmit, if going to an off-site printer.

✎ *Digital files are large and hard to manipulate.*

If using digital photographs, consider holding them as separate files until you are ready to print. Some word processor programs can actually call the file when needed, but otherwise it is not integrated into the file.

Tables

✎ *Tables are a shorthand for presenting information.*

A table is a compact list of details or related facts arranged in an orderly sequence—usually in rows and columns—for convenience of reference. Tables, since they are set in type rather than reproduced from artwork, are not considered illustrations. They are listed separately from figures and are separately numbered. Table numbers and titles are centered at the top of the page or table as shown in figure 5-2. As with figures, table titles are initial caps.

Tables should be used extensively whenever possible. Tables can present an enormous amount of information about a subject that describes the issue better than a narrative explanation. Tables can also be presented in graphic form when the table is presented as a chart or graph of the data. Charts and graphs can quickly depict the data for a reader by showing a line or a bar-chart of the data results. Figure 5-3 presents the same information in figure 5-2 as a graphic illustration.

Covers

It is very useful to have a standard cover that depicts your company logo and product or service. Covers, both front, back, and spine, add a degree of professionalism to your proposal that your competition may not have. Covers can be inserted into a three-ring presentation binder or added to whatever type of binding you are using.

✎ *Cover art gives your proposal a professional touch.*

Cover art can be created electronically and stored on a central server. As suggested in Chapter 2, a cover can be a simple text cover with the essential information or a graphic that in some manner illustrates your product or service.

If you are a small company with limited resources, it may be better to use a plain text-based cover. However, if you have skills and the software to create an appropriate image, it may be worth the time to put together a graphic cover.

Estimates of Paper Volumes by Division

Division	# Files	# Pages	Method
Division 1	12836	351220	Count
Division 2	14967	314311	Count
Division 3	21821	458241	Estimate
Division 4	12836	397916	Estimate
Division 5	579	8685	Count
Division 6	1484	71232	Estimate
Division 7	298	8344	Estimate
Division 8	443	12404	Estimate
Division 9	2819	68482	Count
Division 10	1430	14299	Count
Division 11	16799	203280	Count
Division 12	18975	412419	Estimate
Total:	105287	2320833	

Figure 5-3. *Example Table and Call-outs.*

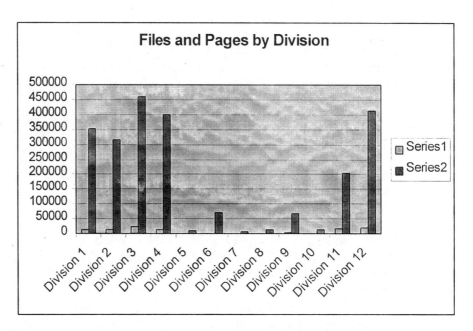

Figure 5-4. *Tabular Information Presented as a Chart*

See Chapter 2, *Proposal Contents: Overview*, for an in-depth discussion of cover suggestions and requirements. Chapter 8, *Printing the Proposal*, explains how to work with printers and how to get the most for your money.

Sources of Ready-to-Use Art

Depending on the size of your company and the departments available to you, there are various sources and types of ready-to-use art in-house and outside, elaborate and simple, conventional and electronic.

✍Build a library of reusable illustrations.

Almost all types of line-drawing illustrations and tables can be created and transmitted electronically. Many companies have a full-time staff devoted just to computer-generated artwork for marketing, engineering, education, and maintenance. Many graphic houses are now employing computer-graphic artists—some graphic houses produce only computer-generated art. So if you are equipped for and knowledgeable in "desktop publishing," consider your electronic options.

If you decide to pursue this avenue, start building a library of icons, or images, to represent various hardware components, products, or equipment, depending on your line of business. These icons can be arranged and rearranged to represent different configurations. Using the same icons for different drawings has the advantage of giving your illustrations uniformity of style. Figure 5-4 is an example of computer-generated art composed of pre-drawn images that have been put together with the graphics program.

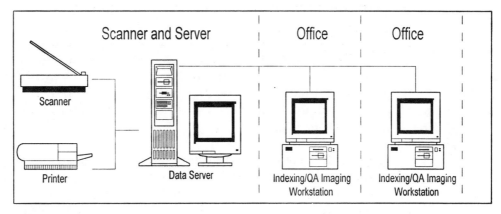

Figure 5-5. *Sample of Computer-generated Artwork*

In-house Sources

If you work in a large company with a technical illustrations department, you can arrange with that department manager to supply boilerplate graphics that you can keep on file. You should have an agreement with the manager early on—the main point of the agreement being that, in addition to supplying you with boilerplate art, you will be requiring a fast, meaning very fast, turnaround time for custom requests. If your art department manager is aware of the quick turnaround times you may require for a proposal, he will be better prepared to give your work priority.

✍ Ensure your in-house sources understand the need for speed.

If your art department manager is not familiar with proposal work, it is best to work closely with him during the initial proposals. Draw the manager into the proposal so that the urgency can be experienced firsthand.

If you do not have a technical illustrations department in your company, or you are in a field sales office without direct access, you might check with your engineering or technical manuals department to see if there are usable drawings of your products that can be added to your boilerplate files. Other internal sources of illustrations are data sheets, technical manuals, and brochures which are produced by marketing.

Clip Art

✎ *Clip art will save you time and expense.*

Electronic clip art consists of electronically drawn images that are available from many sources:

1. The word processor program that you use may have built-in clip art that can be used. This art may range from excellent quality to poor quality. Always insert this art into the page and do a test printing prior to making a final commitment.

2. Clip art can be purchased from companies that specialize only in clip art. These drawings range from excellent to poor. Often, the files also contain photographs and other illustrations in various formats. Before purchasing, ensure that your word processor can read and use the files as they may be stored in some type of proprietary format.

3. Illustration software usually has a large number of pre-drawn illustrations that can be used as a single illustration or grouped together to compete a picture. Before purchasing, ensure that your word processor is able to accept this type of file format.

Once you have decided on an illustrations program, any of the sources above can contribute to your storehouse of electronic images. If you are collecting these images for future use, it may be best to copy them from the original source into a directory that can be easily accessed and cataloged for future use. Additional illustrations can be added at any time and available for use. Even complex drawings from the current proposal may be kept as a separate file instead of redrawing the illustration.

■ ILLUSTRATION FORMATS

When dealing with illustrations and tables, there are a few basic principles regarding treatment that should be mentioned. One of the most important is allowing for ample space around them and providing sufficient space between the illustrations and their titles and/or captions. Keep in mind that for both illustrations and tables, all related information should be the same orientation as the material itself regardless of the type of page it is presented on.

✎ *Remember that illustrations complement text.*

Illustrations are presented in various ways. Ensure that all artwork is properly aligned with the paper edges, and remember that the purpose of the illustrations is to enhance and clarify the text, and therefore they need to be clearly, cleanly, and carefully presented.

Landscape vs. Portrait Orientation

Illustrations can be mounted vertically or horizontally on the page. A horizontal illustration is sometimes called a landscape or a turn-page illustration because it is mounted so that the proposal must be turned in order to see it. This type of illustration is called for if the drawing would have to be reduced so much in order to fit on the page that it may not remain legible. If you have a turn-page, you must also ensure that the illustration fits within the margins. The turn-page illustration should be mounted so that the illustration is readable when the book is turned clockwise. The title should be centered over the illustration along the long side of the paper, not placed as it would be for a vertical illustration. Captions are always vertical like the text.

In-text Graphics

☜ Small in-text graphics help make your point.

An in-text graphic is usually an example of special text or a small illustration that does not warrant being a figure or a table by itself. The example is embedded within a paragraph and separated from the text by spacing. In-text illustrations do not have captions, are not numbered, and do not appear in the list of illustrations. The following paragraph contains an example of in-text graphics:

Developing and maintaining a library of icons, such as the ones shown here, is essential for effective electronic "desktop publishing."

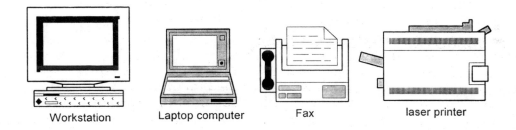

Workstation   Laptop computer   Fax   laser printer

These icons can be combined in many ways to produce a variety of configurations for your product or services.

A second example may be a small table or graph that provides a visual image of the text subject. The text should make a reference to the visual aid such as:

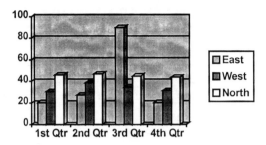

*The graph above shows the spread of document imaging technology throughout the business community. It appears that the Eastern sector of the United States...*Standalone illustrations in text can be put into a number of different positions so that the text wraps around the illustration. If you are doing two-column text, it may be essential to have this type of capability. However, in the interest of time and clarity, the illustration inserted between paragraphs, as above, with adequate spacing is generally good enough.

It is not necessary to make your proposal look like a professionally published magazine or manual (unless that is your product). Clean and readable text is the object of a proposal.

■ ILLUSTRATION STANDARDS

✎ Setting standards makes the proposal look as though it came from one company.

To make it look as though one company submitted the proposal, it is necessary to set illustration standards early. These standards, when followed, will give your illustrations a consistent look and a professional appearance. The standards listed below should be considered, but not necessarily incorporated. The word illustrations refers to both figures and tables.

The suggestions below should be modified according to your own company standards and included in a proposal style sheet. Having your illustrations completed in a consistent fashion will save you many hours at the last minute, when you need the time for final review, not final work.

Boxing Illustrations

There is probably a 50-50 chance that your company places boxes around all illustrations. Boxing illustrations is a convention, but it is not followed industry-wide. If the decision is to box, all illustrations, including tables, must be boxed for consistency.

Type Styles

✍ Consistency of type faces and drawing styles contributes to making a more effective proposal.

Illustrations with many different sizes and styles of type tend to have less impact. A rule of thumb is never use more than three sizes of type or two styles within any given drawing. If you use 12-point Helvetica bold for the title of a table, use 12-point Helvetica bold for all tables. Of course, this is also true for all figures. Use initial capital letters for type within an illustration.

Line Weights

Line weights refer to the thickness of the lines. Generally, lines that are medium-light weight tend to be more pleasing to the eye than heavy, bold lines. However, be sure the lines are not so thin that they will drop out (not reproduce) when printed. As with type styles, the general rule is to use no more than two line weights for any given drawing. Also, try to have all the drawings appear to have the same line weights. In general, try to be consistent.

Figure and Table Numbers

Illustrations are usually assigned two numbers: the section number and the sequential number of the figure within the section. (Chapter 4, Proposal Contents: Boilerplate Files, discusses numbering methods.) Figures are numbered on the bottom while tables are numbered on the top. Callouts are flush left with the margin of the drawing.

Illustration References

✍ Illustrations should be near the text with which they are associated.

Two rules of referencing illustrations are:

- An illustration must be referenced in the text before it appears.
- Illustrations should appear as close to the reference as possible. Do not save all the illustrations and place them at the back of the section or book.

When referencing figures and tables, avoid describing them in the reference when the illustration is obvious: "Table 5-1 is a list of..." The most preferable reference to a figure or table is a simple reference to its number: "See Table 5-1." Remember, the text should not be describing the figure; the figure should be clarifying the text.

Titles and Captions

✎ *The treatment of illustration elements is not dictated by hard and fast rules— it's consistency that counts.*

While there are no "standards" for this type of work, and each company may do things differently, what is important is to have a consistent look and feel to your proposal and the illustrations. Below are suggestions to consider, if your company has a different method, make the changes accordingly and incorporate into a style sheet.

- Use initial capital letters for titles and captions.
- Titles and captions should be separated from the illustration with at least one blank space.
- Titles are centered at the top.
- Captions are flush left at the bottom.
- Titles are the same orientation as the drawing.
- Captions are always vertically oriented.
- Figures and tables are numbered with a separate sequence.

Punctuation

- Figure and table numbers are followed by a period.
- No periods are used in the illustration caption unless it comprises several sentences.

While the above rules could all be incorporated as standards, they need not be. Being flexible but consistent is one key to getting a proposal finished on time in addition to keeping a professional appearance.

Illustration Consistency and Orientation

One potential problem with using illustrations from many different sources is that they may not look the same in terms of line weights, detail, and orientation.

The size of the line used to create the drawing may vary from drawing to drawing So that some drawings look dark and heavy while others are very light. This detail should be reviewed prior to using the drawings.

✎ *Try not to mix drawing styles and programs.*

The amount of detail should be similar among the different packages. Some drawings of a PC may provide the least amount of detail while others may be very detailed. The amount and type of detail should be relatively constant (just like the text of your proposal.).

Consistency may also include orientation of the drawings. Do PCs face head-on or do they face left or right? Do some face left and some face right? Are the views from the top, side, some other view? Readers may notice this type of inconsistency and it may have a negative effect if the differences are too pronounced.

While it may be easy to get and use electronic art, it is somewhat difficult for the average user to make the illustrations look consistent. If you do not have a professional illustrator and/or guidance, use common sense and review your finished product with a critical eye. Having the illustration is worth the time and effort even if they are not perfect.

■ ORGANIZATION

≥Illustration preparation should begin in parallel with writing text.

Using illustrations in a proposal requires a high degree of organization. The more you work with proposals and illustrations, the more you will find that artwork or photographic work must begin in parallel with writing the text. A single drawing may take five full working days to complete. A photograph, even if it is already taken, will require several days of processing time. These illustrations need to be cataloged and kept where they are easily accessible during the proposal preparation process. This section contains suggestions for indexing and tracking your artwork.

The key issue is whether you generate or have boilerplate illustrations in a corporate library or you simply generate illustrations on demand at the time of the proposal effort.

If you do have a library of illustrations, or want to start one, the illustrations should be indexed so that users can peruse the library and download the illustrations required. The library may have a preview function allowing users to see a thumbnail of the illustration or the index must be sufficiently documented to allow the user to get the correct drawing. Users may not want to have to select and download many drawings in order to get just one or two.

Once downloaded, the illustrations can be renamed to reflect the illustration number being assigned in the proposal.

If you do not have a library of illustrations but create them on the fly, they still must be assigned an illustrations number and placed in a directory for ease of access. There may also be a time in which the illustration is "roughed-out" by hand and someone else is in charge of putting the illustration together using an illustrations package.

Numbering and Indexing Artwork

✎ Indexing helps you track and monitor the artwork.

How you number and index your artwork depends on the source of the artwork itself. If you are using illustrations from an existing technical publication or boilerplate artwork supplied from your illustrations department, the art will most likely already have been assigned a number. You may want to keep this number, but it is probably better to assign an index number of your own and cross-reference it to its original number in a log of some sort (in case you want more of the same from the original source). This log is independent of the proposal and is simply a reference for your own convenience. If you are having artwork custom-created, assign your own new index number.

The boilerplate illustration files will now have a unique indexing scheme that allows all users to quickly identify and request art from your files.

✎ Use separate logs for figures and tables.

Figure 5-5 shows an example log form for keeping track of illustrations. The first column is the number for the illustrations library or, a reference to the source document. This is important because you may change the original and want to change it back at some point—or download the original a second time.

The second column is the sequential number assigned to the drawing and is the number put into the blank space left for the drawing if they are not loaded into the text during the writing period. The sequential number is used because the figure or table number may change over time and potentially cause to put the wrong drawing in that place.

The third column is the assigned figure or table number. This number may also change as drawings are inserted before the current number so that figure 5-1 becomes 5-3, etc.

The art log also allows you to see at a glance whether the art has been completed and approved. As the deadline draws near, you will want to hurry the completion of any outstanding illustrations.

The author column should be filled in for quick reference. A large proposal may have several authors working on it and producing illustrations. When a question arises, or an approval is needed, knowing whom to go to is helpful.

The last two columns are self-explanatory. For any given drawing, do not make an entry until work on the drawing has actually begun. You will be able to tell at a glance which illustrations are not being prepared, which are in progress, and which are completed. Note: logged entries should be made in pencil or kept electronically.

This log is only an example. Your log may be more complex and have many more columns for dates and data. You may also want to make a separate log for any tables that are being generated.

Index Number	Ref. Number	Figure Number	Title	Author	Status Draft	Complete
HW027	1	1-1	Hardware Architecture	Bud P-R	6-23	7-3
HW009	2	1-2	Workstation	Bud P-R	6-15	7-3
ED015	3	1-3	Training Schedule	Mike M.	?	??
DI007	4	1-4	Project Org. Chart	Mary E.	6-12	7-3
	5					
	6					

Figure 5-6. *Example Art Log*

Master Proposal Art File

Illustrations should be available over a shared drive or on a server.

After your indexing system is established, the next step is to set up a master proposal art file on your server along with the text. This file is simply a place for the art to reside while the proposal is being developed.

This, of course, hinges on whether you keep the art separate from the proposal, have professional illustrations being created, or just grab some clip art for insertion into your proposal. If the art is being created, there is a good chance that it will change as it is being reviewed and the proposal story unfolds. Therefore, it is best to keep it on a shared drive or accessible over a network by the illustrator and the user. The art log illustrated above could serve as a simple check-in/check-out log. However, more sophisticated document management programs will provide library facilities for both the text and the illustrations.

How and where to keep the files, both text and illustration, must be decided during the initial stages of the proposal development process.

Authors must have access to these files at all times, even when traveling and access over the network.

■ STORAGE OF ILLUSTRATIONS

⚲Final art should be indexed and kept for the next proposal.

Storage is an important part of developing a proposal and a proposal development program. Like boilerplate, if the illustration files cannot be located and used. Developing a file system is necessary for both the large company with a distributed set of offices and the local office with several people using the files.

In addition to locating an illustration file quickly, it allows you to build the files because you have a methodology for storage and retrieval. If we review earlier sections of developing boilerplate, one of the best methods of acquisition is from proposals that are or have been written in the field. If there is no practical method for acquiring, updating, and retrieving new files, the boilerplate will eventually become full of old and outdated material, which is worse than not having the files in the first place.

Illustration files should be categorized and numbered as part of the illustration database. Categorizing will put the file into the proper topic heading such as hardware, software, education, etc. Each major category may have a unique identifier coupled with a sequential number. For example, files in the hardware section may begin with a HW and numbered HW001, HW002, etc. Having unique identifiers allows the user to rapidly identify the files and file type after they have been downloaded from the database.

For the single office or single user, the same system can be employed in order to track illustrations created for other proposals. The database may be nothing more than a spreadsheet, or it may be a more complex library type program. The key is ease of use and access to materials. It is amazing that we spend more time looking for a "lost" illustration in an old proposal than it would have taken to draw a new one.

■ SUMMARY

In a proposal, illustrations are an especially powerful means of communication. Illustrations can mean the difference between a prosaic, but technically accurate proposal, and a sharp, clearly stated document. Good supporting illustrations clarify your text and thus ensure that what is being read is also being understood. Of course, illustrations add a professional touch to your proposal, but their real

✍Illustrations and artwork help bind text and concepts into comprehension for the reader.

function is to help the reader understand complex technical concepts. Illustrations help bind text and concepts into comprehension.

With the excellent illustration programs available today, along with extensive "clip-art" files, there is no reason why proposals should not have strong illustrations. Even a simple drawing will help a reader by breaking up the dense text and allowing the reader to "see" what has just been described. However, be careful not to toss in an illustration that has little or no meaning and does not clarify the text. After a few instances of this, the reader may be annoyed at the superfluous information and not read the illustrations that matter.

In addition to helping the reader, drawing an illustration helps the writer focus on the concept that is being conveyed, which in turn may provide the writer with greater insight into the concept or subject itself. Many large government contractors, with adequate personnel to support the methodology, make their proposal writers concentrate on developing the proposal illustrations before they write the text. This forces the writer to understand the concept first, which leads (one hopes) to better writing in addition to providing illustrations that are excellent counterparts to the text.

Finally, if you are in doubt about the power of illustrations and their place in a proposal, review any technical manual and try to read it without looking at the illustrations. The text becomes cumbersome as you try to visualize what is being described and your focus and attention are diverted from the subject. Also, do you want to chance it that your readers will incorrectly visualize the concept that you are trying to relate?

Notes

Post-proposal Activities

The proposal is not finished when you turn it
in. That is the start of post-proposal work.

Post-proposal Activities

■ INTRODUCTION

✍ There are several important post-proposal activities not required by the RFP.

After the proposal has been written and is ready for submission, there are a number of matters that need to be addressed. Some are required by the RFP, and relate to such activities as ensuring the specified proposal format has been complied with, correctly addressing the proposal package, observing the delivery date, preparing demonstrations, and providing customer references.

Other activities are not required by the RFP, but are just as necessary to complete the proposal development cycle. These include, but are not limited to, establishing and maintaining complete files, planning for negotiations, and continued selling of the solution. Thoughtful attention to these matters is important enough to make the difference between winning or losing the contract. Generally speaking, there are five main areas of concern:

■ Submission criteria
■ Proposal delivery requirements
■ Post-delivery considerations
■ Pre-contract steps
■ Interpreting post-proposal feedback

Review Appendix G, Post-proposal Checklist, for a list of typical activities.

✍ Analyzing why other proposals have been rejected can help you to avoid the same pitfalls.

The following quotation from an RFP lists several reasons why proposals have been disqualified by this company:

Many of the causes for rejection arose from either an incomplete understanding of the competitive bidding process or administrative oversight on the part of the bidders. The following examples are illustrative of the more common causes for rejection of bids:

1. *A bid stated, "This proposal is not intended to be of a contractual nature."*

2. *A bid was submitted which had not been signed by a properly authorized individual.*

3. *A bid was delivered to the wrong office.*

4. *A bid was delivered in an unsealed condition.*

5. *A bid was submitted that was incomplete.*

≈ The same intensive energy as was devoted to the proposal must be directed toward completion of the post-proposal activities.

A careful and experienced proposal writer understands the value and importance of sustaining the proposal effort beyond completion of the proposal itself. It is during the post-proposal period that the proposal team is beginning to break apart. The team members are tired; they are worried about other jobs and assignments now waiting for them; they want to get this proposal behind them. However, if the same amount of time and effort as was given to proposal development is not spent in carefully attending to post-proposal requirements, control over meeting these requirements will be lost if details such as signing the requested documentation, packaging the proposal correctly, or even delivering it to the right address are not properly taken care of.

Also, it is during this time that essential, difficult, and costly tasks, such as writing and building a product demonstration, must be undertaken. The same intensive energy as was devoted to the proposal must be directed toward completion of the post-proposal activities. Lack of this energy and attention to detail will jeopardize the success of the project.

■ SUBMISSION CRITERIA

Most, if not all, RFPs contain simple item-by-item instructions as to the format and content of your proposal. These often are not read until the last minute to find out such information as how many copies of the proposal are required and where they should be sent. The following topics have been taken from RFPs that have listed these instructions:

- Submission Criteria
- Instructions
- Proposal Preparation Instructions (PPI)
- Bidding Instructions
- Responsibilities of Vendor
- Appendix 1-Guidelines for Vendor's Proposal
- Section 11-General Instructions for Bidder
- Appendix B-Instructions for Technical Response

≈ Not reading all the instructions may result in your proposal being disqualified.

These instructions range in scope from very simple — indicating the name, address, and number of copies requested — to very complex. In one RFP, the instructions were contained in an appendix that was over fifty pages long and listed such details as the page length for each section and the size of the type. Missing the instructions or ignoring the submission criteria may result in the proposal being disqualified.

Sometimes the instructions are not found in a single section of the RFP, but are spread throughout the RFP as part of the introductions to each of the major sections. If this is the case, there will be general instructions in the front of the RFP — name, place, time, number — but each section or volume will contain detailed information on the format for that section only. For example, the cost section or volume may contain detailed instructions for submitting costing information on an electronic spreadsheet.

These instructions also provide information about working with the requestor: who the contact person is, how that person may be contacted, when and where the bidder's conference will be held, and if attendance is mandatory. There is usually a paragraph that "expressly prohibits social or after-work invitations to personnel engaged in this Request for Proposals," and that "all questions must be directed through the RFP administrator, (name, address, etc.) and submitted in writing."

✍ *RFPs that require a standard format facilitate evaluation.*

RFPs that require a standard format facilitate evaluation. Without these guidelines, there is often no acceptable method of comparison among the many different proposals submitted. Proposals that follow the format guidelines offer evaluators an apples to apples comparison. This type of comparison allows your features and benefits to be more clearly understood because they can be easily compared to the same proposal from your competition.

General Submission Criteria

✍ *Seek clarification if you are not sure about the submission guidelines.*

Before a proposal undergoes evaluation, it is checked into the system: copies are made, initial adherence to RFP submission criteria is checked, and possibly an initial screening of the contents for conformance to the required standards is made. Listed below are basic submission requirements that apply to all proposals. If proposal submission instructions are not provided, the following information should be requested from the customer:

Response due date and time. If not given, contact the person who released the request. Early submission of your proposal may not, in fact, be beneficial. Some companies or government agencies do not open the proposals or start the evaluation until all proposals are received.

Number of copies. The number of copies required will vary according to each RFP. Some companies will ask for one master and then make their own duplicates of your proposal, and some will request as many as fifteen or more. One RFP released by an international consortium required 125 copies of the proposal.

Address. A common question is: To whom do you address the proposal? Some sales reps have been in contact with a particular department manager but received the RFP from another manager in procurement. Even if you received the RFP because of your conversations with the RFP leader, *send the proposal to the name listed in the RFP.*

Packaging. Depending on the size of your proposal and the number of copies requested, it may be possible to use a large envelope or you may need to use multiple boxes. In all cases, though, the proposal must be sealed; do not submit open binders with your business card stapled to the corner.

≥ Following the submission criteria will prevent the proposal from being misplaced, lost, or otherwise compromised.

Markings. Because most proposals are submitted to a procurement department, and held there until the RFP manager is ready to receive them, it is important to properly mark the proposal package with the RFP number and project name. This will help prevent a proposal from becoming lost or misplaced, as it is possible that proposals for other projects are being submitted to the same office at the same time.

The instructions will normally state: "All responses shall be marked with the solicitation number and the project name: Solicitation 92-057, 'Parts and Inventory Control Project.' Multiple packages shall be marked 'Box 1 of X.'" If you have three boxes, you would mark the first Box 1 of 3, the second Box 2 of 3, and the third, Box 3 of 3.

Cost proposals. Often, but not always, the instructions will request that you separate the technical proposal from the cost proposal and seal each in separate packages. The cost breakdown usually is analyzed by procurement personnel, and in many RFPs, the customer does not want the technical evaluators to be influenced by the cost of the equipment. Unless specifically instructed otherwise, it is generally advisable to submit the cost and technical proposals separately.

Signature. Most RFPs request: "All proposals shall be signed by a duly authorized officer and dated upon execution." The reason for this requirement is that should you win, your proposal will become part of the contract and the contract will be legally binding.

Specific Non-standard Criteria

≥ Submission guidelines are often buried and not picked up in casual reading. Consider a close reading looking just for submission criteria.

The above requirements are basic for all proposals. However, some sections will have additional requirements of their own. Failure to comply with all requirements will result in two possibilities:

You may be disqualified before the evaluation begins.

If accepted for evaluation, your proposal will receive a lower score than those proposals that did follow the preparation instructions.

Below are some specific non-standard requirements taken from actual RFPs:

Vendors are required to submit one complete set of contracts with their proposal. Contracts should include purchase agreements, maintenance contracts, and licensing agreements for software.

One of the most common problems inexperienced people have is not knowing what to look for when reading and outlining an RFP. Often, mandatory requirements are buried in narrative sections of the RFP, and in a casual reading of that section these requirements may not be noted as such.

✎ *Words such as shall or must indicate a requirement in the RFP.*

The stipulation cited above was buried in a general section of the RFP and was not included in the preparation instructions. Often, conditions like this are added at the last minute by the final RFP review team and are not placed in their appropriate sections. Careful reading of the RFP for words such as *required, shall,* or *must* reveals many requirements not apparent at the first reading.

All questions must be answered and cross-referenced to the relevant paragraph number. If a question is not applicable, it should be listed with the notation 'not applicable (N/A)' and a reasonable explanation of the exception included.

Some RFPs are written in a question/answer format. A simple version may be just a list of questions — each question is numbered and accompanied by a corresponding number for your response. Some RFPs are written as a series of paragraphs with blanks for you to fill in. When you find a question or blank that is not applicable, you must give a reasonable explanation. Be as specific as possible.

Often, the instructions are very specific regarding such items as number of volumes or sections, page count, number of copies, and number of binders. In the example cited below,

Proposals will be page-limited to 100 pages, printed one side only, single column with one-inch borders. Type size is limited to ten point Helvetica or similar.

the requestor is specifically limiting the size of the proposal and attempting to keep the use of proposal boilerplate responses to a minimum. However, if a client is trying to limit the size of a proposal and states, "Proposals are limited to 100 pages," you have several devious options for getting around such an ambiguous restriction. For example, you can have the proposal printed on both sides of the page, or you can have it typeset in two columns using eight point type, which compresses about three pages of normal text onto one page.

✑ Don't lose evaluation points because you didn't follow the compliance criteria.

However, to avoid confusion and possibly being disqualified, and to ensure that your proposal receives all evaluation points possible, total compliance with the proposal preparation instructions is strongly recommended.

If, for example, you are page-limited and have exceeded the specified number, include all information that is relevant but not important enough to attach to that section as an appendix. Usually, there is no limit to the amount of information or number of appendices you can submit, but your customer may or may not choose to read everything in your proposal.

■ PROPOSAL DELIVERY REQUIREMENTS

Delivery Date

Delivery dates always should be taken seriously. Following is an example of one RFP's deadline requirements:

All proposals shall be received no later than 4:00 p.m. Pacific Standard Time, Friday, April 1, 19XX. Proposals are to be mailed or delivered to: [the address]

No proposals will be accepted after this date. No exceptions will be allowed.

✑ Proposals generally are not opened until the due date and after all proposals have been submitted.

There have been occasions when weeks of hard work have been in vain because an inexperienced bidder thought the deadline was negotiable. Many companies actually clock proposals in and refuse to accept proposals that are late. However, it is not always advantageous to finish and submit a proposal early; proposals may not be opened until the due date and the evaluation team is assembled and given instructions.

If you find you are not going to meet the deadline, you may ask for a last-minute extension. If you realize only a few days before the proposal is due that you are not going to meet the deadline, call the contact point for the RFP, explain in detail why you are unable to keep your commitment, and inform him of when you can submit your proposal. If the call is made several days or a full week before the deadline, it is a reasonable request. It would not be reasonable to request an extension on the day the proposal is due. Having the request for extension granted depends entirely upon your relationship with the account, the number of other vendors, and the flexibility of the company's procurement department.

For example, a company requested an extension one week before a proposal was due and was turned down. The RFP manager felt no need to grant an extension because all other vendors were able to submit their proposals on time. The company making the request was unable to submit a proposal after three months of dedicated work. Conversely, extensions have been granted on the due date because the requestor was favored and the competition was being used to justify the favored vendor.

Delivery Conditions

Your proposal should be delivered in a sealed envelope or box. The following example is from an RFP which clearly requests that all proposals must be submitted under sealed cover:

All copies of proposals and bids must be under sealed cover which is to be plainly marked with the program name and solicitation number. The sealed cover shall also be clearly marked CONFIDENTIAL and shall state the scheduled date and time for submission. Final bids not received by the date and time specified will be rejected. Proposals and bids submitted under improperly marked covers may be disqualified.

There are many reasons why customers ask that all proposals be delivered in sealed packages. One obvious and primary reason is to prevent accidental loss or disclosure of materials submitted in open packages. In proposal competitions there may be internal backers who favor a particular vendor and are willing to provide information on the other proposals. It is possible that an unsealed proposal may be previewed by unauthorized personnel and information concerning solutions and pricing given to a favored vendor. Proper marking and sealing of the package will help prevent potential problems.

A secondary reason has to do with internal management of the evaluation. Many companies want to hold the proposals in the procurement department until all proposals are checked in, there are no other requests for extension, and other administrative tasks are completed such as checking for documentation that was required to be sent with the proposal. Once the procurement department is satisfied that those proposals received meet the minimum requirements, the evaluation committee is briefed on the proposals, the rules for evaluating the proposals are explained, and questions concerning the proposals are answered.

Delivery Method

Finally, where the proposal is to be delivered and how you will get it there are important considerations. For proposals that are strategic opportunities and very important to your company, delivery in person should be considered. This ensures that your proposal is signed in and you receive a receipt. If you do not verify that your proposal has arrived on time and has been signed in, you may be disqualified for missing the deadline.

Another way of sending your proposal is via an overnight express company. As an added precaution, a separate copy of the proposal is sometimes sent via another courier, airplane, or express delivery service. It is also possible to send one copy on a separate flight using an airline's "counter-to-counter" package service. This copy is then picked up at the airport by another representative of your company and delivered to the customer.

✍ Now is not the time to save pennies at the expense of losing a proposal.

If your proposal does not warrant personal delivery, overnight express services usually provide a safe and convenient method for transporting your proposal—in addition they offer the ability to trace a shipment if it has not arrived. Also, be aware of the check-in time. If proposals are due at 10:00 A.M., and your delivery is afternoon at 3:00 P.M., you may be disqualified. However, even though these services guarantee delivery or your money back, twenty-five or fifty dollars will not compensate you for a contract that you did not win because your proposal was lost en route or delivered late.

■ POST-DELIVERY CONSIDERATIONS

✍ Good housekeeping is essential to proposal follow-up activities.

Once the proposal has been delivered, there is a natural tendency for people to sit back, take a day off, or begin calling on other accounts or working with existing accounts that have been neglected during the proposal writing period. But the job is not over yet. It is during this post-delivery time that many tasks such as organizing and filing all records must be given proper attention.

Instituting good housekeeping practices before, during, and after the proposal is imperative. A filing system should be established and maintained when the proposal is started and could be as simple as folders marked by section and kept in a file cabinet. All information relating to decisions that are made should be kept in a separate folder with minutes of meetings, personal notes, and audit trails that lead to why a decision was made. The types of decisions that need to be tracked would be those that would have to be justified to the customer such as pricing models, equipment configurations, or anything that needs to be tracked internally such as discount information.

As part of the post-proposal cleanup, special attention should be paid to documents that provide:

- Information on why products were chosen
- Why certain products were not chosen
- How the proposed solution was developed
- What trade-offs were made in the development of the solution
- Who participated in these decisions
- How pricing was developed
- Who was responsible for non-standard pricing decisions
- Who was responsible for non-standard discounts
- Who approved non-standard pricing and discounts

These papers and other related materials are collected in preparation for the time when the customer will begin to ask questions and request clarifications of product descriptions, procedures, or prices.

≥ Develop an audit trail by organizing your proposal files and records.

When the proposal is finished, the original RFP and the masters used to photocopy the proposal should be kept together in one file. Added to this file would be any addenda, supplements, questions, answers, or other written communications between you and the customer. The file becomes the master record of the project and will be a duplicate of the file kept by the customer and added to the contract as an exhibit. This file will be the "public" file that would be reviewed by the lawyers during contract negotiations and also serve as the beginning of the project notebook kept by the project leader.

If your proposal wins, it will be copied many times (within your company) as new people are assigned to the project. It is possible that Contracts, Legal, Accounting, Manufacturing, Engineering and Development, Customer Support, and Customer Training will want to have copies of the proposal. This will be a normal request if a department is going to support the project effort. However, without this file, or with an incomplete file, the contract will be subject to the customer's interpretation of the facts. In addition, you will avoid spending many hours trying to re-create and substantiate why equipment or services were proposed.

Depending on your company, it may be a good idea to have your proposal copied and sent to the individual departments that will have a part in the project. Too often the training or service group begins to interact with the customer without having read the proposal. It can be disappointing to your customer to have to read your proposal to your own people.

Another reason for keeping the files in order is to facilitate the ongoing proposal activities before the contract is awarded. In many cases, there will be pre-award steps (described in detail below) such as questions and answers, demonstrations, factory visits, and oral presentations, that will require information from the proposal or even make use of parts of the proposal itself. Quite often illustrations from the proposal are used in the oral presentation instead of being redrawn. (And quite often these drawings are lost or have been so abused that they cannot be used and have to be redrawn.)

✑ Materials from your proposal are often used for the presentation and demos.

Also, as the contract award draws closer, it is possible that the customer will ask you to do some *what-if* projections and calculations. If these are successfully sold, and the customer is willing to accept them, a good audit trail must be established in order to substantiate the what-ifs at the time of the contract award. As an example, the customer might want to increase the number of workstations in order to receive a higher discount.

It is often the case that when a contract is won, the team responsible for the proposal is not able to document why a decision was made and what effect that decision had/has on the current state of the negotiations. Also, it is not uncommon during contract negotiations for members of the proposal team to have either left the company or to have been transferred to another division, and, of course, not leaving notes or other material on why a decision was made.

The following three examples illustrate some problems that can occur by not keeping a well-organized and documented proposal file:

> 1.   A company finished a long and difficult proposal that required the efforts of many people and company resources. The proposal team also included a third-party software supplier. This third-party group was not located in the same city as the proposal effort and therefore made many decisions at their corporate office. No consistent method was developed among the wide diversity of people and companies involved for tracking why certain decisions were made.

Upon notification that they had lost the proposal, no attempt was made to consolidate files or put away all proposal-related material in an orderly fashion. In addition, as proposal members learned of the loss, they threw away personal proposal material as they cleaned house, were transferred, or left the company. Several months after the contract award, the company was notified that the first vendor picked was not able to perform and their company was being asked to negotiate the contract. During the negotiation period, this company was unable to justify several price items in addition to being unable to re-create most of the documentation required. Because of this, the company was not prepared for negotiations and gave the customer a lower price than was originally proposed.

2.　The sales representative who managed a proposal created a project management section along with a project team and quoted a price for these additional people and for installing the equipment. Before the contract was awarded, this sales representative, who had been responsible for writing and pricing the proposal, left the company. During the negotiations, the customer wanted a detailed explanation of why a large project management group was required (and priced) to manage the installation of standard equipment. The customer thought installation of the equipment was covered under the "installation charge" that was separate from the project management charge. Due to lack of documentation, the company was unable to resolve this issue, among others, to the customer's satisfaction, and the contract was awarded to the competitor.

3.　A systems analyst, who was responsible for developing the system configuration (how many CPUs, disk drives, tape drives, etc.), left the company. Due to unforeseen circumstances, the contract award was delayed by several months. Upon award, the winning company belatedly began to develop a project team and organize the effort. Because of a lack of records, the people in charge soon realized they did not understand how the proposed configuration was arrived at and, after much study and embarrassment, had to inform the customer that the configuration proposed did not include enough hardware. Fortunately, the customer changed the requirements and the equipment shortfall was covered under a new agreement.

■ PRE-CONTRACT STEPS

✍ Writing the proposal is only one of the many steps toward winning the contract.

Generally, customers do not make a decision to award a contract based solely on submitted proposals. There are many potential steps before the contract is awarded:

- ■ Question and Answer Period
- ■ Oral Presentation

- Product Demonstration
- Reference Validation
- Reference Site Visits
- Headquarters Visit
- Best and Final Offer (BAFO)
- Contract Negotiations
- Contract Award

Question and Answer Period

✎ Questions from the customer provide valuable feedback on your proposals

While your proposal is being reviewed and evaluated, there will be questions about your solution, products, price, or how you are going to administer the project. If your proposal is going to make the short list, or has made it, the customer will often:

reserve the right to request clarification of vendor responses and request additional information as needed. Questions will be made in writing and responses to questions must be made in writing; oral responses are not acceptable.

In this phase of the proposal evaluation, the customer is looking very seriously at your proposal and will begin to develop a list of questions that you will have to answer. Just as you were allowed to ask questions concerning requirements in the RFP, and perhaps could not go on until you had the answers, customers have the same problem. Usually, you will receive one set of questions from the customer. However, if the proposal is very complex, your answers to the customer's first set of questions may generate more questions on their part.

✎ Questions are a positive reaction from the customer.

Questions from the customer are a positive indication that you are being considered for the short list and that your proposal is being given serious consideration. It is important that you give these questions as much attention as you gave to the original proposal. Because questions indicate that something is not clearly understood, you may lose the award by not being able to give clear, understandable responses.

These questions also are a means of keeping the communication lines open as well as indicating your progress through the evaluation cycle. By analyzing these questions, you will be able to determine what section of your proposal the evaluation team is having problems with and therefore what section you should be prepared to defend. This knowledge may help direct you in preparing for the oral presentation and the system demonstration.

If, for example, the proposal section that described the computer operating system received several questions and a request for additional information, it would be prudent not only to provide as much information as possible, but also to devote additional time to this subject in your oral presentation and demonstration.

Oral Presentation

An oral presentation allows you to clarify any misconceptions and interact directly with the evaluation team.

Being asked to make an oral presentation is a definite sign that your proposal has made the short list:

Selected vendors will be required to make an oral presentation of their proposal. This presentation will be made to the evaluation and executive staff responsible for awarding this contract. This opportunity is given to allow vendors the chance to further define the primary features and benefits of their proposal, allow for clarification of proposal weak areas, and allow for limited questions from the review team. Presentation format is left to the discretion of the vendor; however, presentations should address the proposed solution and not address general marketing features and benefits.

The oral presentation can be a simple affair in which you make a presentation to the evaluation committee and they ask questions about your proposal. Or it can be an elaborate event involving the use of a computer-type presentation and a written script of your presentation. If you are going to make a formal presentation with graphics and handouts, the planning stage must start before the proposal is due. A well-planned formal presentation requires:

Oral presentations require additional planning and resources.

- A clear understanding of your proposal
- Knowledge of your weak areas
- Knowledge of your competition's strong areas
- Knowledge of your competition's weak areas
- Resources to write and produce the presentation
- Hours of rehearsal
- Additional time
- Additional money

Ask the customer what is expected and who should be present for the presentation. Usually the sales representative gives the presentation while a technical representative is present to cover the technical questions during and after the presentation. However, for a more detailed presentation, several people may present to the customer. A typical multi-person presentation may include:

- The sales representative providing introductions and covering the basic business features and benefits, serving as the moderator for your company, and providing a summary and conclusion. If time permits and the occasion warrants, a brief overview of your company and products should be included
- The technical analyst or project manager giving a detailed description of the solution
- A project manager reviewing how the project will be implemented and managed
- A regional manager providing insight into the pricing structure, if required
- The sales representative making the concluding remarks

Oral presentations allow the evaluators to ask questions about your proposal before making a final decision. The presentation also allows the evaluation staff to meet the key participants in the proposal effort and affords them an opportunity to make non-technical assessments of your company and its personnel. If you are running even with a competitor, your presentation, corporate deportment, and personal demeanor could be a deciding factor in winning the contract.

> *Given that two competitors are equal from a technical point of view, many customers begin to look at the vendors from a "Can I work with this company?" point of view. You are always giving the customer subtle hints about yourself and your company when you follow up on time with a request, always appear professional, don't pass the buck or make excuses.*

It cannot be overemphasized that technology is becoming less of a factor in decision making, while company professionalism is becoming more of a factor. In many cases, you and your competition may be bidding many of the same products and it will be your responsibility to convince the customer that your company is a safer choice for on-time installation and project success.

✎ Be sensitive to customer feedback, it will give you hints on how to direct your presentation.

The presentation itself **should not be your standard canned presentation**. The presentation should be customized to the specific opportunity and should re-emphasize your strong points and counter any weaknesses. The presentation should not simply review your proposal, but should review the business issues behind the RFP and how your proposal solves those business issues. If possible, time may be spent on a review of the cost-justification and how confident you are that the numbers represent a true justification. Once the business issues are addressed, it would be proper to spend time on how your proposal technically addresses and solves the business problem.

If you are competing with other companies bidding the same products, time should be spent on your implementation strategy, past successes, and how your understanding of the customer's issues will make your implementation faster, smoother, and trouble free (i.e., you have already experienced and solved problems your competition may not have encountered yet.)

The oral presentation can be either a total success or a miserable failure, depending on how much preparation and effort you have made. Remember, during the presentation you have no place to hide when you don't know the answer. You are on live without the engineering department or marketing department to help. Be prepared by:

1. Knowing what you said in your proposal

2. Knowing your product

3. Knowing the RFP

Product Demonstration

Demonstrations can be costly and time consuming.

In conjunction with the oral presentation, or as a second step in the process, a demonstration of the proposed technology may be requested. This request by the customer may be very specific—asking for a demonstration of product and functionality—or the request might simply state that a demonstration may be required:

This procurement may require a demonstration of the bidder's response to specific requirements (including benchmark requirements) before final selection in order to verify the claims made in the bid, corroborate the evaluation of the bid, and confirm that the hardware and software are actually in operation.

The demonstration is the last phase for technically qualifying your solution and can be a deciding factor in your ability to win this procurement; a successful demonstration will allow you to move to the negotiation phase, but an unsuccessful demonstration may eliminate you from any further participation.

Whether or not you are provided with a detailed script by the customer, the same amount of attention and effort must be given to planning, developing, and executing the demonstration. Some RFPs require that you explain in your proposal how you will demonstrate your offering:

The bidder must prepare and include in his bid a complete Demonstration Plan for the performance of all applicable products. The Plan must include a discussion of applicable hardware, software, and communications in your configuration. Failure of the bidder to demonstrate that the claims made by the bid, in response to the RFP requirements, are in fact true, may be sufficient to cause the bid to be deemed non-responsive.

A typical demonstration may include any or all of the following equipment and physical resources:

- Proposed hardware and software in operation
- Custom-developed demonstration program
- Additional in-house equipment
- Non-standard equipment
- Adequate space to have the demonstration
- Reserved time for setup and rehearsal
- Additional personnel to support the demonstration
- Accelerated product development schedules (to demonstrate a partial solution)
- Sufficient reserve resources to meet unexpected needs

A demonstration for computer systems has the potential for being very costly in terms of facilities, hardware and software, programming resources, and personnel. It is not uncommon for a major demonstration to cost a company $100,000 in equipment, time, and facilities. Before beginning to undertake a major demonstration, your senior management should approve a budget and plan. If adequate resources are not made available or provided, the demonstration is almost certain to be inferior and potentially cause your company to lose the competition.

During the demo there will be constant interaction between you and the customer.

Most proposals are not won outright. During the post-proposal activities, selling, positioning, and negotiating are constantly occurring. During the demonstration there will be constant interaction between you and the customer. This interaction should provide you with some awareness of your position and whether your proposal and demonstration are being accepted by the customer.

For example, in one situation, a company was in the middle of a demonstration when the customer took documentation from his briefcase and asked the vendor to work with this new material instead of the material already selected for the demonstration. The new material was used and the equipment failed to process it as required. The demonstration was stopped and a lengthy meeting ensued. The result of the meeting was that the demonstration was to be rerun at a later date—the first being a "mistrial"—but the second demonstration had to use the new documentation. The second demonstration was successfully run. However, if this company and the customer did not have a good working relationship, and the sales representative did not continue to sell and negotiate, the project would have ended with the failure of the first demonstration.

Demonstration Plan and Agenda

Once you have been selected for a demonstration, it is important that you work with the customer to ensure the customer will see what they expect to see. If the customer has an agenda, follow it and make agreed-upon changes that suit your company and products. Remember, the original agenda was prepared to cover all of the vendors and potential technologies. Your solution may not exactly fit that agenda so don't be shy about speaking up.

✎ *Many customers are naïve in understanding what can be accomplished in a demonstration.*

Also, be cautious about accepting the customer's agenda without careful consideration and review. Many customers naively think that you can demonstrate your whole solution "out-of-the-box" when in fact considerable programming and work has to be done. If you are in a proposal/demonstration situation in which the customer wants you to demonstrate a "solution," you have to explain that that capability is the solution that will take weeks/months to build—i.e., refer to your implementation plan and the amount of time your have proposed to "program the application."

Instead, focus the customer's attention on the functional aspects of your software and hardware. If you state that your scanner can scan 40 documents per minute, the demonstration should prove that functional specification. If your database can handle 200 transactions per minute, set up a demonstration that loads the database with transactions and show the customer some type of report the demonstrates the transaction throughput.

It is important that you and your customer have the same expectation of what your demonstration will accomplish. If this is not negotiated and agreed to up-front, you may severely underestimate what your customer expects and (even wrongly) will be eliminated from the competition.

Reference Validation, Reference Site Visits, and Headquarters Visit

One of the last steps in the proposal review process is to check the references that were listed in your proposal. The evaluators may request a visit to a site where your equipment is installed or a visit to your headquarters and manufacturing areas:

The purpose of the Customer Reference requirement is to provide the evaluation committee with the ability to verify the claims made in the bid by the vendor. The bidder must provide a list of five customers who presently have the proposed equipment installed and operating.

⤢Reference visits are used to verify your claims.

The customer will make contact with your references and usually arrange to visit only one of the sites. The purpose of the reference checking and site visits is twofold: the first is to see and verify that your equipment is working at a customer's site; the second is to speak candidly with your customers about your company's qualifications, reputation, and capabilities.

Customers may also ask for a "factory visit." This request will include a company tour, a meeting with your executives, and an overview of your company and its future directions. In short, the customer is trying to get a first-hand impression of your company and to decide whether or not he wants to do business with you, the sales representative, and your company.

⤢A factory tour will give your potential customers a first-hand impression of your company.

During this visit, the customer will also want to verify that your company is stable and will be able to perform successfully against the contract:

Prior to award of contract, we must be assured that the vendor selected has all of the resources and experience required to successfully perform under this contract. This includes, but is not limited to, personnel in the numbers and with the skills required, equipment of appropriate type and in sufficient quantity, financial resources sufficient to complete performance under the contract, and experience in similar endeavors. If we are unable to assure ourselves of the vendor's ability to perform under this contract, additional information such as credit ratings, credit letters, or performance bonds may be requested. If these are found to be insufficient, we reserve the right to reject the bid and discontinue further negotiations.

Only vendors in the final stages of being accepted will undergo a company visit. This means that the customer is still undecided about two companies (it is usually only two), that the technological solutions are equal, and they are trying to find that "deciding factor." It is at this point that you, the sales rep, and your company can make the decision in your favor by careful attention to detail, professionalism, and business common sense.

Best and Final Offer (BAFO)

The BAFO stage is generally your last chance to change your proposal. The purpose is to allow bidders to review equipment, schedules, management, organization, and pricing in light of changes to requirements and to supplement their proposal one final time. These modifications are allowed because requirements have changed due to:

- The length of the procurement process
- New technology has become available
- Requirements have been modified, by the customer, during the question and answer period
- Original requirements cannot be met
- Contract requirements have changed by the customer

✏Like a presentation and demonstration, the BAFO takes time and resources.

Being invited to a BAFO (pronounced BAFF-O) is another definite sign that you are on the short list or have won given agreement to these final changes. BAFOs are sometimes considered a pre-negotiation stage in which the customer is clearing away any remaining problems that may result in an unsuccessful negotiation. BAFOs are interactive sessions in which the customer will ask a series of questions, make statements about your proposal, define and list any problems with your solution, and finally, tell you if your price is too high.

When you attend a BAFO session, you should have technical and financial representatives who were part of the proposal effort, in addition to your contract negotiator. Generally you are not asked to make decisions at the meeting, but are allowed to respond in writing after a designated time.

Federal and state governments generally have BAFOs. Although unusual, commercial RFPs are beginning to incorporate formal BAFOs as part of the RFP cycle. The difference between a government BAFO and a commercial account BAFO is that the government is bound by the Federal Acquisitions Regulations (FARs) but a commercial customer is not bound by any laws or regulations. Therefore, the federal BAFO is subject to and in compliance with the FARs. If you lose, it is possible to protest the award. Protesting an award of a commercial contract is difficult and generally is without benefit of legal precedent.

It is important to note that you can lose the proposal at this point by not being prepared to respond to BAFO requests, not being prepared for questions raised during the BAFO, and not "reading-between-the-lines" and therefore not providing the correct solution/price answer.

Contract Negotiation

Be flexible, let the customer do the talking because the ball is in their court.

Contract negotiations are the final step before you are awarded the contract. The purpose of this step is to get agreement as to exact and specific work statements that spell out who is responsible for what work and when it will be done. In addition to the work statement, contracts are also concerned with administrative tasks such as the FOB point, payment terms, recourse for mistakes and deficiencies, and how simple paperwork is transmitted between the two companies.

Because negotiation is defined as the bargaining between two parties, it is important to remember that two parties are needed to negotiate. Some customers try to dominate the negotiation session so that any or all concessions are made by you and your company.

The key to successful contract negotiations is to be prepared to explain and defend your solution and price. If you are unable to explain why a project management staff is required or to defend the cost of one, the customer will not buy or allow that portion of the proposal to be part of the contract. On the other hand, if the customer is unable to provide you with specific information that is required to properly size your configuration, he will have to concede to your proposed configuration.

It is important for both parties to understand what is being purchased and what it will or will not do. If this understanding is not reached and agreed to, the contract will be a constant

> *The good news is we won the contract. The bad news is, we won the contract.*
> So goes an old proverb.

problem as both vendor and customer point fingers at each other in an effort to assign blame for products and services that do not perform as expected.

In rare cases, it may be better to not accept a contract if you and your customer do not agree. Generally speaking, the customers are naïve and still may not fully understand the technology and the solution you are proposing. The end result will be a dissatisfied customer and a contract loss for your company. Let the competition have this customer.

As an example, a vendor bid on and won a contract, but the value of the contract was lower than the normal contract expected. To compensate for the low dollar value, the vendor cut corners on the project plan, and overcharged for travel costs. In addition, this contract went to the "bottom of the stack" and higher value contracts were given more attention. Needless to say, the customer balked at this lack of attention and cancelled the contract, forcing the vendor to accept returned equipment in addition to paying for time lost.

The final analysis is: the vendor not only lost a contract, but lost any goodwill and good name recognition with this customer. The customer was one of nine campuses on a state university system and therefore the vendor lost the potential to supply eight other campuses with the same software application.

■ INTERPRETING POST-PROPOSAL DATA

✍ Now is the time to assess the signals and clues given by the customers.

After your proposal is submitted, your oral presentation complete, and your best and final offer is made, your proposal responsibilities are still not over. Now is the time to assess the signals and cues given by the customer. These signals are sometimes obvious but more often are obscure. Sometimes they are called buying signals and indicate the customer is beginning to think of you as the winning vendor.

For example, the customer may be concerned about delivery times and the first possible date for completion of the installation. The customer may be asking if it is possible for a 30- or 60-day delivery instead of the 90 days that were quoted.

Other signals are less apparent, but you may have a general feeling that things are going well—confident that you might win. If it is possible to pinpoint why you have this feeling, you may be able to develop a post-proposal selling plan that capitalizes on your strengths and draws attention away from your weaknesses. Similarly, if you think you are losing the proposal, an analysis of the signs from the customer may reveal your flaws.

Assume you have been given questions to answer and are invited to give a presentation. You receive several questions directed at the management section that ask, more or less, who will actually be responsible for the project and what place that person occupies in the chain of command. It is very possible that the customer is telling you indirectly that the sales representative is not the appropriate person to handle the post-award account.

If you work out of a small office, you might restructure the project so that the technical analyst acts as the project manager and the sales representative continues in his capacity as the account manager. In any event, the correct interpretation of the data is that the potential customer is not satisfied and this may affect the award.

From the beginning of the proposal effort, the sales rep should keep track of the "hints" given by the customer. These generally come from:

1. Questions about your proposed technology
2. Questions about why you chose one product over another
3. Questions about your implementation plan
4. Questions about delivery and installation
5. Questions about your company and its stability

■ SUMMARY

✍ Now is not the time to relax!

If you pay attention to details, it is possible to assemble some facts that will guide you in the post-submission phase. Assuming you put your best effort into the proposal, now is not the time to relax. If anything, hope the competition has reduced their effort while you are still driving home every point whenever possible.

It is this process of continuing to sell and establishing a good working relationship with the customer that will reap the most benefits. The situation in the second example of this chapter, in which the company proposed but could not substantiate a project management price to the customer, could have been turned around if better relations had been established with the customer and the salesman had better data to present. In that particular example, the company writing the proposal had no previous contact with the customer and had no knowledge that an RFP was to be issued. Compounded by the change in sales representatives in the middle of the process, it was not likely the proposal could have won given that set of circumstances.

Many sales representatives find ways to keep in contact with the customer during the post-proposal phase. They use this contact to judge how they are rated against the competition, and try to provide additional information whenever possible. For example, an industry analyst published a false and misleading report about a company that was vying with other vendors for a contract. The competition was quick to capitalize on this by forwarding a copy of the report to the project leader for the RFP. When the company was not invited to provide a demonstration, it asked for a debriefing with the customer and was told that both the product and the company were given low ratings and that the report had influenced their decision.

Of course, the company that had been given the low rating knew of the report; the analyst was notified that he was mistaken and the report was false. The analyst printed a retraction in his next report and this was given to the customer. Not only did the losing company give the customer the retraction, but it used this opportunity to deliver a well-written and very powerful letter from the president of the company. This company was placed back on the potential winners' list, was given the chance to provide a demonstration, and in the end, won the contract.

If your company is in the mist of change, while you have outstanding proposals, be prepared to be proactive and let the customers know what is happening and why. Changes are typically beneficial and these benefits should be brought to the customer's attention. Be prepared to counteract the competition's use of any publicity and change, within your company, to sound the "alarm bell" in the customer's ears, and to implement the FUD principle — *"Fear, Uncertainty, and Doubt."*

We have covered a lot of ground in this chapter. We hope that you will pay as much attention to the post-proposal activities as you did with the proposal itself. The proposal allows you to participate in the post-proposal activities; this means that you are being considered as a candidate. Each step, presentation, demonstration, and negotiation brings you closer to winning. Don't stumble!

Notes

Evaluation

If you understand how your proposal is evaluated, you will be able to gain points by tailoring your proposal.

Evaluation

■ INTRODUCTION

⊠By evaluating your proposal from the customer's point of view, you can gain valuable insights into your proposal.

The evaluation process is a critical step in the proposal development effort. By evaluating your proposal with the customer's point of view in mind, you can gain valuable insight into what the customer's real requirements are and how best to meet them. In order to do this, however, you must be able to answer such questions as these: How will the proposal be evaluated? Who will evaluate it? What criteria will be used? How can you be sure which area, such as pricing, for instance, is most important? Is there anything that can be done to help the evaluation?

Questions like these should be asked the day you receive the RFP. Plan the evaluation as you would all other phases and parts of the proposal, and make this activity a regular item on your proposal checklist. You may greatly enhance your chance of winning by asking and then determining the answers to such questions. Review Appendix E, Evaluation Checklist, for a list of evaluation activities.

As an overview, let's take a brief look at each question stated above:

How will the proposal be evaluated?

Probably the first thing that the evaluators will do is check for the obvious:

■ Were you on time?
■ Did you provide the requested number of copies?
■ Did you follow the suggested format?
■ Did you provide a complete set of data sheets?
■ Is the cost volume separate?
■ Is your price in the ballpark?
■ Did you take exception to every important item requested?

⊠Taking an exception is a risk. You may be non-compliant.

An exception means you are not complying with a requirement in the RFP or that you want to substitute an alternative solution. For example, suppose that the RFP required external modems for a certain workstation configuration. You may make an exception because your workstations are already equipped with internal modems. Or possibly, you may be able to meet the customer's requirements, but in a different way with different, but comparable, equipment in a more cost-effective manner.

These initial checks are to eliminate any proposals that really didn't respond to the RFP or took so many exceptions that what was left wasn't worth considering. After these initial evaluations are made, the proposals that merit an in-depth study are commonly referred to as having made the *short list*.

Who reads the proposals?

The proposals on the short list usually are split apart and given to evaluators who are experts in certain areas. For example, terms and conditions probably will go to the contracts specialist, the management section will go to the project leader, and the technical section could be broken down among many people. A large proposal will not be read by a single person. The evaluation is a group effort, and usually, the winner is not chosen by one person.

What criteria will be used?

✎ *There may be non-written evaluation criteria.*

Naturally, the criteria will vary with each proposal depending on what the customer needs and requires. The evaluation criteria can be separated into two general types: that which is formally stated under headings such as *Evaluation Criteria,* and criteria you learn through account contacts and reading "between the lines" of the RFP.

Generally, the formal evaluation criteria are very broad, and not very informative:

> *General evaluation criteria will be the completeness of the response to this RFP and the ability of the bidder to meet the objectives and requirements.*

This tells virtually nothing that we would not assume on our own. On the other hand, the following quote from another RFP tells us something very different and important. It is the last item under *Evaluation Factors:*

> *The professionalism of the proposal and marketing/technical staff involved will provide valuable insight into each organization's ability and willingness to satisfy our complex and changing needs.*

How can you be sure one area is most important?

Again, read between the lines. When the customer emphasizes a certain requirement, you can be sure this requirement is foremost in his mind. If he emphasizes compatibility with his current equipment, don't try to sell him something at a bargain price that is not compatible. Price is obviously not his major concern.

What can be done to help the evaluation?

The most important way you can help the evaluation is to enlist the best available people to work on the project—from the proposal team manager to the experts in your company—who will review the RFP. Then, questioning the customer as much as possible and reading the RFP thoroughly with the customer's point of view constantly in mind are the next best measures you can take to help the evaluation.

■ IN-HOUSE EVALUATION

✎Don't be shy about asking questions.

The place to start finding out about the evaluation is in the RFP itself. If there is a section on evaluation, read it and make sure the proposal team reads it also. During the proposal kickoff meeting, go over the criteria and ask for questions. Write the questions down and submit them to the customer. Ask that evaluation criteria be part of the agenda for the bidders' conference.

The bidders' conference is hosted by the customer, and all vendors who have received the RFP are expected to attend. At this conference, the customer explains the ground rules, goes over the RFP, and allows procedural questions to be asked. This is the time to ask any questions regarding the evaluation criteria. Technical questions usually have to be written and submitted to the customer. Responses by the customer are in writing also.

Rating the Proposal

For purposes of evaluation, RFPs are broken into sections and each section is given a value or weight. For example, a typical RFP has a management section, a technical section, and a cost section. The customer may assign a total value of 100 points that breaks down as follows:

Management Section = 40 points

Subject Area	Points
Project leadership	10
Implementation schedule	15
Quality control	15

Technical Section = 40 points

Subject Area	Points
Technical approach	5
Design	5
Performance	10
Compatibility	20

Cost Section = 20 points

Subject Area	Points
Hardware price	5
Software price	5
Service price	5
Training	5

✑Understanding evaluation criteria will help direct your efforts and prevent lost time.

Not all RFPs will go into this much detail, but for purposes of illustration, let's assume that you have this information. Looking through the management section, the point spread is fairly close so you would want to pay equal attention to all areas, perhaps spending a little more time on the 15-point areas.

In the technical section, however, we can see clearly where the most time should be spent. Obviously, this customer doesn't care how you do it; he is interested only in whether you can be compatible. The most time and effort in this section should be spent convincing the customer that your product is completely, totally, and without question compatible with his existing equipment.

In the cost section, the customer may not be greatly concerned with the initial purchase investment. What he is really looking for is how much your service and maintenance is going to be. So, in the cost section, you may give standard prices for equipment and not offer a discount. No discount on the equipment price would then enable you to lower the service cost.

It is essential to determine this kind of information as early as possible to prevent you from spending valuable time directing your arguments to the wrong issue. If, in the example above, the proposal team failed to study the evaluation criteria, the assumption might be made that the customer would be attracted to the proposal with the least expensive equipment, which in this case, was not the issue at all.

Developing the Evaluation Criteria

✑ Develop a list of evaluation criteria as soon as possible and pass it on to the proposal team.

Whether a proposal is being prepared by one person or a large team effort is involved, the proposal leader is responsible for developing the proposal evaluation criteria (PEC). There are three good places to start this development:

- Read the evaluation criteria given in the RFP.
- Ask the customer.
- Read between the lines of the RFP.
- Work with the account representative.

From this type of research, you should be able to begin a PEC list of what is important and what is not important to the customer and then begin to direct your proposal accordingly.

Reading between the Lines

An example of reading between the lines would be repeated questions and statements about service and maintenance. If the RFP section on service was very detailed, and reference to long-term service contracts was asked for, you may assume that the customer is placing great weight on the service issues. If you have made this assumption early enough, it would be possible then to direct a question to the customer to test your assumption during the bidders' conference. (But be careful not to tip your hand to other vendors.)

✑ Sometimes the evaluation criteria offer what amounts to conflicting information.

Evaluation criteria are often spread throughout the RFP and sometimes can be confusing and offer what amounts to conflicting information. For example, in the general preparation instructions of one RFP, it states: *"While pricing will be considered competitively, we are not obligated to consider the lowest priced proposal."* Further into the RFP, in the technical overview, pricing is given a little different value: *"Evaluation will be on the basis of two criteria: First is overall price performance of the technical approach and second is the ability of the system to sustain continued growth."* And last, in the proposal evaluation section, pricing is placed last in a list of three criteria: *"The following attributes will form the basis for the overall selection: a. Technical approach, b. Demonstrable history of project management, and c. Price performance tables."*

Reading further in the evaluation section, a recurring theme of simplicity seems to carry weight: *"A simple and straightforward design...."* And on the next page: *"Attention will be given to the simplicity of the program office and its ability...."* And last, these two statements that reflect the need for simplicity: *"The ease with which the overall program can be implemented.... We expect to undergo significant internal change and the ease with which these changes can be accommodated will be a very important criteria for evaluation."*

✎Look for a common thread that runs through the RFP. Think of it as the counterpart to your sales themes.

In this particular RFP, the idea of simplicity and ability to upgrade seems to be a common thread running through both the technical and the management section. An alert reader would home in on this and try to develop themes that reflect this need in the proposal. In the proposal kickoff meeting, these themes would be given to the proposal team with the request that the "simplicity of design" and "standards-based technology" be reiterated whenever possible.

While this was fairly easy to spot, other needs in this RFP were buried. One hidden need was touched on above in that the company expects "to undergo significant change" in a short amount of time. This type of statement should be researched carefully because a drastic change may result in the postponement and eventual cancellation of the project. Such was the case in this RFP. Figure 7-1 is an example of evaluation guidelines from a larger RFP.

Forming an In-house Evaluation Team

✎Separate and objective reviews can only help your proposal.

If your proposal is going to be a winner, you must take the time to have it reviewed and evaluated by a third party. This third party could range from your manager or his manager to a group of people that duplicates the customer's evaluation team. The evaluators need to be identified early and given a copy of the RFP so they can become familiar with the specifications and requirements.

Identify a date for the in-house evaluation and begin working toward producing a rough draft of your proposal for the evaluation team, also known as the *Red Team* (see below). An evaluation checklist such as the one shown in figure 7-2 is a useful tool for the leader of the evaluation team. Explain to the evaluators that on that date you will expect them to have read the RFP or their assigned section, and to be prepared to read your proposal and evaluate it. The evaluation should be from the customer's point of view.

✎Stress that the proposal is to be evaluated from the customer's point of view.

Because the in-house evaluation is done by in-house people, they tend to know the products and therefore are not as objective as they should be. Your manager, who also knows the products and who is evaluating your proposal, might agree with a decision to offer something other than what was asked for instead of questioning your decision. For this reason, stress that the proposal is to be evaluated from the customer's point of view.

I. **PROPOSAL EVALUATION**

    A. Introduction. Proposals will be formally evaluated to determine the responsiveness to the administrative and technical requirements set forth in this Request. The final selection will be made on the basis of the highest composite score for those proposals that meet all of the requirements.

    B. Receipt. Proposals will be dated and time stamped as they are received and verified that they are properly sealed. All proposals will remain sealed until the designated date for opening.

    C. Initial Evaluation. At the designated time of opening, all proposals will have an initial evaluation for the following four items:

        1. Proposal Opening. Proposals received by the specified date will be opened and checked for conformance to the requirements set forth in Volume 1, Section 2, Proposal Preparation Instructions. Proposals not in conformance with the required information will be marked non-responsive and may be rejected.

        2. RFP Requirements. Proposals that are responsive to the above will be checked for compliance to the mandatory requirements as outlined in Volume 2, Section 3, Mandatory Requirements. For proposals not meeting these requirements, the deviation will be defined approved or not approved. If approved, the proposal will be processed and the deviation noted. If not approved. the proposal will be non-responsive and returned to vendor.

        3. References. All references on the customer Reference List will be contacted and interviewed for the following: a. Equipment satisfaction b. Satisfaction with vendor's support c. Ease of installation d. Quality of training and instruction e. Quality of vendor's documentation

        Overall customer satisfaction must be displayed to remain responsive to this Request. Negative responses may be cause for rejection.

        4. Cost Analysis. Proposal costing information will be checked against required format. Cost schedules will be checked for mathematical accuracy and any resulting inconsistencies will be handled according to volume 1, Section 2, Proposal Preparation Instructions.

    D. Evaluation Methodology. Proposals will be evaluated using a weighted score system and must achieve a minimum number of points to be considered responsive to this Request. Proposals meeting or exceeding the minimum acceptable level will be deemed responsive.

    A technical score sheet will be completed for each proposal and points awarded for Mandatory, Desirable, and Variable items as follows:

        1. Mandatory. All requirements described in this Request as being Mandatory will be simply scored as approved or not approved. These mandatory requirements must be _fully_ satisfied or the proposal will be rejected and returned to the vendor.

        2. Desirable. All requirements described in this Request as being Desirable will be assigned a numeric value according to the benefit of that requirement. Desirable requirements can only have a positive effect on the overall score. Absence of Desirable requirements will not incur a negative score.

        3. Variable. All requirements described in this Request as being Variable will be initially scored as approved/not approved. Variable requirements scored as approved will have a proportionate value according to the weight and benefit assigned to each requirement.

    E. Final Selection. A summary score sheet will be completed for each vendor and a composite score for each proposal will be calculated. Selection of vendors for negotiation will be based on the highest composite score achieved. Final award of contract will be based on satisfactory contract negotiation and a successful demonstration.

Figure 7-1. _Evaluation Guidelines_

The Red Team

The in-house evaluation team is known as the Red Team. A Red Team is typically formed at the same time as the regular proposal team and is assigned a team leader. The Red Team's job is to constructively tear your proposal apart and offer advice on how to put it back together. The Red Team is recruited from inside and outside of your company and may contain a recognized expert hired as a consultant. Red Team members should not have had any working position on the proposal itself in order to be as objective as possible.

✎ *The Red Team is the customer.*

The Red Team is established as an equal to the proposal team. It must have the same clout and its recommendations must be taken seriously if it is to serve any useful purpose. The Red Team leader is usually assigned by the same person who assigned the proposal leader. Adequate time must be given for the Red Team review in addition to allowing time for corrections and recommendations to be implemented.

Activity	Notes
❑ Evaluation Team Formed ❑ Technical Team ❑ Management Team ❑ Pricing Team	
❑ Date and Time Established	
❑ RFP Distributed to Team	
❑ Space for Team Established	
❑ In-room Lunch and Coffee Ordered	
❑ Team Assembled for Evaluation	
❑ Proposals Distributed	
❑ Evaluation Form Distributed	
❑ Proposals and Forms Signed	
❑ Debriefing Held	
❑ Proposals and Forms Collected	
❑ Results Determined	
❑ Corrective Action Determined	
❑ Proposals Revised	

Figure 7-2. Evaluation Checklist

Although the results of a Red Team evaluation can be absolutely devastating, there is an excellent chance that the customer would approach the proposal in the same way, finding the same problems and offering the same objections.

■ CUSTOMER EVALUATION

Your proposal is not read by one person but by many. The customer's evaluation team is composed of people similar in make-up to the proposal team. It usually consists of **specialists in the technical fields**, **specialist in project management**, **someone knowledgeable in the competitive market**, and **a finance person**.

✎ For a large proposal, no single person may read the complete proposal.

Often, these people are not familiar with your product or service and may not even know your company existed before looking at your proposal. Nevertheless, their job is to weed out all proposals that are not serious contenders for whatever reason. In one sense, they don't recommend winners so much as point out the losers.

One of the major problems your proposal will encounter is the fact that often no one person on the customer's evaluation team will read the entire proposal, and therefore no one sees the overall picture. Each evaluator is assigned a section and does not have an opportunity to read other sections. Therefore, if you made an exception that was clearly identified and justified in the Executive Summary, and the evaluator that was given the technical section did not see it, he will give you fewer points for not complying with all the equipment requirements.

Below is a list of typical evaluation criteria that will help you and your evaluation team evaluate your own proposal from the customer's point of view. Not all of these will always apply.

■ Are the basic criteria in the RFP followed? Did you follow the basic instructions for formatting?
■ Is the proposal well organized and responsive to the basic specifications?
■ Does the proposal demonstrate a grasp of the overall problem or does it focus on individual parts that are not connected?
■ Does the proposal address the major issues of the RFP with equal weight?
■ Is the proposal's solution spelled out clearly?
■ Is the proposal's solution believable?
■ Is the proposal's delivery schedule believable?
■ Is the proposal responsive to terms and conditions?
■ Does the proposal demonstrate the capability to perform?

- Does the proposal demonstrate technical capability?
- Is this capability believable?
- Are the vendor's facilities adequate?
- Are the vendor's personnel resources adequate?
- Does the vendor have related experience?
- Is there a demonstrable past performance?
- Can the vendor supply non-product-related deliverables such as documentation, manuals, training?
- Is the vendor's company stable financially?
- Is the costing reasonable?
- Is the cost broken down or lump sum?
- Is the costing method believable?

There are also judgment criteria that will never appear in writing. These criteria reflect personal biases, personal dislikes or likes, past performance problems, job-related fears, threats from above, and so on. In other words, they are intangible.

Following are some examples of intangible criteria:

- An RFP might be written using the incumbent's terminology in an attempt to lock in the incumbent and lock out everyone else.
- The incumbent's proposal guarantees additional jobs in the customer's city and the competing proposal doesn't add any jobs.
- A small company in California bidding on a service contract in Florida makes the evaluators feel uncomfortable with their inability to respond to day-to-day problems. (Local presence!)
- If a proposal wins, it will jeopardize the jobs of a manager and his department. (Reengineering the workplace)
- A proposal may be a threat to one of the prospective customer's departments that has used a certain product for many years, and all of the people in the department are satisfied with the product. (The incumbent has the upper hand)

Although it is possible for upper management to go against a recommendation on the part of the evaluation team, giving you the contract instead of the company that had the most points in the evaluation, it isn't something you would want to rely on. When this happens, most likely the decision to award the contract to a certain vendor was made long before the RFP was written.

The Evaluation Board

Following is a simple diagram of a typical proposal evaluation board. The actual evaluation takes place with the people below the RFP director, who is responsible for the proposed project and may become the project leader after selection is made.

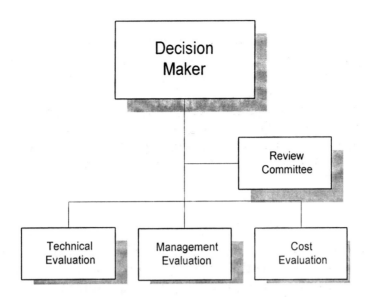

The evaluators read sections according to their expertise and make their recommendations to the RFP director. These, in turn, are organized and the points or comments compiled into a recommendation that is passed up to the decision maker. This person may have formed a review committee that would look at the recommendation, possibly alter it, and submit a recommendation of its own. The decision maker may accept the committee's recommendation or choose to go along with the initial recommendation made by the evaluation team, thus, in a sense, rubber stamping the RFP director's decision.

The final decision is generally a team decision.

In either case, it is important to remember that the RFP director usually cannot make the final decision. This adds another dimension to the proposal process. If it is the president or senior vice president who will make the decision, how can you reach this person in order to sell your proposal?

You may not need to. The decision maker of a company that has gone to the trouble of writing an RFP and setting up a committee to evaluate the responses will most likely follow the recommendation made by the evaluation team. The decision maker is someone who has the interest of the company as a whole in mind, not just this particular project.

However, it is just because the decisionmaker has the company's interests at heart that he may not follow the recommendation. If he becomes aware of some development that was unknown to the RFP director, such as a dramatic rise in the price of oil or an environmental issue that affects the company as a whole, he may decide to put the procurement on hold until the matter can be studied; or the award may be made to a company that anticipated the problem and presented an alternate proposal.

In other words, major dollar decisions are, or can be, major political issues. This is where the account representative earns his or her dollar. Without the account rep's opinion and guidance, in a major RFP, you should carefully consider whether to continue.

■ SUMMARY

Of the many factors and variables that go into making a proposal, paying attention to the evaluation process can contribute as much to winning as a competitive price, a brilliant technical approach, and a masterful management section. The in-house evaluation should be given as much attention as was given to writing the technical section. Finding out how the customer is going to evaluate your proposal and what the political climate is, is as important as driving the cost down to its absolute lowest.

In-house evaluation will increase your chances of winning.

Proper evaluation practices will enhance your proposal's chances for winning. This is a two-step process that begins with selecting an in-house evaluation team. Selection of the team or person should be done with as much care as selecting a proposal manager. It is essential to give the in-house evaluation proper acknowledgment and support, otherwise everyone's time will be wasted. In fact, you must be willing and prepared to stand behind the Red Team and its verdict, even if you do not agree with its decision.

Don't rely solely on the RFP for evaluation criteria.

The second phase in the evaluation process is to begin questioning the customer and getting as much information as possible on evaluation criteria. Most customers will respond to direct questions. They may not tell you everything, and sometimes what they don't tell you is just as important. Remember, the customer has spent a great deal of time, money, and effort writing the RFP. It is to his advantage to let you know as closely as possible what he wants to see and what he doesn't.

In other words, sell the customer what he wants to buy, not what you think he should buy. In the proposal business this means read the RFP with a critical eye, pay close attention to the evaluation criteria, question the customer, and read between the lines. Your rewards in new business will be well worth the effort.

Printing the Proposal

High quality printing will make your
proposal look professional and add value.

Printing the Proposal

■ INTRODUCTION

⌦Printing also requires planning and resources.

Printing is the last step in producing your proposal. In some ways, printing is also one of the most difficult steps because of limited time and, usually, an inflexible due date. Even though you may have planned thoroughly in the beginning when the original schedule was made, there is always some time slippage as the proposal progresses—unforeseen problems are invariably encountered. Sometimes the four or five days you may have originally planned for become an overnight effort.

This section is devoted to familiarizing you with the printing process so you can complete this phase as quickly and efficiently as possible:

- Methods of printing and binding
- What parts of the proposal are specially printed, including a discussion of binder tabs
- Selecting a printer and knowing what is expected of you as well as what you can expect from him
- How to physically organize and assemble the proposal

See Appendix D, Printing, for a checklist of activities.

■ METHODS OF PRINTING

The vocabulary of different industries is important to understand. A familiar story concerns a man who had never been to an auction before and inadvertently bought a $5,000 vase when he scratched his head. I encountered a similar situation at one of our field offices. The first day I arrived, the sales personnel and I had a meeting with the printer they had selected. As we talked, it seemed we were talking about the same thing—but not the same thing! We soon discovered the printer was a book publisher and was treating our 250-page proposal as if it were a book, including a first run of 5,000 copies. (We only wanted 15 copies made.) When he came up with his rock bottom price of $30,000 for the typesetting, we stopped right there. He didn't understand what a sales proposal was and the field office people knew nothing about printing.

In the context of proposals, the word printer is used loosely to mean anyone who agrees to reproduce your proposal regardless of the method used. It is unlikely that you will use the services of a printer as that term normally implies, i.e., a company that uses large letterpress or offset printing equipment. If you do not have special requirements for such items as photographs or continuous tone artwork (i.e., artwork that has graduated fine shading), you will probably use printing processes such as photocopying or laser printing.

Therefore, we will spend most of our time on photocopy-type reproduction or the office laser printer. However, there are a few pieces that you might consider having professionally printed, such as the cover, tabs, and other color inserts.

■ SPECIALTY PRINTING

✍ Covers and tabs may require special printing.

Certain parts of the proposal may need to be specially printed by a vendor other than a photocopy shop such as proposal covers and binder tabs (also called index tabs).

Covers. If you have original art drawn for a cover, by an illustrator, it is best to have the cover art and the text handled professionally. The proposal cover may require the most amount of time to print; therefore, it should be taken to the printer as soon as the information for the cover is determined. The cover text will need to be typeset, proofread, possible corrections made, and approved before the final copies are printed. Information and suggestions for covers can be found in Chapter 2, Proposal Contents: Overview. This only applies if you have had original artwork created for your covers, whether it be a one-time only or covers used as boilerplate.

If your cover art is done on a PC or graphics workstation, it may be printed on a color printer (laser or inkjet) or the electronic file transferred via modem or taken to a color reproduction shop.

The above also applies to any binder spines that are being created. Binder spines are strips of paper that are slid into the presentation binder spine. The spine usually has the customer's project name or your company name printed. The spines will need to be cut to fit the binder and you will need to know the size of the binder (1/2", 1", 1 ½", etc.).

Having a printed cover and spine gives your proposal a professional appearance. In the example below, created from a commercial drawing software program, the cover is a grouping of computers because the project is a computer system. The printed spine could either be "ERMS" or your company name AJAX CORP.

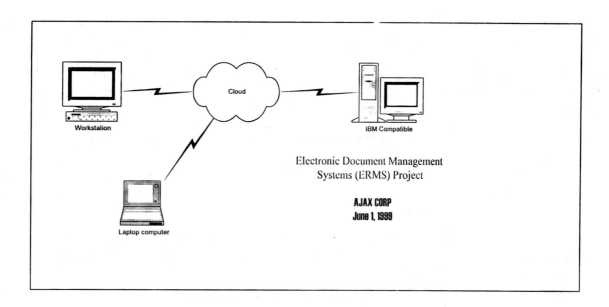

Electronic Document Management
Systems (ERMS) Project

AJAX CORP
June 1, 1999

Binder Tabs

Custom-printed binder tabs are very professional in appearance but are the most expensive and time-consuming to prepare. Following is a more complete discussion of other alternatives as well as what is involved in ordering custom-printed tabs. Binder tabs are available in several formats. Below are listed the most common types:

- *Preprinted.* These are available at most stationery stores and are the least expensive and most convenient to use as no preparation is required. They consist of a package of preprinted tabs with numbers or letters and are simply inserted in front of the appropriate section after the proposal is complete. The main drawback is they do not indicate the titles of the sections. Also, refrain from using colored tabs and stick with black and white.

- *Blank tabs.* You can buy blank manila tabs from a good office supply store and then type right on the tab. This allows you to specify section titles and gives the proposal a custom feel. You can also purchase stick-on labels that are printed with your laser printer and placed on the tab. However, they are much more work—especially if you have to submit multiple copies.

- *Clear plastic tabs.* You can buy tabs with clear or colored plastic holders in which you insert a typed piece of paper with the section number and title. However, these are not very professional in appearance and tend to look amateurish.

- *Professionally printed tabs.* The most professional looking are custom-printed tabs. A very important proposal is worth the extra money. If you decide to use this type, be sure to allow enough time to have them printed; tabs should be turned in to the printer at the same time as the cover. Below is an example.

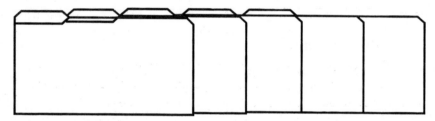

General Information

Binder tabs are called out by cuts. The cuts indicate how many tabs appear across. Tabs usually come in standard three-cut, five-cut, or seven-cut banks (sets). A five-cut bank is shown here.

A three-cut gives you the most room to type information, but a five- or seven-cut may be better for very large proposals. The information on a tab is the section number and title as shown below.

Ordering Tabs

There is a surprising amount of information the printer needs to know about your tabs. You can save yourself and the printer a great deal of time and grief if you specify all the required information at the time of the order. The information must fall into three general categories: identity of the printer; your identity; and the actual specifications (called specs, a contraction for specifications). Prepare a form or checklist (see figure 8-1) that you can use over and over. Be sure to make a copy of the completed form for your files in the event of a dispute between you and the printer.

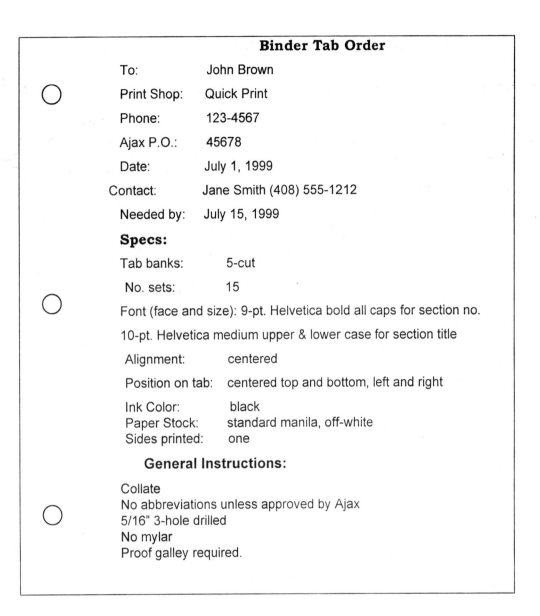

Binder Tab Order

To: John Brown

Print Shop: Quick Print

Phone: 123-4567

Ajax P.O.:   45678

Date: July 1, 1999

Contact: Jane Smith (408) 555-1212

Needed by: July 15, 1999

Specs:

Tab banks: 5-cut

No. sets: 15

Font (face and size): 9-pt. Helvetica bold all caps for section no.

10-pt. Helvetica medium upper & lower case for section title

Alignment: centered

Position on tab: centered top and bottom, left and right

Ink Color: black
Paper Stock: standard manila, off-white
Sides printed: one

General Instructions:

Collate
No abbreviations unless approved by Ajax
5/16" 3-hole drilled
No mylar
Proof galley required.

Figure 8-1. *Binder Tab Order Checklist*

Note the request at the bottom of the checklist shown in figure 8-1: *Proof galley required.* The galley is the typeset text that will be printed on the tabs. It is very important to proof it for typographical errors and conformance with your requirements before it is printed on the tabs.

Tabs are often given a coat of clear mylar to protect and strengthen them. Unless offered at no extra cost, this is really not needed as proposals have a very limited shelf life.

In addition to the specific information on your checklist, you may be asked by the printer to fill out additional information. Note: If your company has an in-house print shop, check with them first to see if they can print the tabs for you rather than ordering them outside; most company print shops can handle this kind of job.

Preparing Instructions for the Printer

The following instructions apply if you are reproducing the proposal at a print or photocopy shop. It is important that they have specific instructions and can copy the proposal according to your needs.

✇Ensure you outline your instructions to the printer.

This may not appear to be too difficult, but in some cases the pagination can be complex if you are printing on two sides. Briefly, you would want your first section page to start as a "right" page. If you look at this book, the first page is a section title page, next is an index to the section and the first page of the section starts on the right. Also notice that a right page is an odd number and left pages are even numbered.

Because the last printed page may be a right page, the printer needs to know to insert a blank left page as the next page, otherwise, your next section would printed on the backside of the last section. This may not be consistent as some sections may end on a left page.

Printing One-Sided or Two

The first consideration will be whether the proposal pages will be printed on one or two sides. Several factors should be taken into account. If your proposal is long, printing on two sides will cut the actual size in half. If your proposal is only fifty pages, you may want to print one side only. Printing two-sided gives your proposal a more professional appearance, but one-sided is usually acceptable. Occasionally, the RFP will specify whether you must print one- or two-sided.

If not, the decision should be based on the need, time, expense, binding method, and your own experience. In most cases, printing on two sides is preferable. If you choose this format, some of the page information will need special attention. For example, if you normally print your page number on the bottom right, when you print two-sided, the page number on the back side will appear on the bottom near the binding, rather than on the bottom left where it should be. Also, the margins must be alternated if you have the margin near the spine wider than the margin at the outside of the page. Centering the text on the page and centering the page number at the bottom of the page eliminates these problems. Most word processors today have the ability to alternate "left" and "right" pages and, when selected, will automatically set the page margins, headers, and footers for left and right printing.

Preparing the Dummy

The next step is to complete what is called a printer's dummy. As shown in figure 8-2, the dummy gives the printer a road map of how you want your proposal printed. It also tells him how many pages there are in each section, as well as how many and where tabs, photos or other artwork will be inserted. Without this information, the printer or you may lose a sheet unknowingly.

✍ The dummy sheet provides the printer with a road map to your proposal.

By convention, pages on the right side of a book are odd numbered and are called front pages; those on the left side are even numbered and are known as back pages. Look at figure 8-2. This illustration shows how to fill in the dummy layout of a book that is to be printed on both sides of the page. At the top of the form is general information. The page ___ of___ is important to fill in because this indicates how many pages of the dummy there are. For example, if your dummy is five pages long, you would write page 1 of 5, page 2 of 5, etc. Remember, once you turn the material in to a print shop, they will not have time to call you and ask for such information as how many pages are in each section or whether you have a one- or three-page dummy sheet.

Following the blocks across the page from left to right, you will see that the first page is a right page and is indicated as the cover. The 0 at the bottom means there is no page number, and even though the top of the form calls for two-sided printing, a slash is drawn through the back page to reinforce that there is nothing printed on the back. The next page, a right page, is the title page with nothing printed on the back, and also has no page number. The third page starts the table of contents; notice that it is paginated by using Roman numerals, not Arabic numerals.

The proposal proper starts with the first section. Generally the section begins with a tab followed by a section title page, although both are not needed. Sometimes, in very long proposals, a mini table of contents for that section only is printed on the back of the tab or on the section title page. Page 1-4 is the last page of Section 1.For long proposals, you do not need to actually indicate each page. Notice in figure 8-2 that the beginning of section 2 starts on page 2-1 and goes in order through pages 2-22.

If there were special printing requirements or pages, they would be called out on the dummy as "foldout page" or "photograph" to alert the printer.

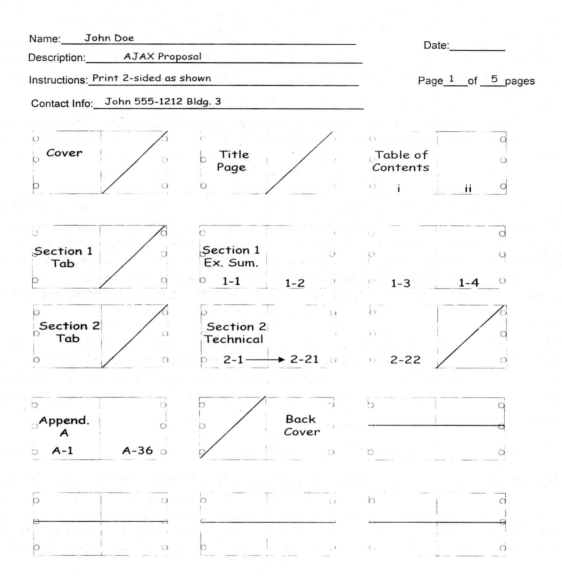

Figure 8-2. *Sample Dummy Sheet*

An appendix is paginated by using the appendix letter followed by a dash and the normal sequence of numbers. For instance, Appendix A is paginated A-i, etc. The last block on the dummy indicates to the printer that there is a back cover with nothing printed on the inside. The remaining pages are lined out so that every page on the dummy is accounted for.

Special Treatment

If you have special illustrations, photographs, foldouts, or anything that is out of the ordinary, be sure to alert the printer as well as indicating it on the dummy. The printer may need to subcontract such work as half-toning a photograph. In the case of foldouts, the print shop will separate them from the rest of the material and print them on a special machine. The dummy then helps in reassembling the proposal.

For reasons of cost, suppose you are going to assemble the proposal yourself and are not asking the printer to insert tabs, foldouts, etc., or place the completed proposal in a binder. You will get a separate stack of foldouts from the printer that may not be collated. To help you put the foldouts in the text, colored paper called **slip sheets** can be used. Indicate on the dummy where slip sheets are to be inserted so the printer can prepare the manuscript accordingly.

✐ *Check with your printer first for his version of the dummy.*

Most printers have their own version of the dummy sheet and may want you to use the ones they provide. Also, each printer will have different customs and methods for indicating special needs. The best approach is to discuss the entire job with the printer before preparing the dummy.

■ TYPES OF BINDING

Before having your proposal printed, you must consider how it will be bound. In Chapter 2, Proposal Contents: Overview, a three-ring binder is recommended for its ease of use. However, there are several methods commonly used that are just as acceptable depending on your situation. The following is a list and explanation of the types of binding that are suitable for proposal work:

Three-Ring Binder

The three-ring binder is probably the easiest binding method and also allows for instant change when needed. In addition, it has the advantage of standing up on a shelf; if you have your company's name and the requester's name on the spine, it will be easy for the evaluator to pick out your proposal from the others. Also, it lies flat when open, which is convenient for the evaluators.

✐ *3-ring binders are recommended.*

If you use a binder, it is best to use a presentation or view binder that has clear plastic slip pockets on the front, spine, and back. With the slip pocket, you can insert custom covers and put your company's name on the spine. However, for a really special proposal, you can contact a company that makes binders and have your logo, proposal project name, and other information, including an illustration, printed right on the binder itself, although this is costly and time-consuming.

Generally on the inside front cover of a presentation binder there is a plastic half-slip pocket that can be used to insert additional preprinted material such as an annual report, data sheets, brochures, reprint articles, or your business card.

Binders usually come in one-half inch increments starting at one-half inch and going to three inches. Anything more than three inches is not advisable as the sheer weight of that much paper becomes a problem to work with. Binders generally hold 100 sheets of paper (including binder tabs) per one-half inch. As a tip, if you do decide to use a three-ring binder, ask the printer to punch your paper with the larger five-sixteenths inch hole rather than the standard one-quarter inch. This larger hole makes the pages easier to turn and helps prevent tearing around the holes.

Any binders other than three-ring are not recommended. There are binders with more than three rings, but if you use these, you will encounter problems when making corrections unless you have a 16- or 32-hole punch.

ACCO® Fastener

The ACCO type of binding is a two-piece metal fastener that uses three-hole punched paper. ACCO binding is almost as flexible as the three-ring binder, allowing spot changes to be made. Like the three ring binder, ACCO allows you to assemble the proposal in your office instead of paying a printer to do the assembly work.

ACCO binding does lack several key features of the binder:

- Does not have a spine on which your company name and the proposal program name can be printed
- Will not stand on a shelf
- Does not permit pages to lie flat when open
- Does not have the substantial feel of a binder

Plastic Comb Binding

The plastic comb is a spiral strip of plastic with teeth that are inserted into the page and bind the paper by means of a variety of methods. Perhaps the most commonly known type is made by the General Binding Corporation (GBC). It is commonly referred to as the GBC 19-hole, or simply comb binding.

This type of binding is more permanent than the first two because the pages cannot easily be separated once bound. Also, unless you own a machine, the proposal will have to be assembled and bound by the printer. Once this is done, the proposal can only be changed at additional expense and time as the old comb will have to be cut and a new one inserted. It is possible to remove the comb yourself and change pages, if the new pages are punched and you are willing to spend some time inserting the comb by hand.

Comb binding will give your proposal a professional look and you will be able to use your custom-made covers. However, comb bindings normally do not have information printed on the spine, although it is possible to have your company name and logo printed specially if you are ordering large quantities. Comb bindings do not stand upright on a shelf.

■ SELECTING A PRINTER OR REPRODUCTION SHOP

The printer you select will depend on your location and the type of proposal you are writing. For many people, the company reproduction department will more than satisfy their needs. However, in a field sales office with an important account, the office copy machine may not do. It would be possible to print the whole proposal on the office laser printer, but this may be time consuming and costly when printing 200 pages and 6 copies.

Start by looking up several printers in the telephone book yellow pages under Printers. Choose those that are close to your office. Driving across town in rush-hour traffic to get your proposal or make last-minute changes before the printer closes is much too risky.

If your proposal is basically simple and small, a quick print shop is adequate. The quick print shops, also called instant press shops, are not equipped to provide services other than high-speed photocopy reproduction from your masters.

For more complex requirements, select full service printers that are capable of providing typesetting, photographic work, paste-up, offset printing, binding, and possibly two-color work, in addition to special handling for covers and assembly.

Once you have selected several printers, arrange to visit their shops. Have them show you around and explain how they operate. Ask what they expect you to provide and what things cause them problems. Have them show you samples of their work. If they have an illustration department, ask to see it and meet the illustrators and typesetters.

Some of the basic qualities to look for in a printer and his printing are:

■ Can the printer handle all of your needs such as typesetting, binder tabs, photographic work, and complicated reproduction work for covers and special artwork?

- Is the printer well organized and able to meet your deadlines? It is critical that the printer understand up front the importance of having your job done on time.
- Is the print itself clear and sharp?
- Is the paper clean with no roller marks or shadow lines?
- Are halftones sharp with good contrast?
- Can the printer provide the appropriate type of paper for your job?
- Does the printer offer advice and assistance in preparing the job?
- Does the printer suggest cost-saving alternatives for reproduction?
- Is the printer willing to handle small jobs? Some printers may believe that your small jobs are not a cost-effective way for him to do business.
- Is the printer willing to work overtime or on weekends if necessary?

Finding and keeping a good printer will be invaluable to you. For most non-deadline work, such as printing in-house forms or making copies of expendable data sheets, almost any printer is probably satisfactory. However, for proposals you need to establish a good rapport with a printer who is willing to hold his press run for an incoming job that might be several hours late, or will add extra pages at the last minute for an additional unexpected appendix. You need someone who will do favors for you, and be willing to put up with totally outrageous demands and deadlines. If you are lucky enough to find a printer like this, do everything in your power to show your appreciation—just paying rush charges is not enough.

■ FINAL ASSEMBLY

If you, and not the printer, will be doing the final assembly for multiple copies, here are some suggestions to make the job easier. The assumption is you will be using three-ring binders.

Open all the binders and lay them out on a large table. Stack all the special graphics, foldouts, photos, etc., in sets in the order in which they will appear in the proposal. Stack all the binder tabs in sets. Organize the proposal by sections (front matter, main sections, appendices) in individually labeled folders and stack these in the same manner.

Insert the front, back, and spine first as binders may get heavy after they have been stuffed. Place the front matter in all the binders. Next, insert each section with its binder tab. When all the printed matter is inserted, take each set of graphics, foldouts, photos, etc., and go through the binders one at a time inserting this material where it belongs. By setting up this assembly-line procedure, you are less likely to overlook some material in some of the binders. The more methodical you are, the less likely you are to leave something out.

Finally, if possible, have another person check the binders for completeness. Often, a "fresh pair of eyes" can spot something you overlooked. At this point, you can't be too careful. After all, this is the final moment when you are ready to present the winning proposal you have worked so hard to develop and prepare.

Notes

Proposal
Checklists

Checklists are invaluable to
ensure everything has been
completed.

■ Introduction to Appendices

The checklists that follow are very detailed and may include items you would not consider or include. As such, these are reminders and you should use what is needed or create your own checklists.

A. General Pre-proposal Checklist

B. Proposal Writing Checklist

C. Pre-submission Checklist

D. Printing Checklist

E. Evaluation Checklist

F. Proposal Submission Checklist

G. Post-proposal Checklist

H. Proposal Bid No-Bid Checklist

I. Proposal Status Checklist

A. General Pre-proposal Checklist	
Item	**Notes**
❑ RFI/RFP Received	
❑ Qualify Opportunity	
❑ First Analysis of RFP Opportunity	
❑ Acknowledge Receipt of RFP	
❑ Attend Bidders' Conference	
❑ Support	
❑ Sales Support	
❑ Technical Support	
❑ Management Support	
❑ Copy RFP and Distribute	
❑ Bid/No-bid Decision	
❑ Technical	
❑ Marketing	
❑ Cost	
❑ Timing	
❑ Send No-bid Letter?	
❑ Send Intent to Bid Letter?	

A. General Pre-proposal Checklist (continued)	
Item	**Notes**
☐ Establish Proposal Schedule	
☐ Internal Management Presentation	
☐ Terms and Conditions to Contracts	
☐ Outline RFP	
☐ Standard Equipment	
☐ Standard Service	
☐ Custom Equipment	
☐ Custom Services	
☐ Plan Kickoff Meeting	
☐ Establish Proposal Resources	
☐ Sales and Marketing	
☐ Technical/Engineering	
☐ Project Management	
☐ Service and Maintenance	
☐ Education and Training	
☐ Legal Review	
☐ Editing and Illustrations	

A. General Pre-proposal Checklist (continued)	
Item	**Notes**
❑ Reproduction	
❑ Word Processing	
❑ Secure Working Space	
❑ Warroom	
❑ PCs	
❑ Software	
❑ Materials	
❑ Assign Cost/Pricing Team	
❑ Standard Equipment	
❑ Standard Services	
❑ Custom Equipment	
❑ Custom Services	
❑ Assign Internal Review Team	
❑ Technical	
❑ Management	
❑ Cost	
❑ Sales and Marketing	

A. General Pre-proposal Checklist (continued)	
Item	**Notes**
❑ Do Competitive Analysis	
❑ Develop Marketing Strategy	
❑ Customer Politics	
❑ Primary Business Problem	
❑ Develop Marketing Themes	
❑ Develop Technical Approach	
❑ Marketing Strategy Approval	
❑ Technical Approach Approval	
❑ Develop First RFP Questions	
❑ Hold Kickoff Meeting	

B. Proposal Writing Checklist	
Item	**Notes**
❏ Cover Letter	
❏ Executive Summary	
❏ Marketing Themes	
❏ Technical Approach	
❏ Assumptions	
❏ Implementation Schedule	
❏ Project Management	
❏ Facilities and Capabilities	
❏ Service & Support Themes	
❏ Educational Themes	
❏ Company History	
❏ Exceptions to Requirements	
❏ Develop Illustrations	
❏ Technical Volume	
❏ Technical Themes	
❏ List of Assumptions	
❏ Product Descriptions	

B. Proposal Writing Checklist (continued)	
Item	**Notes**
❑ Implementation Schedule	
❑ Quality Control	
❑ Subcontractor's Role	
❑ Subcontractor's Products	
❑ Exceptions to Requirements	
❑ Develop Illustrations	
❑ Management Volume	
❑ Marketing Themes	
❑ Resumes of Key Personnel	
❑ Facilities & Capabilities	
❑ Related Experience	
❑ Subcontractor's Role	
❑ Service and Support	
❑ Education	
❑ Exception to Requirements	
❑ Develop Illustrations	
❑ Cost Volume	

B. Proposal Writing Checklist (continued)	
Item	**Notes**
❑ Introduction to Cost	
❑ Equipment Totals & Summary	
❑ Standard Hardware	
❑ Standard Software	
❑ Custom Hardware	
❑ Custom Software	
❑ Project Management	
❑ Service	
❑ Education	
❑ Installation	
❑ Licenses	
❑ Payment Schedules	
❑ Discounts	
❑ Tax	

C. Pre-submission Checklist	
Item	**Notes**
☐ Proposal Cover	
☐ Title Page	
☐ Proprietary Notice	
☐ Signature Papers	
☐ Bid Bond	
☐ Performance Bond	
☐ Buy USA Statement	
☐ EEO Documentation	
☐ Small Business Qualification	
☐ Minority Business Qualification	
☐ Table of Contents	
☐ List of Illustrations	
☐ Proposal Road Map	
☐ Executive Summary	
☐ Technical Volume	
☐ Management Volume	
☐ Cost Volume	

C. Pre-submission Checklist (continued)	
Item	**Notes**
❑ Glossary	
❑ Appendices	
❑ Compliance Matrix	
❑ Exceptions List	
❑ Supporting Brochures	
❑ Data Sheets	
❑ Annual Report	
❑ Supporting Manuals	
❑ Supplementary Tech. Data	
❑ Industry White Papers	

D. Printing Checklist	
Item	**Notes**
❑ Printer/Reproduction Selected	
❑ Cover Sent to Printer	
❑ Tabs Sent to Printer	
❑ Printing Format Selected	
❑ Binding Method Selected	
❑ Three-ring Binder	
❑ ACCO Fastener	
❑ Comb Binding	
❑ Other	
❑ Final Art Prepared for Printing	
❑ Final Text Master Printed	
❑ Dummy Sheet Prepared	
❑ Page Masters to Printer	
❑ Proposal Assembled	
❑ Cover Illustrations Inserted	
❑ Final Review	

E. Evaluation Checklist for Proposal Team	
Item	**Notes**
❑ Evaluation Team Formed	
❑ Sales and Marketing	
❑ Technical/Engineering	
❑ Project Management	
❑ Pricing Team	
❑ Date and Time Established	
❑ RFP Distributed to Team	
❑ Space Established	
❑ Team Assembled for Evaluation	
❑ Proposal Distributed	
❑ Evaluation Forms Distributed	
❑ Review Debriefing	
❑ Evaluations Reviewed	
❑ Results Reviewed	
❑ Proposal Revised	

E. Evaluation Checklist for Proposal Team (continued)	
Item	**Notes**
❑ Evaluation Criteria Determined	
❑ RFP Stated Criteria	
❑ Sales Reps Input	
❑ Engineering Input	
❑ Team's Input	
❑ Evaluation Criteria Reviewed	
❑ Evaluation "Weights" Posted	
❑ Estimated Technical Points	
❑ Estimated Management Points	
❑ Estimated Pricing Points	
❑ Total Estimate Points Awarded	
❑ Proposal Scoring Reviewed	
❑ Proposal Scoring Accepted/Not Accepted & Proposed Changes	
❑ Competitor 1 Estimated	
❑ Competitor 2 Estimated	
❑ Competitor 3 Estimated	

F. Proposal Submission Checklist	
Item	**Notes**
❑ Proposal Instructions Reviewed	
❑ Due Date & Time	
❑ Number of Copies	
❑ Address & Name	
❑ Sealed Wrapping	
❑ Box Markings	
❑ Delivery Method Established	
❑ Authorized Signature on Proposal	
❑ Signature Papers Included	
❑ Separate Cost Volume?	
❑ Final Review	
❑ Submit Proposal	
❑ Proposal Party	

G. Post-proposal Checklist

Item	Notes
❏ Store Proposal & Documentation	
❏ Respond to Customer Questions	
❏ Prepare for Customer Demonstration	
❏ Demo Room and Facilities	
❏ Demo Equipment	
❏ Demo Script Prepared	
❏ Prepare for Headquarters Visit	
❏ Prepare Presentation	
❏ Prepare for Reference Site Visit	
❏ Respond to Contract Questions	
❏ Prepare for Negotiations	
❏ Prepare Contracts	
❏ Make Requested Proposal/Contract Changes	
❏ Make Requested Price Changes	
❏ Negotiate Contract	
❏ New Account Celebration	

H. Bid/No-Bid Checklist – Account Information	
Item	**Notes**
❏ Account Information	
❏ Sales Rep in Acct?	
❏ How Long in Acct?	
❏ Did We Help Write the RFP?	
❏ What Dept. is the RFP From?	
❏ Who are the Decision makers?	
❏ Is the Project Funded?	
❏ What is the Funding Amount?	
❏ Account Technology Base	
❏ Has a Study Been Completed?	
❏ Who did the Study?	
❏ Do We have a Copy?	
❏ Are Consultants Involved?	
❏ Is the Account Knowledgeable?	
❏ Are Other Vendors Installed?	
❏ Who are the Vendors?	
❏ Describe Current System?	

H. Bid/No-Bid Checklist – Bidding Strategies	
Item	**Notes**
☐ Competition	
☐ List the Competition?	
☐ Did They Write the RFP?	
☐ What are Their Strengths?	
☐ What are Their Weaknesses?	
☐ Why Should We Bid on this RFP?	
☐ What is the RFPs Application?	
☐ Can We Use Std. Products?	
☐ What Custom Work is Needed?	
☐ Is this a Technology Fit?	
☐ Is this a Strategic Opportunity?	
☐ Any Negative Possibilities?	
☐ List Negatives and Comment?	
☐ What is Our Bid Strategy?	
☐ What is Our Leverage?	
☐ What are Our Strengths?	
☐ What are Our Weaknesses?	

H. Bid/No-Bid Checklist – Solutions Strategies	
Item	**Notes**
❑ Describe Basic Solution	
❑ Std. Hardware	
❑ Std. Software	
❑ Custom Hardware	
❑ Custom Software	
❑ Scope of Development	
❑ Std. Maintenance?	
❑ Std. Education?	
❑ Contract	
❑ Contract with RFP?	
❑ If not, can We Get a Copy?	
❑ Std. Contract?	
❑ Describe Unusual Terms	
❑ Can these be Negotiated?	
❑ Overall Opinion of Opportunity?	
❑ Recommendations	
❑ Bid or No-bid?	

H. Bid/No-Bid Checklist – Proposal Development Costs	
Item	**Notes**
❑ Proposal Resources Outlined	
❑ Proposal Manager	
❑ Technical Team	
❑ Management Team	
❑ Sales/Marketing	
❑ Pricing	
❑ Administrative Resources	
❑ Word Processing	
❑ Illustrations	
❑ Admin Support	
❑ Facilities Resources	
❑ Warroom Required	
❑ Equipment	
❑ Software	
❑ Site Visits?	
❑ Headquarters' Visit?	

Appendix I
Proposal Status Sheet

Customer Information

Customer Name: _____

Project Name: _____

Project Description: _____

_____

_____

Proposal Team Information

Salesman: _____

System Analyst: _____

Manager: _____

Key RFP Dates

RFP Issued:_____   RFP Due: _____

RFP Extension: _____   Questions Due:_____

Bid Conference:_____   Oral Presentation:_____

Demonstration: _____   Benchmark: _____

RFP Award: _____   First Ship: _____

Initial Revenue $:_____   Total Revenue $: _____

Key Proposal Dates

Activity	Date	Room	Who
Planning Mting:	_____	_____	_____
Bid/No-bid Mting:	_____	_____	_____
Kickoff Mting:	_____	_____	_____
First Review:	_____	_____	_____
Final Review:	_____	_____	_____
Ship Date:	_____	_____	_____

Appendix I
Technical and Business Review

Client: _____

Sales Rep:_____   Date:_____

Comments: _____

_____

_____

Sales Analyst: _____   Date:_____

Comments: _____

_____

_____

Marketing: _____   Date:_____

Comment: _____

_____

_____

Engineering: _____   Date:_____

Comments: _____

_____

_____

Decision

Refer to Bid/No-bid Committee:_____   Date:_____

No Bid Letter:_____   Date:_____

Comments: _____

_____

_____

Appendix I
Proposal Sign-Off

Client: _____

Sales Rep:_____   Date:_____

Comments: _____

_____

_____

Sales Analyst: _____   Date:_____

Comments: _____

_____

_____

V.P. Sales:_____   Date:_____

Comments: _____

_____

V.P. Marketing: _____   Date:_____

Comment: _____

_____

V.P. Engineering:_____   Date:_____

Comments: _____

_____

V.P. Finance:_____   Date:_____

Comments: _____

_____

Appendix I
Proposal Disposition

Client: _____

Win/Loss Review: _____   Date:_____

Sales Rep:_____   Date:_____

Comments: _____

Sales Analyst: _____   Date:_____

Comments: _____

Primary Win/Loss Factors

Business Solution:_____

_____

Technical Solution: _____

_____

Pricing:_____

_____

Project Management: _____

_____

Maintenance:_____

_____

Education: _____

_____

Exceptions: _____

Appendix I
Proposal Disposition

Win/Loss Review Notes:

_____

_____

_____

_____

_____

_____

_____

_____

Corrective Recommendations:

_____

_____

_____

_____

_____

_____

_____

Appendix I
Proposal Disposition

Customer Comments:

_____

_____

_____

_____

_____

_____

_____

_____

_____

_____

_____

_____

_____

_____

_____

_____

_____

ESTABLISH A FRAMEWORK
FOR EXCELLENCE
WITH THE OASIS PRESS ®

OASIS PRESS BOOKS & SOFTWARE

Celebrating 25 Years

THE OASIS PRESS°

PSI RESEARCH

P.O. BOX 3727

CENTRAL POINT, OR

97502·0032

Fastbreaking changes in technology and the global marketplace continue to create unprecedented opportunities for businesses through the '90s and into the new millennium. However with these opportunities will also come many new challenges. Today, more than ever, businesses, especially small businesses, need to excel in all areas of operation to complete and succeed in an ever-changing world.

The Successful Business Library takes you through the '90s and beyond, helping you solve the day-to-day problems you face now, and prepares you for the unexpected problems you may be facing down the road. With any of our products, you will receive up-to-date and practical business solutions, which are easy to use and easy to understand. No jargon or theories, just solid, nuts-and-bolts information.

Whether you are an entrepreneur going into business for the first time or an experienced consultant trying to keep up with the latest rules and regulations, The Successful Business Library provides you with the step-by-step guidance, and action-oriented plans you need to succeed in today's world. As an added benefit, PSI Research/The Oasis Press® unconditionally guarantees your satisfaction with the purchase of any book or software application in our catalog.

More than a marketplace for our products, we actually provide something that many business Web sites tend to overlook... useful information!

It's no mystery that the World Wide Web is a great way for businesses to promote their products, however most commercial sites stop there. We have always viewed our site's goals a little differently. For starters, we have applied our 25 years of experience providing hands-on information to small businesses directly to our Web site. We offer current information to help you start your own business, guidelines to keep it up and running, useful federal and state-specific information (including addresses and phone numbers to contact these resources), and a forum for business owners to communicate and network with others on the Internet. We would like to invite you to check out our Web site and discover the information that can assist you and your small business venture.

ALL MAJOR CREDIT CARDS ACCEPTED

CALL TO PLACE AN ORDER
— *or* —
TO RECEIVE A FREE CATALOG **1-800-228-2275**

International Orders (541) 479-9464
Web site http://www.psi-research.com
Fax Orders (541) 476-1479
Email sales@psi-research.com

PSI Research P.O. Box 3727 Central Point, Oregon 97502 U.S.A.

The Oasis Press Online
http://www.psi-research.com

From The Leading Publisher of Small Business Information
Books that save you time and money.

Pursuing a high-tech business has never been more opportune, however the competition in the industry is downright grueling. Author Richard Manweller brings a smart, in-depth strategy with motivational meaning. It will show you how to tailor your strategy to gain investor's attention. If you are looking for a financial angel, *Funding High Tech Ventures* is the guidance your need to make the right match.

Funding High-Tech Ventures   **Pages: 160**
Paperback: $21.95   ISBN: 1-55571-405-6

Essential techniques to successfully identify, approach, attract, and manage sources of financing. Shows how to gain the full benefits of debt financing while maintaining its risks. Outlines all types of financing and carefully walks you through the process — from evaluating short-term credit options to negotiating a long-term loan, to deciding whether to go public.

Financing Your Small Business   **Pages: 274**
Paperback: $19.95   ISBN: 1-55571-160-X

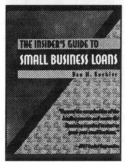

Essential for the small business operator in search of capital, this helpful, hands-on guide simplifies the loan application process as never before. The Insider's Guide to Small Business Loans is an easy-to-follow road map designed to help you cut through the red tape and show you how to prepare a successful loan application. Several chapters are devoted to helping you secure a loan guaranty from the Small Business Administration.

The Insider's Guide to Small Business Loans   **Pages: 200**
Paperback: $19.95   ISBN: 1-55571-429-3
Binder: $29.95   ISBN: 1-55571-378-5

Anyone who has ever listened to a banker and not understood a word will do well to read this guide. It explains the basic principles of finance, from realizing that business is all about making the most money possible with the least investment to understanding cash flow. Learn how to analyze financial statements, how debt is used to a business' advantage, and how to understand stock pricing. Business segment accounting, mergers and acquisitions, currency hedging, and incorporation, are outlined as well.

Financial Decisionmaking   **Pages: 230**
Paperback: $19.95   ISBN: 1-55571-435-8

ALL MAJOR CREDIT CARDS ACCEPTED

CALL TO PLACE AN ORDER
— or —
TO RECEIVE A FREE CATALOG   1-800-228-2275

International Orders (541) 479-9464   *Fax Orders* (541) 476-1479
Web site http://www.psi-research.com   *Email* sales@psi-research.com

PSI Research   P.O. Box 3727   Central Point, Oregon   97502   U.S.A.

HOW TO ORDER

Mail: Send this completed order form and a check, money order or credit card information to: PSI Research/The Oasis Press®, P.O. Box 3727, Central Point, Oregon 97502-0032

Fax: Available 24 hours a day, 7 days a week at **1-541-476-1479**

Email: info@psi-research.com (Please include a phone number, should we need to contact you.)

Web: Purchase any of our products online at our Website at **http://www.psi-research.com/oasis.htm**

Inquiries and International Orders: Please call **1-541-479-9464**

Indicate the quantity and price of the titles you would like:

5/99

TITLE	ISBN	BINDER	PAPERBACK	QTY.	TOTAL
Advertising Without An Agency	1-55571-429-3		☐ 19.95		
Before You Go Into Business Read This	1-55571-481-1		☐ 17.95		
Bottom Line Basics	1-55571-329-7 (B) ■ 1-55571-330-0 (P)	☐ 39.95	☐ 19.95		
BusinessBasics	1-55571-430-7		☐ 16.95		
The Business Environmental Handbook	1-55571-304-1 (B) ■ 1-55571-163-4 (P)	☐ 39.95	☐ 19.95		
Business Owner's Guide to Accounting and Bookkeeping	1-55571-381-5		☐ 19.95		
businessplan.com	1-55571-455-2		☐ 19.95		
Buyer's Guide to Business Insurance	1-55571-310-6 (B) ■ 1-55571-162-6 (P)	☐ 39.95	☐ 19.95		
California Corporation Formation Package	1-55571-368-8 (B) ■ 1-55571-464-1 (P)	☐ 39.95	☐ 29.95		
Collection Techniques for a Small Business	1-55571-312-2 (B) ■ 1-55571-171-5 (P)	☐ 39.95	☐ 19.95		
College Entrepreneur Handbook	1-55571-503-6		☐ 16.95		
A Company Policy & Personnel Workbook	1-55571-364-5 (B) ■ 1-55571-486-2 (P)	☐ 49.95	☐ 29.95		
Company Relocation Handbook	1-55571-091-3 (B) ■ 1-55571-092-1 (P)	☐ 39.95	☐ 19.95		
CompControl	1-55571-356-4 (B) ■ 1-55571-355-6 (P)	☐ 39.95	☐ 19.95		
Complete Book of Business Forms	1-55571-107-3		☐ 19.95		
Connecting Online	1-55571-403-X		☐ 21.95		
Customer Engineering	1-55571-360-2 (B) ■ 1-55571-359-9 (P)	☐ 39.95	☐ 19.95		
Develop and Market Your Creative Ideas	1-55571-383-1		☐ 15.95		
Developing International Markets	1-55571-433-1		☐ 19.95		
Doing Business in Russia	1-55571-375-0		☐ 19.95		
Draw the Line	1-55571-370-X		☐ 17.95		
The Essential Corporation Handbook	1-55571-342-4		☐ 21.95		
Essential Limited Liability Company Handbook	1-55571-362-9 (B) ■ 1-55571-361-0 (P)	☐ 39.95	☐ 21.95		
Export Now	1-55571-192-8 (B) ■ 1-55571-167-7 (P)	☐ 39.95	☐ 24.95		
Financial Decisionmaking	1-55571-435-8		☐ 19.95		
Financial Management Techniques	1-55571-116-2 (B) ■ 1-55571-124-3 (P)	☐ 39.95	☐ 19.95		
Financing Your Small Business	1-55571-160-X		☐ 19.95		
Franchise Bible	1-55571-366-1 (B) ■ 1-55571-367-X (P)	☐ 39.95	☐ 24.95		
The Franchise Redbook	1-55571-484-6		☐ 34.95		
Friendship Marketing	1-55571-399-8		☐ 18.95		
Funding High-Tech Ventures	1-55571-405-6		☐ 21.95		
Home Business Made Easy	1-55571-428-5		☐ 19.95		
Improving Staff Productivity	1-55571-456-0		☐ 16.95		
Information Breakthrough	1-55571-413-7		☐ 22.95		
Insider's Guide to Small Business Loans	1-55571-488-9		☐ 19.95		
InstaCorp™ Book & Software	1-55571-382-3		☐ 29.95		
Joysticks, Blinking Lights, and Thrills	1-55571-401-3		☐ 18.95		
Keeping Score: An Inside Look at Sports Marketing	1-55571-377-7		☐ 18.95		
Know Your Market	1-55571-341-6 (B) ■ 1-55571-333-5 (P)	☐ 39.95	☐ 19.95		
Leader's Guide: 15 Essential Skills	1-55571-434-X		☐ 19.95		
Legal Expense Defense	1-55571-349-1 (B) ■ 1-55571-348-3 (P)	☐ 39.95	☐ 19.95		
Legal Road Map for Consultants	1-55571-460-9		☐ 18.95		
Location, Location, Location	1-55571-376-9		☐ 19.95		
Mail Order Legal Guide	1-55571-193-6 (B) ■ 1-55571-190-1 (P)	☐ 45.00	☐ 29.95		
Managing People: A Practical Guide	1-55571-380-7		☐ 21.95		
Marketing for the New Millennium	1-55571-432-3		☐ 19.95		
Marketing Mastery	1-55571-358-0 (B) ■ 1-55571-357-2 (P)	☐ 39.95	☐ 19.95		
Money Connection	1-55571-352-1 (B) ■ 1-55571-351-3 (P)	☐ 39.95	☐ 24.95		
Moonlighting: Earning a Second Income at Home	1-55571-406-4		☐ 15.95		
Navigating the Marketplace: Growth Strategies for Small Business	1-55571-458-7		☐ 21.95		
No Money Down Financing for Franchising	1-55571-462-5		☐ 19.95		
Not Another Meeting!	1-55571-480-3		☐ 17.95		
People-Centered Profit Strategies	1-55571-517-6		☐ 18.95		

Sub-total for this side:

Order Directly From **The Oasis Press**®

Call, Mail, Email, or Fax Your Order to: PSI Research, P.O. Box 3727, Central Point, OR 97502

Order Phone USA & Canada: +1 800 228-2275   Email: info@psi-research.com   Fax: +1 541 476-1479

Includes
Titles Through
Winter 1999

TITLE	✔ BINDER	✔ PAPERBACK	QUANTITY	COST
Advertising Without An Agency: A Comprehensive Guide to Radio, Television, Print...		❑ $19.95		
Bottom Line Basics: Understand and Control Your Finances	❑ $39.95	❑ $19.95		
BusinessBasics: A Microbusiness Startup Guide		❑ $16.95		
The Business Environmental Handbook	❑ $39.95	❑ $19.95		
Business Owner's Guide to Accounting & Bookkeeping		❑ $19.95		
businessplan.com: how to write a web-woven strategic business plan		❑ $19.95		
Buyer's Guide to Business Insurance	❑ $39.95	❑ $19.95		
California Corporation Formation Package		❑ $29.95		
Collection Techniques for a Small Business	❑ $39.95	❑ $19.95		
A Company Policy and Personnel Workbook	❑ $49.95	❑ $29.95		
Company Relocation Handbook	❑ $39.95	❑ $19.95		
CompControl: The Secrets of Reducing Workers' Compensation Costs	❑ $39.95	❑ $19.95		
Complete Book of Business Forms		❑ $19.95		
Connecting Online: Creating a Successful Image on the Internet		❑ $21.95		
Customer Engineering: Cutting Edge Selling Strategies	❑ $39.95	❑ $19.95		
Develop & Market Your Creative Ideas		❑ $15.95		
Developing International Markets: Shaping Your Global Presence		❑ $19.95		
Doing Business in Russia: Basic Facts for the Pioneering Entrepreneur		❑ $19.95		
Draw The Line: A Sexual Harassment Free Workplace		❑ $17.95		
Entrepreneurial Decisionmaking: A Survival Manual for the Next Millennium		❑ $21.95		
The Essential Corporation Handbook		❑ $21.95		
The Essential Limited Liability Company Handbook	❑ $39.95	❑ $21.95		
Export Now: A Guide for Small Business	❑ $39.95	❑ $24.95		
Financial Decisionmaking: A CPA/Attorney's Perspective		❑ $19.95		
Financial Management Techniques for Small Business	❑ $39.95	❑ $19.95		
Financing Your Small Business: Techniques for Planning, Acquiring, & Managing Debt		❑ $19.95		
Franchise Bible: How to Buy a Franchise or Franchise Your Own Business	❑ $39.95	❑ $24.95		
Friendship Marketing: Growing Your Business by Cultivating Strategic Relationships		❑ $18.95		
Funding High-Tech Ventures		❑ $21.95		
Home Business Made Easy		❑ $19.95		
Information Breakthrough: How to Turn Mountains of Confusing Data into Gems of Useful Information		❑ $22.95		
Improving Staff Productivity: Ideas to Increase Profits		❑ $16.95		
The Insider's Guide to Small Business Loans		❑ $19.95		
InstaCorp – Incorporate In Any State (Book & Software)		❑ $29.95		
Joysticks, Blinking Lights and Thrills		❑ $18.95		
Keeping Score: An Inside Look at Sports Marketing		❑ $18.95		
Know Your Market: How to Do Low-Cost Market Research	❑ $39.95	❑ $19.95		
The Leader's Guide: 15 Essential Skills		❑ $19.95		
Legal Expense Defense: How to Control Your Business' Legal Costs and Problems	❑ $39.95	❑ $19.95		
Legal Road Map for Consultants		❑ $18.95		
Location, Location, Location: How to Select the Best Site for Your Business		❑ $19.95		
Mail Order Legal Guide	❑ $45.00	❑ $29.95		
Managing People: A Practical Guide		❑ $21.95		
Marketing for the New Millennium: Applying New Techniques		❑ $19.95		
Marketing Mastery: Your Seven Step Guide to Success	❑ $39.95	❑ $19.95		
The Money Connection: Where and How to Apply for Business Loans and Venture Capital	❑ $39.95	❑ $24.95		
Moonlighting: Earn a Second Income at Home		❑ $15.95		
Navigating the Marketplace: Growth Strategies For Your Business		❑ $21.95		
No Money Down Financing for Franchising		❑ $19.95		
People Investment: How to Make Your Hiring Decisions Pay Off For Everyone	❑ $39.95	❑ $19.95		
Power Marketing for Small Business	❑ $39.95	❑ $19.95		
Profit Power: 101 Pointers to Give Your Business a Competitive Edge		❑ $19.95		
Proposal Development: How to Respond and Win the Bid	❑ $39.95	❑ $21.95		
Public Relations Marketing: Making a Splash Without Much Cash		❑ $19.95		
Raising Capital: How to Write a Financing Proposal		❑ $19.95		
Renaissance 2000: Liberal Arts Essentials for Tomorrow's Leaders		❑ $22.95		
Retail in Detail: How to Start and Manage a Small Retail Business		❑ $15.95		
Secrets of High Ticket Selling		❑ $19.95		
Secrets to Buying and Selling a Business		❑ $24.95		
Secure Your Future: Financial Planning at Any Age	❑ $39.95	❑ $19.95		
Selling Services: A Guide for the Consulting Professional		❑ $18.95		
The Small Business Insider's Guide to Bankers		❑ $18.95		
BOOK SUB-TOTAL (Additional titles on other side)				